שַׁעֲרֵי הַבַּיִת

GATES OF THE HOUSE

כה אמר יי: עשו משפט וצדקה, והצילו גזול מיד עשוק, וגר, יתום
ואלמנה אל־תנו אל־תחמסו, ודם נקי אל־תשפכו במקום הזה. כי
אם־עשו תעשו את־הדבר הזה, ובאו בשערי הבית הזה מלכים ישבים
לדוד על־כסאו . . .

Thus says the Eternal One: Do justice and right; deliver the
wronged from the hand of the oppressor; do not exploit or
harm the stranger, the widow, or the orphan; and hold life
sacred in this place. For if you faithfully fulfill this word, then
those who enter the gates of this house shall be of David's
royal line . . .

—Jeremiah 22.3–4a.

שַׁעֲרֵי הַבַּיִת

GATES OF THE HOUSE

The New Union Home Prayerbook

Prayers and Readings
for Home and Synagogue

CENTRAL CONFERENCE OF AMERICAN RABBIS

5737 New York 1977

Contents

Index to Psalms

This index cites Psalms appearing in whole or in substantial part

Introduction

The Central Conference of American Rabbis presents *Shaarei Habayit*, *Gates of the House: The New Union Home Prayerbook*. It carries forward our intention to provide for the Jewish community a liturgy for the individual and the family, as well as for the synagogue and the worshipping congregation.

Gates of the House is a companion-volume to *Gates of Prayer*. Taken together, and supplemented by *Tadrich Leshabbat: A Shabbat Manual* (C.C.A.R., 1972), these volumes point out a way to hallow life on weekdays, Sabbaths, and Festivals, and in times of joy and sorrow.

This volume includes prayers and meditations for private devotion; services for familial and communal occasions; and Notes to identify the sources of its contents. Many of the prayers, poems, and meditations may also be used to enrich the congregational service.

Gates of the House expresses in contemporary terms the classic themes of Judaism. We pray that it will contribute to the further development of the spiritual life of the House of Israel. If our labors lead to a growing love of God, Israel, and Torah, we shall rejoice. May our homes always be miniature sanctuaries, enclaves of holiness where the distressed may find refuge, the weary find strength, and all who enter, peace. Now, as in days gone by, may the bonds of kinship and affection uphold the children of Sarah and Abraham.

אם־יי לא יבנה בית, שוא עמלו בוניו בו.

ערב שבת קדש 'ואתחנן' תשל"ו

Chaim Stern

10 Av 5736

CHAPPAQUA, NEW YORK

vii

A Note on Usage

This volume is intended primarily for the home, although it may also be used in the synagogue as a source of supplementary readings and prayers for its companion-volume, *Shaarei Tefillah, Gates of Prayer*.

The type-face is intended to suggest how group worship might be conducted. In place of the conventional rubrics, 'Reader,' 'All Reading,' 'Singing,' and the like, we employ Roman type for 'Reader,' *italics* for 'All Reading,' and sans serif (in the English) for Hebrew passages that will usually be sung. These are, of course, suggestions. Families and groups assembled for worship may choose to experiment with different patterns.

Acknowledgments

The Central Conference of American Rabbis is grateful to all who helped shape the contents of this volume. Many suggestions were received during the course of its preparation; each was carefully considered, and many were accepted.

The Conference is especially indebted to a number of individuals. Rabbi Chaim Stern served as Editor of *Gates of the House*. He prepared the various drafts, compiling and shaping their contents, translating the Hebrew, writing many new prayers, and adapting many others. He wishes to record his special gratitude to Rabbi A. Stanley Dreyfus (Chairman of the Liturgy Committee), who was his indispensable co-worker. At all times Rabbi Dreyfus was the source of valuable comments and suggestions. In the latter stages of this volume's preparation, they were partners in the work of preparing the manuscript for publication.

The Conference wishes to thank Rabbi Harvey J. Fields and Dr. Edward Graham (who served on the Liturgy Committee as delegate from the American Conference of Cantors) for their help. Rabbi Robert I. Kahn, who served as Chairman of the Liturgy Committee until 1973, contributed leadership, energy, and devotion to the work which led to the creation of this prayerbook. Rabbi Malcolm Stern served as Secretary of the Committee and as a most helpful advisor. Mr. Andor Braun's work on the design of *Gates of Prayer* served as the model for the design of *Gates of the House*. The Hebrew caligraphy was the work of Mr. Ismar David. Rabbi James R. Michaels assisted the Editor and Rabbi Dreyfus with the proofreading in the early stages of the work. Rabbi Elliot Stevens was most helpful in a number of matters related to preparation of the volume for publication. Rabbi Joseph B. Glaser was always available for counsel and assistance. All these have earned the gratitude of the Conference.

In addition to those named in *Shaarei Tefillah*, pp. xvi–xvii, the Committee and Conference thank the following persons, whose suggestions were helpful to the Editor: Rabbis Philip Horowitz, Simeon J. Maslin, W. Gunther Plaut, and Bernard Taylor; Mr. Michael Isaacson.

◆ ◆

The present volume owes much to two previous works: *Service of the Heart* (Union of Liberal and Progressive Synagogues, London, 1967, edited by John Rayner and Chaim Stern), especially to the section entitled 'Supplements for Home and Synagogue'; and *The Union Home Prayerbook* (Central Conference of American Rabbis, 1951).

✦ ✦

Every effort has been made to ascertain the owners of copyrights for the selections used in this volume, and to obtain permission to reprint copyrighted passages. For the use of the passages indicated, the Central Conference of American Rabbis expresses its gratitude to those whose names appear below. The Conference will be pleased, in subsequent editions, to correct any inadvertent errors or omissions that may be pointed out.

A. S. BARNES AND COMPANY, INC.: From *The Golden Peacock: A Worldwide Treasury of Yiddish Poetry*, compiled, translated and edited by Dr. Joseph Leftwich. Reprinted by permission.

ATHENEUM PUBLISHERS: From *The Hard Hours*, by Anthony Hecht. Copyright © 1967 by Anthony E. Hecht. Reprinted by permission of Atheneum Publishers.

BLANK, AMY K.: "I will lift my hands unto thee, O my God!" Used by permission.

CAMBRIDGE UNIVERSITY PRESS: From *The New English Bible*. Copyright © The Delegates of the Oxford University Press and the Syndics of the Cambridge University Press 1961, 1970. Reprinted by permission.

COLLINS PUBLISHERS, LTD.: From *Ardours and Endurance*, by Robert Nichols, 1917.

FARRAR, STRAUSS & GIROUX, INC.: From *O The Chimneys*, by Nelly Sachs, Copyright, 1967, poems on pp. 3, 9, 29–30, 61, 65–66.

HARCOURT BRACE JOVANOVITCH, INC.: "i thank you god." Copyright, 1950, by E. E. Cummings. Reprinted from his volume, *Complete Poems 1913–1962*, by permission of Harcourt Brace Jovanovitch, Inc.

HARVARD UNIVERSITY PRESS: Reprinted by permission of the publishers from Theodore Spencer, *An Act Of Life*, Cambridge, Mass.: Harvard University Press, Copyright 1944, by the President and Fellows of Harvard College; © 1972, by Eloise Spencer Bender.

THE JEWISH PUBLICATION SOCIETY OF AMERICA: From *The Torah* and *Psalms* for occasional use of the translation.

KNOPF, ALFRED A., INC.: "Now from the world the light of God is gone..." is reprinted from *A Winter Tide*, by Robert Nathan, by permission of Alfred A. Knopf, Inc., 1939.

ACKNOWLEDGMENTS

MACMILLAN PUBLISHING CO. INC.: From *Poems* by John Masefield. Copyright 1916 by John Masefield, renewed 1944 by John Masefield; reprinted by permission of Macmillan Publishing Co. Inc.

McGRAW-HILL, INC.: From *I Never Saw Another Butterfly*, copyright © 1964 by McGraw-Hill, Inc. Used by permission of McGraw-Hill, Inc.

THE NATIONAL COUNCIL OF CHURCHES: *Revised Standard Version of the Bible*, for occasional use of the translation.

NEW DIRECTIONS PUBLISHING CORPORATION: Denise Levertov, *The Jacob's Ladder*. Copyright 1961 by Denise Levertov Goodman, and Charles Reznikoff, *By the Waters of Manhattan*. Copyright 1951 by Charles Reznikoff. Both selections reprinted by permission of New Directions Publishing Corporation and the San Francisco Review.

THE RABBINICAL ASSEMBLY: "This Is My Prayer," by Hillel Bavli, translated by Norman Tarnor, in *Selihot*, copyright © 1964 by The Rabbinical Assembly, reprinted by permission of The Rabbinical Assembly.

RANDOM HOUSE, INC.: "I think continually of those . . ." is reprinted from *Selected Poems*, by Stephen Spender, by permission of Random House, Inc., 1934.

THE UNIVERSITY OF CALIFORNIA PRESS: From *Modern Hebrew Poetry*, selected and translated by Ruth Finer Mintz, copyright © 1966. Originally published by the University of California Press; reprinted by permission of The Regents of the University of California.

שערי הבית

GATES OF THE HOUSE

תפלות וקריאות שונות
Prayers and Readings

Evening and Morning Prayers

FOR CHILDREN

Evening Prayer

Lord God, Creator of day and night, thank You for this good world. Thank You for the day. I was so busy! Now I am tired, and I thank You for sleep.

Bless my family and friends, all those I love, all who love me. May my dreams be pleasant ones, and may I wake up with a smile, ready for the new day.

For all that I have learned this day I thank and praise You. So twice each day, early and late, morning and evening, I say:

Morning Prayer

מוֹדֶה אֲנִי לְפָנֶיךָ . . .

Mo·deh a·ni le·fa·ne·cha . . .

Lord, I thank You for the morning, for the new day in which I may learn and play and laugh. I thank You for all the day's goodness — for the love of my family, the beautiful world which has awakened with me, and for Your Torah which teaches me how to live.

Today I will show my love for my parents and all my family. I will be kind to my friends. I will be gentle with animals. I will do my best to learn, to be helpful, to be a good person. For the power to grow, I thank You. So twice each day, early and late, morning and evening, I say:

שְׁמַע יִשְׂרָאֵל: יְיָ אֱלֹהֵינוּ, יְיָ אֶחָד!

Hear, O Israel: the Lord is our God, the Lord is One!

Blessed is His glorious kingdom for ever and ever.

בָּרוּךְ שֵׁם כְּבוֹד מַלְכוּתוֹ לְעוֹלָם וָעֶד.

You shall love the Lord your God with all your mind, with all your strength, with all your being.

וְאָהַבְתָּ אֵת יְיָ אֱלֹהֶיךָ בְּכָל־לְבָבְךָ וּבְכָל־נַפְשְׁךָ וּבְכָל־מְאֹדֶךָ.

3

Set these words, which I command you this day, upon your heart. Teach them faithfully to your children; speak of them at home and away, when you lie down and when you rise up.

וְהָיוּ הַדְּבָרִים הָאֵלֶּה, אֲשֶׁר אָנֹכִי מְצַוְּךָ הַיּוֹם, עַל־לְבָבֶךָ. וְשִׁנַּנְתָּם לְבָנֶיךָ, וְדִבַּרְתָּ בָּם בְּשִׁבְתְּךָ בְּבֵיתֶךָ, וּבְלֶכְתְּךָ בַדֶּרֶךְ, וּבְשָׁכְבְּךָ וּבְקוּמֶךָ.

Bind them as a sign upon your hand; let them be a symbol before your eyes; inscribe them on the doorposts of your house, and on your gates.

וּקְשַׁרְתָּם לְאוֹת עַל־יָדֶךָ, וְהָיוּ לְטֹטָפֹת בֵּין עֵינֶיךָ, וּכְתַבְתָּם עַל־מְזֻזוֹת בֵּיתֶךָ, וּבִשְׁעָרֶיךָ.

Be mindful of all My Mitzvot, and do them: so shall you consecrate yourselves to your God. I, the Lord, am your God who led you out of Egypt to be your God; I, the Lord, am your God.

לְמַעַן תִּזְכְּרוּ וַעֲשִׂיתֶם אֶת־כָּל־מִצְוֹתָי, וִהְיִיתֶם קְדֹשִׁים לֵאלֹהֵיכֶם. אֲנִי יְיָ אֱלֹהֵיכֶם, אֲשֶׁר הוֹצֵאתִי אֶתְכֶם מֵאֶרֶץ מִצְרַיִם לִהְיוֹת לָכֶם לֵאלֹהִים. אֲנִי יְיָ אֱלֹהֵיכֶם.

◆ ◆

FOR ADULTS

Evening Prayer

Lord, Your touch unseen brings sleep upon my eyes, You make my lids grow heavy with the night. Grant that I may lie down in peace, and rise up to life renewed. Let Your majesty and beauty be in my thought at end of day, and at the moment of my awakening!

Lord, Guardian of Israel, You neither slumber nor sleep. Blessed are You by day, and blessed by night; blessed when we lie down, blessed when we rise up. For in Your hands are the souls of all the living and the spirits of all flesh.

May angels' wings caress me all through the night; let Your good presence hover at my side. Lord, spread the shelter of Your peace upon me, my dear ones, and all Your children.

4

שְׁמַע יִשְׂרָאֵל: יְיָ אֱלֹהֵינוּ, יְיָ אֶחָד!

Hear, O Israel: the Lord is our God, the Lord is One!

בָּרוּךְ שֵׁם כְּבוֹד מַלְכוּתוֹ לְעוֹלָם וָעֶד!

Blessed is His glorious kingdom for ever and ever!

Ve·a·hav·ta, page 3, may be recited here.

בְּיָדוֹ אַפְקִיד רוּחִי, בְּעֵת אִישָׁן וְאָעִירָה.
וְעִם רוּחִי גְּוִיָּתִי, יְיָ לִי, וְלֹא אִירָא.

Into Your hands I commend my body and my spirit, both when
I sleep and when I wake. In Your presence, I cast off fear and
lie down to restful sleep.

◆ ◆

Morning Prayer

Blessed is the Eternal our God, who has awakened me to the
new day, made me a Jew, called me to be free, and formed me
in the Divine Image. Blessed is the One who opens the eyes of
the blind, who provides clothes for the naked, who brings freedom to the captive, and whose power lifts up the fallen.

Blessed is the Eternal our God, Ruler of the universe, who re-
moves sleep from the eyes, slumber from the eyelids. Help me,
Lord, to be awake this day to the wonders that surround me,
alive to beauty and love, aware that all being is precious, that
we walk on holy ground, wherever we go.

שְׁמַע יִשְׂרָאֵל: יְיָ אֱלֹהֵינוּ, יְיָ אֶחָד!

Hear, O Israel: the Lord is our God, the Lord is One!

בָּרוּךְ שֵׁם כְּבוֹד מַלְכוּתוֹ לְעוֹלָם וָעֶד!

Blessed is His glorious kingdom for ever and ever!

Ve·a·hav·ta, page 3, may be recited here.

Lift up my eyes, Lord, beyond the day's routine, to see the
glory of all creation; make my day a song of praise and thanksgiving for all this grandeur, and its wondrous Source!

5

Blessings before and after Meals

Before meals

Ha·mo·tsi le·chem min ha·a·rets,

הַמּוֹצִיא לֶחֶם מִן־הָאָרֶץ,

We give thanks to God for bread.
Our voices rise in song together,
As our joyful prayer is said:

בָּרוּךְ אַתָּה, יְיָ אֱלֹהֵינוּ, מֶלֶךְ הָעוֹלָם, הַמּוֹצִיא לֶחֶם
מִן־הָאָרֶץ.

Ba·ruch a·ta, A·do·nai E·lo·hei·nu, me·lech ha·o·lam, ha·mo·tsi
le·chem min ha·a·rets.

Blessed is the Lord our God, Ruler of the universe, who causes
bread to come forth from the earth.

◆ ◆

After meals

ON SHABBAT AND YOM TOV

Psalm 126

A SONG OF ASCENTS.

שִׁיר הַמַּעֲלוֹת.

בְּשׁוּב יְיָ אֶת־שִׁיבַת צִיּוֹן, הָיִינוּ כְּחֹלְמִים. אָז יִמָּלֵא שְׂחוֹק פִּינוּ, וּלְשׁוֹנֵנוּ
רִנָּה. אָז יֹאמְרוּ בַגּוֹיִם: 'הִגְדִּיל יְיָ לַעֲשׂוֹת עִם־אֵלֶּה.' הִגְדִּיל יְיָ לַעֲשׂוֹת
עִמָּנוּ, הָיִינוּ שְׂמֵחִים! שׁוּבָה יְיָ אֶת־שְׁבִיתֵנוּ כַּאֲפִיקִים בַּנֶּגֶב. הַזֹּרְעִים
בְּדִמְעָה, בְּרִנָּה יִקְצֹרוּ. הָלוֹךְ יֵלֵךְ וּבָכֹה, נֹשֵׂא מֶשֶׁךְ־הַזָּרַע, בֹּא־יָבֹא
בְרִנָּה נֹשֵׂא אֲלֻמֹּתָיו.

When the Lord restores the exiles to Zion, it will seem like a dream.
Then our mouths will fill with laughter, our tongues with joyful song.
Then they will say among the nations: 'The Lord has done great
things for them.' It is for us that the Lord is doing great things: we
will rejoice. Lord, restore our fortunes, as streams revive the desert.
Then those who sow in tears shall reap in joy. Those who go forth
weeping, bearing sacks of seeds, shall come home with shouts of
joy, bearing their sheaves.

◆ ◆

6

After all meals

Let us praise God.

רַבּוֹתַי, נְבָרֵךְ!

יְהִי שֵׁם יְיָ מְבֹרָךְ מֵעַתָּה וְעַד עוֹלָם!

Praised be the name of God, now and for ever!

בִּרְשׁוּת מָרָנָן וְרַבָּנָן וְרַבּוֹתַי, נְבָרֵךְ אֱלֹהֵינוּ שֶׁאָכַלְנוּ מִשֶּׁלּוֹ.

Blessed is our God, of whose abundance we have eaten.

בָּרוּךְ אֱלֹהֵינוּ שֶׁאָכַלְנוּ מִשֶּׁלּוֹ וּבְטוּבוֹ חָיִינוּ.

Blessed is our God, of whose abundance we have eaten, and by whose goodness we live.

בָּרוּךְ הוּא, וּבָרוּךְ שְׁמוֹ!

Blessed is the One-Who-Is!

בָּרוּךְ אַתָּה, יְיָ אֱלֹהֵינוּ, מֶלֶךְ הָעוֹלָם, הַזָּן אֶת־הָעוֹלָם כֻּלּוֹ
בְּטוּבוֹ. בְּחֵן בְּחֶסֶד וּבְרַחֲמִים הוּא נוֹתֵן לֶחֶם לְכָל־בָּשָׂר,
כִּי לְעוֹלָם חַסְדּוֹ. וּבְטוּבוֹ הַגָּדוֹל תָּמִיד לֹא חָסַר לָנוּ, וְאַל
יֶחְסַר לָנוּ מָזוֹן לְעוֹלָם וָעֶד, בַּעֲבוּר שְׁמוֹ הַגָּדוֹל. כִּי הוּא
אֵל זָן וּמְפַרְנֵס לַכֹּל וּמֵטִיב לַכֹּל וּמֵכִין מָזוֹן לְכָל־בְּרִיּוֹתָיו
אֲשֶׁר בָּרָא. בָּרוּךְ אַתָּה, יְיָ, הַזָּן אֶת־הַכֹּל.

Blessed is the Lord our God, Ruler of the universe, whose goodness sustains the world. The God of grace, love, and compassion is the Source of food for all who live — for God's love is everlasting. Through God's great goodness we do not lack and will not ever lack. For God is in the goodness that sustains and nourishes all, providing food enough for every living being. Blessed is the Lord, Source of food for all who live.

• •

נוֹדֶה לְךָ, יְיָ אֱלֹהֵינוּ, עַל שֶׁהוֹצֵאתָנוּ מֵאֶרֶץ מִצְרַיִם,
וּפְדִיתָנוּ מִבֵּית עֲבָדִים, וְעַל תּוֹרָתְךָ שֶׁלִּמַּדְתָּנוּ, וְעַל חֻקֶּיךָ
שֶׁהוֹדַעְתָּנוּ, וְעַל חַיִּים חֵן וָחֶסֶד שֶׁחוֹנַנְתָּנוּ, וְעַל אֲכִילַת
מָזוֹן שָׁאַתָּה זָן וּמְפַרְנֵס אוֹתָנוּ תָּמִיד בְּכָל־יוֹם וּבְכָל־עֵת
וּבְכָל־שָׁעָה.

For leading us out of Egypt, delivering us from the house of bondage, we give thanks to You, Lord our God. And we thank

You for the laws and commandments that You have taught us; for Your gracious gifts of life and steadfast love; and for the food that sustains us each and every day.

On Chanukah or Purim, continue on page 14 or 16.

וְעַל הַכֹּל, יְיָ אֱלֹהֵינוּ, אֲנַחְנוּ מוֹדִים לָךְ, וּמְבָרְכִים אוֹתָךְ.
יִתְבָּרַךְ שִׁמְךָ בְּפִי כָּל־חַי תָּמִיד לְעוֹלָם וָעֶד, כַּכָּתוּב:
"וְאָכַלְתָּ וְשָׂבָעְתָּ, וּבֵרַכְתָּ אֶת־יְיָ אֱלֹהֶיךָ עַל־הָאָרֶץ הַטֹּבָה
אֲשֶׁר נָתַן־לָךְ."

בָּרוּךְ אַתָּה, יְיָ, עַל־הָאָרֶץ וְעַל־הַמָּזוֹן.

For all these things, O Lord our God, we thank and bless You. Let Your name be blessed continually by every living creature, as it is written: "When you have eaten and are satisfied, then bless the Lord your God, who has given you this good land." Blessed is the Lord, for the land and for the food.

❖ ❖

רַחֵם, יְיָ אֱלֹהֵינוּ, עַל יִשְׂרָאֵל עַמֶּךָ, וְעַל יְרוּשָׁלַיִם עִירֶךָ,
וְעַל צִיּוֹן מִשְׁכַּן כְּבוֹדֶךָ, וְעַל מַלְכוּת בֵּית דָּוִד מְשִׁיחֶךָ.
אֱלֹהֵינוּ אָבִינוּ, רְעֵנוּ זוּנֵנוּ, פַּרְנְסֵנוּ וְכַלְכְּלֵנוּ וְהַרְוִיחֵנוּ,
וְהַרְוַח לָנוּ, יְיָ אֱלֹהֵינוּ, מְהֵרָה מִכָּל צָרוֹתֵינוּ. וְנָא, אַל
תַּצְרִיכֵנוּ, יְיָ אֱלֹהֵינוּ, לֹא לִידֵי מַתְּנַת בָּשָׂר וָדָם וְלֹא לִידֵי
הַלְוָאָתָם, כִּי אִם לְיָדְךָ הַמְּלֵאָה הַפְּתוּחָה, הַגְּדוּשָׁה
וְהָרְחָבָה, שֶׁלֹּא נֵבוֹשׁ וְלֹא נִכָּלֵם לְעוֹלָם וָעֶד.

Lord our God, show compassion for Israel Your people, Jerusalem Your city, Zion, the ancient dwelling-place of Your glory, and the kingdom of Your anointed David's royal line. O God, Source of our being, guide and sustain us in all our habitations, and be a help to us in all our troubles. Lord our God, let us not be dependent on mortals and on their gifts; teach us, rather, O Holy One, to rely on Your open and generous bounty: then we shall never be put to shame.

❖

ON SHABBAT

רְצֵה וְהַחֲלִיצֵנוּ, יְיָ אֱלֹהֵינוּ, בְּמִצְוֹתֶיךָ וּבְמִצְוַת יוֹם הַשְּׁבִיעִי הַשַּׁבָּת הַגָּדוֹל וְהַקָּדוֹשׁ הַזֶּה, כִּי יוֹם זֶה גָּדוֹל וְקָדוֹשׁ הוּא לְפָנֶיךָ, לִשְׁבָּת־בּוֹ וְלָנְוּחַ בּוֹ בְּאַהֲבָה כְּמִצְוַת רְצוֹנֶךָ. וּבִרְצוֹנְךָ הָנַח לָנוּ, יְיָ אֱלֹהֵינוּ, שֶׁלֹּא תְהֵא צָרָה וְיָגוֹן וַאֲנָחָה בְּיוֹם מְנוּחָתֵנוּ. וְהַרְאֵנוּ, יְיָ אֱלֹהֵינוּ, בְּנֶחָמַת צִיּוֹן עִירֶךָ וּבְבִנְיַן יְרוּשָׁלַיִם עִיר קָדְשֶׁךָ, כִּי אַתָּה הוּא בַּעַל הַיְשׁוּעוֹת וּבַעַל הַנֶּחָמוֹת.

O Lord our God, strengthen our resolve to obey Your Mitzvot, and especially the Mitzvah of the Seventh Day, the great and holy Sabbath, the day of rest and serenity, of loving reflection upon Your will. May this, our day of rest, be free of sorrow, anguish, and pain; and grant — for You are Lord of deliverance and Master of consolation — that we may see that redemption of which the consolation of Zion is a token, that deliverance of which the renewal of Jerusalem, Your holy city, is a symbol.

◆

ON ROSH CHODESH AND YOM TOV

אֱלֹהֵינוּ וֵאלֹהֵי אֲבוֹתֵינוּ, יַעֲלֶה וְיָבֹא וְיִזָּכֵר זִכְרוֹנֵנוּ וְזִכְרוֹן כָּל־עַמְּךָ בֵּית יִשְׂרָאֵל לְפָנֶיךָ, לְטוֹבָה לְחֵן לְחֶסֶד וּלְרַחֲמִים, לְחַיִּים וּלְשָׁלוֹם בְּיוֹם

Our God and God of all ages, be mindful of Your people Israel on this

First day of the new month,	רֹאשׁ הַחֹדֶשׁ הַזֶּה.
Day of Remembrance,	הַזִּכָּרוֹן הַזֶּה.
Feast of Sukkot,	חַג הַסֻּכּוֹת הַזֶּה.
Feast of Atzeret-Simchat Torah,	הַשְּׁמִינִי חַג הָעֲצֶרֶת הַזֶּה.
Feast of Pesach,	חַג הַמַּצּוֹת הַזֶּה.
Day of Independence,	הָעַצְמָאוּת הַזֶּה.
Feast of Shavuot,	חַג הַשָּׁבֻעוֹת הַזֶּה.

and renew in us love and compassion, goodness, life, and peace.

זָכְרֵנוּ, יְיָ אֱלֹהֵינוּ, בּוֹ לְטוֹבָה. אָמֵן.

This day remember us for well-being. Amen.

וּפָקְדֵנוּ בוֹ לִבְרָכָה. אָמֵן.

This day bless us with Your nearness. Amen.

וְהוֹשִׁיעֵנוּ בוֹ לְחַיִּים. אָמֵן.

This day help us to a fuller life. Amen.

וּבִדְבַר יְשׁוּעָה וְרַחֲמִים חוּס וְחָנֵּנוּ, וְרַחֵם עָלֵינוּ וְהוֹשִׁיעֵנוּ.

Compassionate and redeeming God, show us love and grace,
and be our Help.

◆

ON ALL OCCASIONS

וּבְנֵה יְרוּשָׁלַיִם עִיר הַקֹּדֶשׁ בִּמְהֵרָה בְיָמֵינוּ. בָּרוּךְ אַתָּה, יְיָ,
בּוֹנֵה בְרַחֲמָיו יְרוּשָׁלָיִם. אָמֵן.

O let Jerusalem, the holy city, be renewed in our time. Blessed
is the Lord, by whose compassion we will see Jerusalem renewed and at peace. Amen.

◆ ◆

בָּרוּךְ אַתָּה, יְיָ אֱלֹהֵינוּ, מֶלֶךְ הָעוֹלָם, הָאֵל אָבִינוּ מַלְכֵּנוּ,
אַדִּירֵנוּ, בּוֹרְאֵנוּ, גֹּאֲלֵנוּ, יוֹצְרֵנוּ, קְדוֹשֵׁנוּ קְדוֹשׁ יַעֲקֹב,
רוֹעֵנוּ רוֹעֵה יִשְׂרָאֵל, הַמֶּלֶךְ הַטּוֹב וְהַמֵּטִיב לַכֹּל, שֶׁבְּכָל־
יוֹם וָיוֹם הוּא הֵטִיב, הוּא מֵטִיב, הוּא יֵיטִיב לָנוּ. הוּא גְמָלָנוּ,
הוּא גוֹמְלֵנוּ, הוּא יִגְמְלֵנוּ לָעַד, לְחֵן לְחֶסֶד וּלְרַחֲמִים
וּלְרֶוַח, הַצָּלָה וְהַצְלָחָה, בְּרָכָה וִישׁוּעָה, נֶחָמָה, פַּרְנָסָה
וְכַלְכָּלָה וְרַחֲמִים וְחַיִּים וְשָׁלוֹם וְכָל־טוֹב, וּמִכָּל־טוֹב אַל־
יְחַסְּרֵנוּ.

Blessed is the Lord our God, our divine Maker and King, mighty
Creator and Redeemer, the Holy One of Jacob, the Shepherd of
Israel, Source of goodness for all the world. Show us kindness
and love in the future as in the past. Grant us grace and compassion, freedom and deliverance, prosperity and blessing, life
and peace; withhold no good thing from us.

הָרַחֲמָן, הוּא יִמְלוֹךְ עָלֵינוּ לְעוֹלָם וָעֶד.

May the Merciful One reign over us for ever.

הָרַחֲמָן, הוּא יִתְבָּרַךְ בַּשָּׁמַיִם וּבָאָרֶץ.

May the Merciful One be blessed in heaven and earth.

הָרַחֲמָן, הוּא יִשְׁתַּבַּח לְדוֹר דּוֹרִים, וְיִתְפָּאַר בָּנוּ לָנֶצַח
נְצָחִים, וְיִתְהַדַּר בָּנוּ לָעַד וּלְעוֹלְמֵי עוֹלָמִים.

Let all generations extol the Merciful One; let us proclaim
God's glory and majesty for all time.

הָרַחֲמָן, הוּא יְפַרְנְסֵנוּ בְּכָבוֹד.

May the Merciful One help us to sustain ourselves in honor.

הָרַחֲמָן, הוּא יִשְׁבּוֹר עֻלֵנוּ מֵעַל צַוָּארֵנוּ.

May the Merciful One break the yoke of exile and oppression
from off our necks and the necks of all the living.

הָרַחֲמָן, הוּא יִשְׁלַח בְּרָכָה מְרֻבָּה בַּבַּיִת הַזֶּה, וְעַל שֻׁלְחָן
זֶה שֶׁאָכַלְנוּ עָלָיו.

May the Merciful One bless this house, and this table at which
we have eaten.

הָרַחֲמָן, הוּא יִשְׁלַח לָנוּ אֶת אֵלִיָּהוּ הַנָּבִיא, זָכוּר לַטּוֹב,
וִיבַשֶּׂר-לָנוּ בְּשׂוֹרוֹת טוֹבוֹת, יְשׁוּעוֹת וְנֶחָמוֹת.

May the Merciful One send us Elijah the prophet (whose memory be for good) with good tidings of deliverance and comfort.

הָרַחֲמָן, הוּא יְבָרֵךְ אוֹתָנוּ וְאֶת־כָּל־אֲשֶׁר לָנוּ, כְּמוֹ שֶׁנִּתְבָּרְכוּ
אֲבוֹתֵינוּ אַבְרָהָם, יִצְחָק וְיַעֲקֹב בַּכֹּל מִכֹּל כֹּל, כֵּן יְבָרֵךְ
אוֹתָנוּ כֻּלָּנוּ יַחַד בִּבְרָכָה שְׁלֵמָה, וְנֹאמַר: אָמֵן.

Merciful God, bless us and all our dear ones; as You blessed our
ancestors, Abraham, Isaac, and Jacob, so may You abundantly
bless us, one and all; and let us say: Amen.

בַּמָּרוֹם יְלַמְּדוּ עָלֵינוּ זְכוּת שֶׁתְּהֵא לְמִשְׁמֶרֶת שָׁלוֹם;
וְנִשָּׂא בְרָכָה מֵאֵת יְיָ, וּצְדָקָה מֵאֱלֹהֵי יִשְׁעֵנוּ, וְנִמְצָא־חֵן
וְשֵׂכֶל טוֹב בְּעֵינֵי אֱלֹהִים וְאָדָם.

Let our merit be rehearsed on high and lead to enduring peace;
may we receive blessings from the Lord, and justice from God
our Help, and may divine and human grace and favor descend
upon us all.

ON SHABBAT

הָרַחֲמָן, הוּא יַנְחִילֵנוּ יוֹם שֶׁכֻּלּוֹ שַׁבָּת.

May the Merciful One help us to see the coming of a time that
is all Shabbat.

ON ROSH CHODESH

הָרַחֲמָן, הוּא יְחַדֵּשׁ עָלֵינוּ אֶת־הַחֹדֶשׁ הַזֶּה לְטוֹבָה וְלִבְרָכָה.

May the Merciful One bring us a month of renewed good and
blessing.

ON YOM TOV

הָרַחֲמָן, הוּא יַנְחִילֵנוּ יוֹם שֶׁכֻּלּוֹ טוֹב.

May the Merciful One help us to see the coming of a time of
infinite good.

ON YOM HA-ATSMA-UT

הָרַחֲמָן, הוּא יָאִיר אוֹר חָדָשׁ עַל צִיּוֹן וְנִזְכֶּה כֻלָּנוּ לְאוֹרוֹ.

May the Merciful One shed radiance upon Zion, and may it be
our blessing to see its splendor.

ON ROSH HASHANAH

הָרַחֲמָן, הוּא יְחַדֵּשׁ עָלֵינוּ אֶת־הַשָּׁנָה הַזֹּאת לְטוֹבָה וְלִבְרָכָה.

May the Merciful One bring us a year of renewed good and
blessing.

ON ALL OCCASIONS

הָרַחֲמָן, הוּא יְזַכֵּנוּ לִימוֹת הַמָּשִׁיחַ וּלְחַיֵּי הָעוֹלָם הַבָּא.

May the Merciful One find us worthy of witnessing the time
of redemption and of attaining eternal life.

◆ ◆

Any or all of the following may be added here.

הָרַחֲמָן, הוּא קֶרֶן לְעַמּוֹ יָרִים.

Merciful One: give strength to Your people.

הָרַחֲמָן, הוּא יִשְׁלַח בְּרָכָה וְהַצְלָחָה בְּכָל־מַעֲשֵׂי יָדֵינוּ.

Merciful One: bless and prosper the work of our hands.

הָרַחֲמָן, הוּא יִרְפָּאֵנוּ רְפוּאָה שְׁלֵמָה, רְפוּאַת הַנֶּפֶשׁ וּרְפוּאַת
הַגּוּף.

Merciful One: grant us perfect healing of body and spirit.

הָרַחֲמָן, הוּא יִפְרֹשׂ עָלֵינוּ סֻכַּת שְׁלוֹמוֹ.

Merciful One: spread over us the shelter of Your peace.

הָרַחֲמָן, הוּא יִטַּע תּוֹרָתוֹ וְאַהֲבָתוֹ בְּלִבֵּנוּ וְיָאִיר עֵינֵינוּ
בִּמְאוֹר תּוֹרָתוֹ.

Merciful One: implant Your Teaching and Your love in our
hearts and illumine our eyes with the light of Your Torah.

הָרַחֲמָן, הוּא יְמַלֵּא מִשְׁאֲלוֹת לִבֵּנוּ לְטוֹבָה.

Merciful One: fulfill for good the desires of our hearts.

◆ ◆

13

עֹשֶׂה שָׁלוֹם בִּמְרוֹמָיו, הוּא יַעֲשֶׂה שָׁלוֹם עָלֵינוּ, וְעַל־כָּל־
יִשְׂרָאֵל, וְאִמְרוּ: אָמֵן.

May He who causes peace to reign in His high heavens, let
peace descend on us, on all Israel, and all the world.

יְראוּ אֶת יְיָ, קְדֹשָׁיו, כִּי אֵין מַחְסוֹר לִירֵאָיו. כְּפִירִים רָשׁוּ
וְרָעֵבוּ, וְדֹרְשֵׁי יְיָ לֹא יַחְסְרוּ כָל טוֹב. הוֹדוּ לַיְיָ כִּי טוֹב, כִּי
לְעוֹלָם חַסְדּוֹ. פּוֹתֵחַ אֶת יָדֶךָ, וּמַשְׂבִּיעַ לְכָל חַי רָצוֹן.
בָּרוּךְ הַגֶּבֶר אֲשֶׁר יִבְטַח בַּיְיָ, וְהָיָה יְיָ מִבְטַחוֹ. נַעַר הָיִיתִי
גַּם זָקַנְתִּי, וְלֹא רָאִיתִי צַדִּיק נֶעֱזָב, וְזַרְעוֹ מְבַקֶּשׁ־לָחֶם.

יְיָ עֹז לְעַמּוֹ יִתֵּן, יְיָ יְבָרֵךְ אֶת־עַמּוֹ בַשָּׁלוֹם.

Revere the Lord, you who would be holy, for those who revere
God suffer no want. Lions may go hungry, but those who seek
the Lord have all that is good. Give thanks to the Lord, who is
good, whose love is everlasting. You open Your hand and show
favor to every living being. Blessed is the one who trusts in
the Lord, whose trust the Lord is. I have been young and now
I am old; yet never have I seen the righteous so forsaken that
their descendants must beg for bread.

The Lord give strength unto His people, the Lord bless His
people with peace.

✦ ✦

ON CHANUKAH

עַל הַנִּסִּים וְעַל הַפֻּרְקָן, וְעַל הַגְּבוּרוֹת וְעַל הַתְּשׁוּעוֹת, וְעַל
הַמִּלְחָמוֹת, שֶׁעָשִׂיתָ לַאֲבוֹתֵינוּ בַּיָּמִים הָהֵם בַּזְּמַן הַזֶּה.

בִּימֵי מַתִּתְיָהוּ בֶּן־יוֹחָנָן כֹּהֵן גָּדוֹל, חַשְׁמוֹנַי וּבָנָיו, כְּשֶׁעָמְדָה
מַלְכוּת יָוָן הָרְשָׁעָה עַל־עַמְּךָ יִשְׂרָאֵל לְהַשְׁכִּיחָם תּוֹרָתֶךָ,
וּלְהַעֲבִירָם מֵחֻקֵּי רְצוֹנֶךָ.

וְאַתָּה בְּרַחֲמֶֽיךָ הָרַבִּים עָמַֽדְתָּ לָהֶם בְּעֵת צָרָתָם. רַֽבְתָּ
אֶת־רִיבָם, דַּֽנְתָּ אֶת־דִּינָם, מָסַֽרְתָּ גִבּוֹרִים בְּיַד חַלָּשִׁים,
וְרַבִּים בְּיַד מְעַטִּים, וּטְמֵאִים בְּיַד טְהוֹרִים, וּרְשָׁעִים בְּיַד
צַדִּיקִים, וְזֵדִים בְּיַד עוֹסְקֵי תוֹרָתֶֽךָ.

וּלְךָ עָשִֽׂיתָ שֵׁם גָּדוֹל וְקָדוֹשׁ בְּעוֹלָמֶֽךָ, וּלְעַמְּךָ יִשְׂרָאֵל עָשִֽׂיתָ
תְּשׁוּעָה גְדוֹלָה וּפֻרְקָן כְּהַיּוֹם הַזֶּה.

וְאַחַר כֵּן בָּֽאוּ בָנֶֽיךָ לִדְבִיר בֵּיתֶֽךָ, וּפִנּוּ אֶת־הֵיכָלֶֽךָ, וְטִהֲרוּ
אֶת־מִקְדָּשֶֽׁךָ, וְהִדְלִֽיקוּ נֵרוֹת בְּחַצְרוֹת קָדְשֶֽׁךָ, וְקָבְעוּ שְׁמוֹנַת
יְמֵי חֲנֻכָּה אֵֽלוּ לְהוֹדוֹת וּלְהַלֵּל לְשִׁמְךָ הַגָּדוֹל.

We give thanks for the redeeming wonders and the mighty
deeds by which, at this season, our people was saved in days
of old.

In the days of the Hasmoneans, a tyrant arose against our ancestors, determined to make them forget Your Torah, and to
turn them away from obedience to Your will. But You were
at their side in time of trouble. You gave them strength to
struggle and to triumph, that they might serve You in freedom.

Through the power of Your spirit the weak defeated the strong,
the few prevailed over the many, and the righteous were triumphant.

Then Your children returned to Your house, to purify the
sanctuary and kindle its lights. And they dedicated these days
to give thanks and praise to Your great name.

Continue with ve·al ha·kol, page 8.

◆ ◆

ON PURIM

עַל הַנִּסִּים וְעַל הַפֻּרְקָן, וְעַל הַגְּבוּרוֹת וְעַל הַתְּשׁוּעוֹת, וְעַל הַמִּלְחָמוֹת, שֶׁעָשִׂיתָ לַאֲבוֹתֵינוּ בַּיָּמִים הָהֵם בַּזְּמַן הַזֶּה.

בִּימֵי מָרְדְּכַי וְאֶסְתֵּר בְּשׁוּשַׁן הַבִּירָה, כְּשֶׁעָמַד עֲלֵיהֶם הָמָן הָרָשָׁע, בִּקֵּשׁ לְהַשְׁמִיד לַהֲרוֹג וּלְאַבֵּד אֶת־כָּל־הַיְּהוּדִים, מִנַּעַר וְעַד־זָקֵן, טַף וְנָשִׁים, בְּיוֹם אֶחָד, בִּשְׁלוֹשָׁה עָשָׂר לְחֹדֶשׁ שְׁנֵים־עָשָׂר, הוּא־חֹדֶשׁ אֲדָר, וּשְׁלָלָם לָבוֹז.

וְאַתָּה בְּרַחֲמֶיךָ הָרַבִּים הֵפַרְתָּ אֶת־עֲצָתוֹ, וְקִלְקַלְתָּ אֶת־מַחֲשַׁבְתּוֹ.

We give thanks for the redeeming wonders and the mighty deeds by which, at this season, our people was saved in days of old.

In the days of Mordecai and Esther, the wicked Haman arose in Persia, plotting the destruction of all the Jews. He planned to destroy them in a single day, the thirteenth of Adar, and to permit the plunder of their possessions.

But through Your great mercy his plan was thwarted, his scheme frustrated. We therefore thank and bless You, O great and gracious God!

Continue with ve·al ha·kol, page 8.

❖ ❖

Grace after Meals (short form)

Leader:

רַבּוֹתַי נְבָרֵךְ.

Response:

יְהִי שֵׁם יְיָ מְבֹרָךְ מֵעַתָּה וְעַד עוֹלָם.

Leader:

בִּרְשׁוּת מָרָנָן וְרַבָּנָן וְרַבּוֹתַי, נְבָרֵךְ אֱלֹהֵינוּ שֶׁאָכַלְנוּ מִשֶּׁלּוֹ.

Response:

בָּרוּךְ אֱלֹהֵינוּ שֶׁאָכַלְנוּ מִשֶּׁלּוֹ וּבְטוּבוֹ חָיִינוּ.

Together:

בָּרוּךְ אַתָּה, יְיָ אֱלֹהֵינוּ, מֶלֶךְ הָעוֹלָם, הַזָּן אֶת הָעוֹלָם כֻּלּוֹ
בְּטוּבוֹ. בְּחֵן, בְּחֶסֶד וּבְרַחֲמִים הוּא נוֹתֵן לֶחֶם לְכָל בָּשָׂר,
כִּי לְעוֹלָם חַסְדּוֹ. וּבְטוּבוֹ הַגָּדוֹל תָּמִיד לֹא חָסַר לָנוּ, וְאַל
יֶחְסַר לָנוּ מָזוֹן לְעוֹלָם וָעֶד, בַּעֲבוּר שְׁמוֹ הַגָּדוֹל. כִּי הוּא
אֵל זָן וּמְפַרְנֵס לַכֹּל וּמֵטִיב לַכֹּל וּמֵכִין מָזוֹן לְכָל־בְּרִיּוֹתָיו
אֲשֶׁר בָּרָא.
בָּרוּךְ אַתָּה, יְיָ, הַזָּן אֶת־הַכֹּל.
וּבְנֵה יְרוּשָׁלַיִם עִיר הַקֹּדֶשׁ בִּמְהֵרָה בְיָמֵינוּ. בָּרוּךְ אַתָּה,
יְיָ, בּוֹנֶה בְרַחֲמָיו יְרוּשָׁלָיִם. אָמֵן.

On Shabbat

הָרַחֲמָן, הוּא יַנְחִילֵנוּ יוֹם שֶׁכֻּלּוֹ שַׁבָּת.

◆

עֹשֶׂה שָׁלוֹם בִּמְרוֹמָיו, הוּא יַעֲשֶׂה שָׁלוֹם עָלֵינוּ וְעַל־כָּל־
יִשְׂרָאֵל, וְאִמְרוּ אָמֵן.

יְיָ עֹז לְעַמּוֹ יִתֵּן, יְיָ יְבָרֵךְ אֶת־עַמּוֹ בַשָּׁלוֹם.

TRANSLITERATION OF THE GRACE AFTER MEALS (SHORT FORM):

Leader:
Ra·bo·tai ne·va·reich.

Response:
Ye·hi sheim A·do·nai me·vo·rach mei·a·ta ve·ad o·lam!

Leader:
Bi·re·shut ma·ra·nan ve·ra·ba·nan ve·ra·bo·tai, ne·va·reich E·lo·hei·nu she·a·chal·nu mi·she·lo.

Response:
Ba·ruch E·lo·hei·nu she·a·chal·nu mi·she·lo u·ve·tu·vo cha·yi·nu.

Together:
Ba·ruch a·ta, A·do·nai E·lo·hei·nu, me·lech ha·o·lam, ha·zan et ha·o·lam ku·lo be·tu·vo. Be·chein, be·che·sed, u·ve·ra·cha·mim hu no·tein le·chem le·chol ba·sar, ki le·o·lam chas·do. U·ve·tu·vo ha·ga·dol ta·mid lo cha·sar la·nu, ve·al yech·sar la·nu ma·zon le·o·lam va·ed, ba·a·vur she·mo ha·ga·dol. Ki hu Eil zan u·me·far·neis la·kol u·mei·tiv la·kol u·mei·chin ma·zon le·chol be·ri·yo·tav a·sher ba·ra.
Ba·ruch a·ta, A·do·nai, ha·zan et ha·kol.

✦

U·ve·nei Ye·ru·sha·la·yim ir ha·ko·desh bi·me·hei·ra be·ya·mei·nu.
Ba·ruch a·ta, A·do·nai, bo·neh be·ra·cha·mav Ye·ru·sha·la·yim, A·mein·

✦

ON SHABBAT

Ha·ra·cha·man, hu yan·chi·lei·nu yom she·ku·lo sha·bat.

✦

O·seh sha·lom bi·me·ro·mav, hu ya·a·seh sha·lom a·lei·nu, ve·al kol Yis·ra·eil, ve·i·me·ru, A·mein.

✦

A·do·nai oz le·a·mo yi·tein, A·do·nai ye·va·reich et a·mo va·sha·lom.

Blessings in Praise of Life and Its Creator

Over bread

בָּרוּךְ אַתָּה, יְיָ אֱלֹהֵינוּ, מֶלֶךְ הָעוֹלָם, הַמּוֹצִיא לֶחֶם מִן הָאָרֶץ.

Blessed is the Lord our God, Ruler of the universe, who causes bread to come forth from the earth.

Over wine

בָּרוּךְ אַתָּה, יְיָ אֱלֹהֵינוּ, מֶלֶךְ הָעוֹלָם, בּוֹרֵא פְּרִי הַגָּפֶן.

Blessed is the Lord our God, Ruler of the universe, Creator of the fruit of the vine.

Over pastry

בָּרוּךְ אַתָּה, יְיָ אֱלֹהֵינוּ, מֶלֶךְ הָעוֹלָם, בּוֹרֵא מִינֵי מְזוֹנוֹת.

Blessed is the Lord our God, Ruler of the universe, Creator of many kinds of food.

Over fruits that grow on trees

בָּרוּךְ אַתָּה, יְיָ אֱלֹהֵינוּ, מֶלֶךְ הָעוֹלָם, בּוֹרֵא פְּרִי הָעֵץ.

Blessed is the Lord our God, Ruler of the universe, Creator of the fruit of the tree.

Over fruits and vegetables that grow in the soil

בָּרוּךְ אַתָּה, יְיָ אֱלֹהֵינוּ, מֶלֶךְ הָעוֹלָם, בּוֹרֵא פְּרִי הָאֲדָמָה.

Blessed is the Lord our God, Ruler of the universe, Creator of the fruit of the earth.

Over food other than bread, fruits, or vegetables, and over
liquids other than wine

בָּרוּךְ אַתָּה, יְיָ אֱלֹהֵינוּ, מֶלֶךְ הָעוֹלָם, שֶׁהַכֹּל נִהְיָה בִּדְבָרוֹ.

Blessed is the Lord our God, Ruler of the universe, by whose
word all things come into being.

On an occasion of joy

בָּרוּךְ אַתָּה, יְיָ אֱלֹהֵינוּ, מֶלֶךְ הָעוֹלָם, שֶׁהֶחֱיָנוּ וְקִיְּמָנוּ
וְהִגִּיעָנוּ לַזְּמַן הַזֶּה.

Blessed is the Lord our God, Ruler of the universe, for giving
us life, for sustaining us, and for enabling us to reach this
season.

On seeing lightning or other natural wonders

בָּרוּךְ אַתָּה, יְיָ אֱלֹהֵינוּ, מֶלֶךְ הָעוֹלָם, עֹשֶׂה מַעֲשֵׂה בְרֵאשִׁית.

Blessed is the Lord our God, Ruler of the universe, the Source
of creative power.

On hearing thunder

בָּרוּךְ אַתָּה, יְיָ אֱלֹהֵינוּ, מֶלֶךְ הָעוֹלָם, שֶׁכֹּחוֹ וּגְבוּרָתוֹ מָלֵא
עוֹלָם.

Blessed is the Lord our God, Ruler of the universe, whose
power and might pervade the world.

On seeing the ocean

בָּרוּךְ אַתָּה, יְיָ אֱלֹהֵינוּ, מֶלֶךְ הָעוֹלָם, שֶׁעָשָׂה אֶת הַיָּם
הַגָּדוֹל.

Blessed is the Lord our God, Ruler of the universe, Maker of
the great sea.

20

On seeing the beauties of nature

בָּרוּךְ אַתָּה, יְיָ אֱלֹהֵינוּ, מֶלֶךְ הָעוֹלָם, שֶׁכְּכָה לוֹ בְּעוֹלָמוֹ.

Blessed is the Lord our God, Ruler of the universe, whose
world is filled with beauty.

On seeing a rainbow

בָּרוּךְ אַתָּה, יְיָ אֱלֹהֵינוּ, מֶלֶךְ הָעוֹלָם, זוֹכֵר הַבְּרִית וְנֶאֱמָן
בִּבְרִיתוֹ וְקַיָם בְּמַאֲמָרוֹ.

Lord our God, Ruler of the universe, You are the Blessed One.
You keep faith with us, and, true to Your word, You remember
Your covenant with creation.

On seeing trees in blossom

בָּרוּךְ אַתָּה, יְיָ אֱלֹהֵינוּ, מֶלֶךְ הָעוֹלָם, שֶׁלֹּא חִסַּר בְּעוֹלָמוֹ
דָּבָר, וּבָרָא בוֹ בְּרִיּוֹת טוֹבוֹת וְאִילָנוֹת טוֹבִים לְהַנּוֹת בָּהֶם
בְּנֵי אָדָם.

Lord our God, Ruler of the universe, You are the Blessed One.
Your world lacks nothing needful; You have fashioned goodly
creatures and lovely trees that enchant the heart.

On seeing a great Torah scholar

בָּרוּךְ אַתָּה, יְיָ אֱלֹהֵינוּ, מֶלֶךְ הָעוֹלָם, שֶׁחָלַק מֵחָכְמָתוֹ
לִירֵאָיו.

Lord our God, Ruler of the universe, we bless You, for You
share Your wisdom with those who revere You.

On seeing a great scholar

בָּרוּךְ אַתָּה, יְיָ אֱלֹהֵינוּ, מֶלֶךְ הָעוֹלָם, שֶׁנָּתַן מֵחָכְמָתוֹ לְבָשָׂר
וָדָם.

Lord our God, Ruler of the universe, we bless You, for You
give of Your wisdom to flesh and blood.

❖ ❖

*Upon recovery from serious illness or upon escape
from danger*

לְדֹ־אֶזְבַּח זֶבַח תּוֹדָה, וּבְשֵׁם יְיָ אֶקְרָא.

I offer You my tribute of thanksgiving, and glorify Your name,
O Lord!

בָּרוּךְ אַתָּה, יְיָ אֱלֹהֵינוּ, מֶלֶךְ הָעוֹלָם, שֶׁגְּמָלַנִי כָּל־טוֹב.

Blessed is the Lord our God, Ruler of the universe, who bestows great goodness upon me.

בָּרוּךְ אַתָּה, יְיָ אֱלֹהֵינוּ, מֶלֶךְ הָעוֹלָם, שֶׁהֶחֱיָנוּ וְקִיְּמָנוּ וְהִגִּיעָנוּ
לַזְּמַן הַזֶּה.

Blessed is the Lord our God, Ruler of the universe, for giving us
life, for sustaining us, and for enabling us to reach this day.

*If this prayer is recited at a synagogue service, the
congregation responds*

מִי שֶׁגְּמָלְךָ כָּל־טוֹב, הוּא יִגְמָלְךָ כָּל־טוֹב סֶלָה.

May the One who has been gracious to you continue to favor
you with all that is good.

◆ ◆

On hearing of the death of a dear one

בָּרוּךְ אַתָּה, יְיָ אֱלֹהֵינוּ, מֶלֶךְ הָעוֹלָם, דַּיַּן הָאֱמֶת.

Blessed is the Lord our God, Ruler of the universe, the righteous Judge.

◆ ◆

On hearing good tidings

בָּרוּךְ אַתָּה, יְיָ אֱלֹהֵינוּ, מֶלֶךְ הָעוֹלָם, הַטּוֹב וְהַמֵּטִיב.

Blessed is the Lord our God, Ruler of the universe, the Good
One, the Source of good.

◆ ◆

Before a Journey

"יְיָ יִשְׁמָר צֵאתְךָ וּבוֹאֶךָ מֵעַתָּה וְעַד עוֹלָם."

"The Lord shall guard your coming and your going from this time forth and for ever."

Lord of the universe, the whole world is full of Your glory. Wherever I go, You are near to me. "If I take up the wings of the morning, and dwell on the ocean's farthest shore, even there Your hand will lead me, Your right hand will hold me."

You have always been a light to my path. Now that I begin a new journey, I turn to You in confidence and trust. Protect me from the perils of the way. May I go forth in health and safely reach my destination. May this journey not be in vain; let its purpose be fulfilled; let me return in contentment to my dear ones. Then shall I know Your blessing in all my travels. Amen.

For a Pilgrimage to Israel

From Psalm 122

שָׂמַחְתִּי בְּאֹמְרִים לִי: בֵּית יְיָ נֵלֵךְ.
עֹמְדוֹת הָיוּ רַגְלֵינוּ בִּשְׁעָרַיִךְ, יְרוּשָׁלָםִ!

I rejoiced when they said to me: Let us go up to the House of
the Lord.

Now we stand within your gates, O Jerusalem!

יְרוּשָׁלַםִ הַבְּנוּיָה! כְּעִיר שֶׁחֻבְּרָה־לָּהּ יַחְדָּו!
יְרוּשָׁלַםִ, הַבְּנוּיָה כְּעִיר שֶׁחֻבְּרָה־לָּהּ יַחְדָּו.

Jerusalem restored! The city united and whole!

Jerusalem, built to be a city where people come together as one.

שַׁאֲלוּ שְׁלוֹם יְרוּשָׁלָםִ: יִשְׁלָיוּ אֹהֲבָיִךְ!
יְהִי־שָׁלוֹם בְּחֵילֵךְ, שַׁלְוָה בְּאַרְמְנוֹתָיִךְ.

Pray for the peace of Jerusalem: may those who love you
prosper!

Let there be peace in your homes, safety within your borders.

לְמַעַן אַחַי וְרֵעָי אֲדַבְּרָה־נָּא שָׁלוֹם בָּךְ.
לְמַעַן בֵּית יְיָ אֱלֹהֵינוּ, אֲבַקְשָׁה טוֹב לָךְ.

For the sake of my people, my friends, I pray you find peace.

For the sake of the house of the Lord our God, I will seek your
good.

❖ ❖

יְבָרֶכְנוּ יְיָ מִצִּיּוֹן, וּרְאֵה בְּטוּב יְרוּשָׁלָםִ.

May the Lord bless us from Zion, and let us see the good of
Jerusalem.

שָׁלוֹם עַל יִשְׂרָאֵל.

Peace be upon Israel.

❖ ❖

24

For the New Moon

When the New Moon is first visible

From Psalm 148

הַלְלוּיָהּ! הַלְלוּ אֶת־יְיָ מִן־הַשָּׁמַיִם, הַלְלוּהוּ בַּמְּרוֹמִים!
הַלְלוּהוּ שֶׁמֶשׁ וְיָרֵחַ!
הַלְלוּהוּ כָּל־כּוֹכְבֵי אוֹר!
הַלְלוּ אֶת־יְיָ מִן־הָאָרֶץ.

Praise the Lord! Praise God in the high heavens, give praise
in deep space!

Give praise, O sun and moon!
Give praise, you shining stars!
Let the earth resound with God's praise.

תַּנִּינִים וְכָל־תְּהֹמוֹת, אֵשׁ וּבָרָד, שֶׁלֶג וְקִיטוֹר, רוּחַ, סְעָרָה,
עֹשָׂה דְבָרוֹ.
הֶהָרִים וְכָל־גְּבָעוֹת, עֵץ פְּרִי וְכָל־אֲרָזִים.

Teeming oceans, fire and hail, snow and mist, storm and wind,
obeying God's will;

Mountains and hills, fruit-trees and cedars;

הַחַיָּה וְכָל־בְּהֵמָה, רֶמֶשׂ וְצִפּוֹר כָּנָף.
מַלְכֵי־אֶרֶץ וְכָל־לְאֻמִּים, שָׂרִים וְכָל־שֹׁפְטֵי אָרֶץ.

Wild beasts and cattle, reptiles and birds;

Kings of all nations, princes and rulers;

בַּחוּרִים וְגַם בְּתוּלוֹת, זְקֵנִים עִם־נְעָרִים:
יְהַלְלוּ אֶת־שֵׁם יְיָ,

Women and men, young and old:

Let all give praise to the Lord,

25

כִּי־נִשְׂגָּב שְׁמוֹ לְבַדּוֹ,
הוֹדוֹ עַל־אֶרֶץ וְשָׁמָיִם.

Whose name alone is exalted,
Whose glory covers earth and sky.

כִּי הוּא צִוָּה וְנִבְרָאוּ, וַיַּעֲמִידֵם לָעַד לְעוֹלָם.
הַלְלוּיָהּ!

For the divine command caused them to be; God sustains them
by law for ever.

Halleluyah! Praise the Lord!

∴

בָּרוּךְ אַתָּה, יְיָ אֱלֹהֵינוּ, מֶלֶךְ הָעוֹלָם, אֲשֶׁר בְּמַאֲמָרוֹ בָּרָא
שְׁחָקִים, וּבְרוּחַ פִּיו כָּל־צְבָאָם.

Blessed is the Lord our God, Ruler of the universe, at whose
word the heavens were made, at whose command the galaxies
were born.

חֹק וּזְמַן נָתַן לָהֶם, שֶׁלֹּא יְשַׁנּוּ אֶת־תַּפְקִידָם. שָׂשִׂים וּשְׂמֵחִים
לַעֲשׂוֹת רְצוֹן קוֹנָם, פּוֹעֵל אֱמֶת, שֶׁפְּעֻלָּתוֹ אֱמֶת.

Their cycles are fixed by God's law, their orbits can never be
altered. They delight to do their Maker's will, that faithful
Creator whose deeds endure.

וְלַלְּבָנָה אָמַר שֶׁתִּתְחַדֵּשׁ; עֲטֶרֶת תִּפְאֶרֶת לַעֲמוּסֵי בֶטֶן,
שֶׁהֵם עֲתִידִים לְהִתְחַדֵּשׁ כְּמוֹתָהּ, וּלְפָאֵר לְיוֹצְרָם עַל־שֵׁם
כְּבוֹד מַלְכוּתוֹ.

To the moon You say: Renew yourself; to us You are a crown
of glory, sustaining us from the day of birth.

Like the moon, may we be renewed in time to come, to honor
You, our Maker, and Your glorious kingdom.

בָּרוּךְ אַתָּה, יְיָ, מְחַדֵּשׁ חֳדָשִׁים.

Blessed is the Lord, who renews the months.

26

SABBATHS, FESTIVALS,
HOLY DAYS

Welcoming Shabbat

*It is customary, before the beginning of Shabbat, for each member
of the household to contribute to some worthy cause.*

"Happy are those who consider the poor."

Eternal God, we hereby vow to fulfill the Mitzvah of Tzedakah
as we begin this day of holiness. We shall not forget the words
of Your prophet, who called us to share our bread with the
hungry, to clothe the naked, and never to hide ourselves from
our own kin.

*May we, together with the whole House of Israel, be mindful
of the needs of others, sharing with them the fruits of our labor,
helping to sustain them in body and soul. For all, may Your
promise be fulfilled: "Then shall your light blaze forth like the
dawn, and your wounds shall quickly heal; your righteousness
shall walk before you, the glory of the Lord shall follow you."*

◆ ◆

שָׁלוֹם עֲלֵיכֶם, מַלְאֲכֵי הַשָּׁרֵת, מַלְאֲכֵי עֶלְיוֹן,
מִמֶּלֶךְ מַלְכֵי הַמְּלָכִים, הַקָּדוֹשׁ בָּרוּךְ הוּא.

Peace be to you, O ministering angels, messengers of the Most
High, the supreme King of kings, the Holy One, blessed is He.

בּוֹאֲכֶם לְשָׁלוֹם, מַלְאֲכֵי הַשָּׁלוֹם, מַלְאֲכֵי עֶלְיוֹן,
מִמֶּלֶךְ מַלְכֵי הַמְּלָכִים, הַקָּדוֹשׁ בָּרוּךְ הוּא.

Enter in peace, O messengers of peace, messengers of the Most
High, the supreme King of kings, the Holy One, blessed is He.

בָּרְכוּנִי לְשָׁלוֹם, מַלְאֲכֵי הַשָּׁלוֹם, מַלְאֲכֵי עֶלְיוֹן,
מִמֶּלֶךְ מַלְכֵי הַמְּלָכִים, הַקָּדוֹשׁ בָּרוּךְ הוּא.

Bless me with peace, O messengers of peace, messengers of the
Most High, the supreme King of kings, the Holy One, blessed is He.

צֵאתְכֶם לְשָׁלוֹם, מַלְאֲכֵי הַשָּׁלוֹם, מַלְאֲכֵי עֶלְיוֹן,
מִמֶּלֶךְ מַלְכֵי הַמְּלָכִים, הַקָּדוֹשׁ בָּרוּךְ הוּא.

Depart in peace, O messengers of peace, messengers of the
Most High, the supreme King of kings, the Holy One, blessed is He.

For transliteration, see page 36.

◆ ◆

הדלקת הנרות

As these Shabbat candles give light to all who behold them,
so may we, by our lives, give light to all who behold us.

As their brightness reminds us of the generations of Israel who
have kindled light, so may we, in our own day, be among
those who kindle light.

◆ ◆

בָּרוּךְ אַתָּה, יְיָ אֱלֹהֵינוּ, מֶלֶךְ הָעוֹלָם,
אֲשֶׁר קִדְּשָׁנוּ בְּמִצְוֹתָיו וְצִוָּנוּ לְהַדְלִיק נֵר שֶׁל שַׁבָּת.

Blessed is the Lord our God. Ruler of the universe, by whose
Mitzvot we are hallowed, who commands us to kindle the
lights of Shabbat.

May we be blessed with Shabbat joy.
May we be blessed with Shabbat peace.
May we be blessed with Shabbat light.

◆ ◆

We thank You, O God, for the many generations of our people
who have hallowed the Sabbath. Their faith and wisdom kept
our people alive, so that we, their children, can celebrate this
Sabbath day in our home. Blessed is the home in which the
hearts of the children are turned to the parents, and the hearts

of the parents to the children. Blessed is the home filled with light and gladness, the spirit of Shabbat.

We give thanks, O God, for family and home. May it be warm with love and companionship. Here may we always find rest from the day's work, and refuge from cares; may our joys be deepened and our griefs softened by the love we give and receive.

◆ ◆

The following may be read in praise of a wife or mother

From Proverbs 31

A woman of valor—seek her out,
for she is to be valued above rubies.
Her husband trusts her,
and they cannot fail to prosper.
All the days of her life
she is good to him.
She opens her hands to those in need
and offers her help to the poor.
Adorned with strength and dignity,
she looks to the future with cheerful trust.
Her speech is wise,
and the law of kindness is on her lips.
Her children rise up to call her blessed,
her husband likewise praises her:
'Many women have done well,
but you surpass them all.'
Charm is deceptive and beauty short-lived,
but a woman loyal to God has truly earned praise.
Give her honor for her work;
her life proclaims her praise.

◆ ◆

The following may be read in praise of a husband or father

From Psalm 112

Blessed is the man who reveres the Lord,
who greatly delights in God's commandments!
His descendants will be honored in the land:

the generation of the upright will be blessed.
His household prospers,
and his righteousness endures for ever.
Light dawns in the darkness for the upright;
for the one who is gracious, compassionate, and just.
He is not afraid of evil tidings;
his mind is firm, trusting in the Lord.
His heart is steady, he will not be afraid.
He has distributed freely, he has given to the poor;
his righteousness endures for ever;
his life is exalted in honor.

◆ ◆

The parents bless the children

May God bless you and guide you. Be strong for the truth, charitable
in your words, just and loving in your deeds. A noble heritage has
been entrusted to you; guard it well.

For a boy

For a girl

יְשִׂמְךָ אֱלֹהִים כְּאֶפְרַיִם וְכִמְנַשֶּׁה. יְשִׂמֵךְ אֱלֹהִים כְּשָׂרָה, רִבְקָה,
רָחֵל, וְלֵאָה.

May God inspire you to live in
the tradition of Ephraim and
Menasheh, who carried forward
the life of our people.

May God inspire you to live in the
tradition of Sarah and Rebekah,
Rachel and Leah, who carried forward the life of our people.

יְבָרֶכְךָ יְיָ וְיִשְׁמְרֶךָ,
יָאֵר יְיָ פָּנָיו אֵלֶיךָ וִיחֻנֶּךָּ,
יִשָּׂא יְיָ פָּנָיו אֵלֶיךָ וְיָשֵׂם לְךָ שָׁלוֹם.

The Lord bless you and keep you;
The Lord look kindly upon you and be gracious to you;
The Lord bestow His favor upon you and give you peace. Amen.

◆ ◆

*There might now be a moment of silence, during which all present
think of one another with blessing.*

◆ ◆

32

Kiddush

For the Eve of Shabbat

"Six days shall you labor and do all your work, but the seventh day is consecrated to the Lord your God." With wine, our symbol of joy, we celebrate this day and its holiness. We give thanks for all our blessings, for life and health, for work and rest, for home and love and friendship. And on Shabbat, eternal sign of creation, we rejoice that we are created in the divine image.

◆

For transliteration, see page 58.

וַיְכֻלּוּ הַשָּׁמַיִם וְהָאָרֶץ וְכָל־צְבָאָם. וַיְכַל אֱלֹהִים בַּיּוֹם
הַשְּׁבִיעִי מְלַאכְתּוֹ אֲשֶׁר עָשָׂה; וַיִּשְׁבֹּת בַּיּוֹם הַשְּׁבִיעִי מִכָּל־
מְלַאכְתּוֹ אֲשֶׁר עָשָׂה. וַיְבָרֶךְ אֱלֹהִים אֶת־יוֹם הַשְּׁבִיעִי וַיְקַדֵּשׁ
אֹתוֹ, כִּי בוֹ שָׁבַת מִכָּל־מְלַאכְתּוֹ אֲשֶׁר־בָּרָא אֱלֹהִים לַעֲשׂוֹת.

Now the whole universe — sky, earth, and all their array — was
completed. With the seventh day God ended His work of creation;
on the seventh day He rested, with all His work completed. Then
God blessed the seventh day and called it holy, for with this day He
had completed the work of creation.

◆

בָּרוּךְ אַתָּה, יְיָ אֱלֹהֵינוּ, מֶלֶךְ הָעוֹלָם, בּוֹרֵא פְּרִי הַגָּפֶן.

בָּרוּךְ אַתָּה, יְיָ אֱלֹהֵינוּ, מֶלֶךְ הָעוֹלָם, אֲשֶׁר קִדְּשָׁנוּ בְּמִצְוֹתָיו
וְרָצָה בָנוּ, וְשַׁבַּת קָדְשׁוֹ בְּאַהֲבָה וּבְרָצוֹן הִנְחִילָנוּ, זִכָּרוֹן
לְמַעֲשֵׂה בְרֵאשִׁית. כִּי הוּא יוֹם תְּחִלָּה לְמִקְרָאֵי קֹדֶשׁ, זֵכֶר
לִיצִיאַת מִצְרָיִם. כִּי־בָנוּ בָחַרְתָּ וְאוֹתָנוּ קִדַּשְׁתָּ מִכָּל־הָעַמִּים,

33

וְשַׁבַּת קָדְשְׁךָ בְּאַהֲבָה וּבְרָצוֹן הִנְחַלְתָּנוּ. בָּרוּךְ אַתָּה, יְיָ,
מְקַדֵּשׁ הַשַּׁבָּת.

Blessed is the Lord our God, Ruler of the universe, Creator of the fruit of the vine.

Blessed is the Lord our God, Ruler of the universe, who hallows us with His Mitzvot and takes delight in us. In His love and favor He has made His holy Sabbath our heritage, as a reminder of the work of creation. It is first among our sacred days, and a remembrance of the Exodus from Egypt.

O God, You have chosen us and set us apart from all the peoples, and in love and favor have given us the Sabbath day as a sacred inheritance. Blessed is the Lord, for the Sabbath and its holiness.

✦ ✦

בָּרוּךְ אַתָּה, יְיָ אֱלֹהֵינוּ, מֶלֶךְ הָעוֹלָם, הַמּוֹצִיא לֶחֶם מִן
הָאָרֶץ.

Blessed is the Lord our God, Ruler of the universe, who causes bread to come forth from the earth.

✦ ✦

34

Kiddush

For the Morning of Shabbat

וְשָׁמְרוּ בְנֵי־יִשְׂרָאֵל אֶת־הַשַּׁבָּת,
לַעֲשׂוֹת אֶת־הַשַּׁבָּת לְדֹרֹתָם בְּרִית
עוֹלָם. בֵּינִי וּבֵין בְּנֵי יִשְׂרָאֵל אוֹת
הִיא לְעֹלָם, כִּי שֵׁשֶׁת יָמִים עָשָׂה יְיָ
אֶת־הַשָּׁמַיִם וְאֶת־הָאָרֶץ, וּבַיּוֹם
הַשְּׁבִיעִי שָׁבַת וַיִּנָּפַשׁ.

Ve·sha·me·ru ve·nei Yis·ra·eil et ha·sha·bat,
la·a·sot et ha·sha·bat le·do·ro·tam, be·rit
o·lam. Bei·ni u·vein be·nei Yis·ra·eil ot
hi le·o·lam, ki shei·shet ya·mim a·sa A·do·nai
et ha·sha·ma·yim ve·et ha·a·rets, u·va·yom
ha·she·vi·i sha·vat va·yi·na·fash.

The people of Israel shall keep the Sabbath, observing the Sabbath
in every generation as a convenant for all time. It is a sign for ever
between Me and the people of Israel, for in six days the Eternal
God made heaven and earth, and on the seventh day He rested
from His labors.

עַל־כֵּן בֵּרַךְ יְיָ אֶת־יוֹם הַשַּׁבָּת וַיְקַדְּשֵׁהוּ.

Al kein bei·rach A·do·nai et yom ha·sha·bat va·ye·ka·de·shei·hu.
Therefore the Lord blessed the seventh day and called it holy.

◆ ◆

בָּרוּךְ אַתָּה, יְיָ אֱלֹהֵינוּ, מֶלֶךְ הָעוֹלָם, בּוֹרֵא פְּרִי הַגָּפֶן.

Blessed is the Lord our God, Ruler of the universe, Creator of the
fruit of the vine.

◆ ◆

בָּרוּךְ אַתָּה, יְיָ אֱלֹהֵינוּ, מֶלֶךְ הָעוֹלָם, הַמּוֹצִיא לֶחֶם מִן
הָאָרֶץ.

Blessed is the Lord our God, Ruler of the universe, who causes
bread to come forth from the earth.

35

Songs for Shabbat

Gates of Prayer and the C.C.A.R. Shabbat Manual contain additional songs.

SHALOM ALEICHEM

שלום עליכם

Sha·lom a·lei·chem, mal·a·chei ha·sha·reit, mal·a·chei El·yon,	שָׁלוֹם עֲלֵיכֶם, מַלְאֲכֵי הַשָּׁרֵת, מַלְאֲכֵי עֶלְיוֹן,
mi·me·lech ma·le·chei ha·me·la·chim,	מִמֶּלֶךְ מַלְכֵי הַמְּלָכִים,
ha·ka·dosh ba·ruch Hu.	הַקָּדוֹשׁ בָּרוּךְ הוּא.
Bo·a·chem le·sha·lom, mal·a·chei ha·sha·lom, mal·a·chei El·yon,	בּוֹאֲכֶם לְשָׁלוֹם, מַלְאֲכֵי הַשָּׁלוֹם, מַלְאֲכֵי עֶלְיוֹן,
mi·me·lech ma·le·chei ha·me·la·chim,	מִמֶּלֶךְ מַלְכֵי הַמְּלָכִים,
ha·ka·dosh ba·ruch Hu.	הַקָּדוֹשׁ בָּרוּךְ הוּא.
Ba·re·chu·ni le·sha·lom, mal·a·chei ha·sha·lom, mal·a·chei El·yon,	בָּרְכוּנִי לְשָׁלוֹם, מַלְאֲכֵי הַשָּׁלוֹם, מַלְאֲכֵי עֶלְיוֹן,
mi·me·lech ma·le·chei ha·me·la·chim,	מִמֶּלֶךְ מַלְכֵי הַמְּלָכִים,
ha·ka·dosh ba·ruch Hu.	הַקָּדוֹשׁ בָּרוּךְ הוּא.
Tsei·te·chem le·sha·lom, mal·a·chei ha·sha·lom, mal·a·chei El·yon,	צֵאתְכֶם לְשָׁלוֹם, מַלְאֲכֵי הַשָּׁלוֹם, מַלְאֲכֵי עֶלְיוֹן,
mi·me·lech ma·le·chei ha·me·la·chim,	מִמֶּלֶךְ מַלְכֵי הַמְּלָכִים,
ha·ka·dosh ba·ruch Hu.	הַקָּדוֹשׁ בָּרוּךְ הוּא.

The translation of Shalom Aleichem is on page 29.

◆

COME, O HOLY SABBATH EVENING

Come, O holy Sabbath evening,
Crown our toil with well earned rest;
Bring us hallowed hours of gladness,
Day of days beloved and blest.

Weave your mystic spell around us
With the glow of Sabbath light:

36

As we read the ancient wisdom,
Learn its laws of truth and right.

Come, O holy Sabbath spirit,
Radiant shine from every eye;
Lending us your benediction,
Filling every heart with joy.

◆

KI ESHMERA SHABBAT

Ki esh·me·ra Sha·bat
Eil yIsh·me·rei·ni.
Ot hi le·o·le·mei ad
bei·no u·vei·ni.

כי אשמרה שבת

כִּי אֶשְׁמְרָה שַׁבָּת
אֵל יִשְׁמְרֵנִי.
אוֹת הִיא לְעָלְמֵי עַד
בֵּינוֹ וּבֵינִי.

If I keep Shabbat, God keeps me. It is a sign for ever between God and me.

◆

YAH RIBON

Yah ri·bon a·lam ve·al·ma·ya,
ant Hu mal·ka, me·lech mal·cha·ya.
O·vad ge·vur·teich, ve·tim·ha·ya,
she·far ko·da·mai, le·ha·cha·va·ya.

Yah ri·bon . . .

יה רבון

יָהּ רִבּוֹן עָלַם וְעָלְמַיָּא,
אַנְתְּ הוּא מַלְכָּא, מֶלֶךְ מַלְכַיָּא.
עוֹבַד גְּבוּרְתֵּךְ, וְתִמְהַיָּא,
שְׁפַר קֳדָמַי לְהַחֲוָיָה.

יָהּ רִבּוֹן עָלַם וְעָלְמַיָּא,
אַנְתְּ הוּא מַלְכָּא מֶלֶךְ מַלְכַיָּא.

She·va·chin a·sa·deir, tsaf·ra
    ve·ram·sha,
lach, E·la·ha ka·di·sha, di ve·ra chol
    naf·sha.
I·rin ka·di·shin, u·ve·nei e·na·sha,
chei·vat ba·ra, ve·o·fei she·ma·ya.

Yah ri·bon . . .

שְׁבָחִין אֲסַדֵּר, צַפְרָא וְרַמְשָׁא,
לָךְ, אֱלָהָא קַדִּישָׁא דִּי בְרָא כָל־
נַפְשָׁא.
עִירִין קַדִּישִׁין, וּבְנֵי אֱנָשָׁא,
חֵיוַת בָּרָא, וְעוֹפֵי שְׁמַיָּא.

יָהּ רִבּוֹן עָלַם וְעָלְמַיָּא,
אַנְתְּ הוּא מַלְכָּא מֶלֶךְ מַלְכַיָּא.

37

Rav·re·vin o·ve·dach, ve·ta·ki·fin,

רַבְרְבִין עוֹבְדָיךְ, וְתַקִּיפִין,

ma·cheich ra·ma·ya ve·za·keif ke·fi·fin,

מָכֵךְ רָמַיָּא וְזָקֵף כְּפִיפִין,

Lu ye·chei ge·var she·nin a·le·fin,

לוּ יְחֵא גְבַר שְׁנִין אַלְפִין,

la yei·ol ge·vur·teich be·chush·be·na·ya.

לָא יֵעַל גְּבוּרְתֵּךְ בְּחֻשְׁבְּנַיָּא.

Yah ri·bon . . .

יָהּ רִבּוֹן עָלַם וְעָלְמַיָּא,
אַנְתְּ הוּא מַלְכָּא מֶלֶךְ מַלְכַיָּא.

Lord God of this and all worlds, You are supreme, the Sovereign
God. Your mighty, wondrous work moves my heart to praise You.
Evening and morning I praise You, Holy God who forms all beings:
angels and mortals, beasts and birds. Great are Your works, and
mighty; You humble the proud, and lift up those who are bowed
down. Were we to live a thousand years, there would not be time
enough to tell of Your might!

◆

YOM ZEH MECHUBAD
יום זה מכבד

Yom zeh me·chu·bad mi·kol ya·mim,

יוֹם זֶה מְכֻבָּד מִכָּל־יָמִים,

ki vo sha·vat tsur o·la·mim.

כִּי בוֹ שָׁבַת צוּר עוֹלָמִים.

Shei·shet ya·mim a·sei me·lach·te·cha,

שֵׁשֶׁת יָמִים עֲשֵׂה מְלַאכְתֶּךָ,

ve·yom ha·she·vi·i lei·lo·he·cha,

וְיוֹם הַשְּׁבִיעִי לֵאלֹהֶיךָ.

Sha·bat lo ta·a·seh vo me·la·cha,

שַׁבָּת לֹא תַעֲשֶׂה בוֹ מְלָאכָה,

ki chol a·sa shei·shet ya·mim.

כִּי כֹל עָשָׂה שֵׁשֶׁת יָמִים.

Yom zeh . . .

יוֹם זֶה . . .

Ha·sha·ma·yim me·sa·pe·rim ke·vo·do,

הַשָּׁמַיִם מְסַפְּרִים כְּבוֹדוֹ,

ve·gam ha·a·rets ma·le·a chas·do,

וְגַם הָאָרֶץ מָלְאָה חַסְדּוֹ,

re·u kol ei·leh a·se·ta ya·do,

רְאוּ כָל־אֵלֶּה עָשְׂתָה יָדוֹ,

ki Hu ha·tsur po·o·lo ta·mim.

כִּי הוּא הַצּוּר פָּעֳלוֹ תָמִים.

Yom zeh . . .

יוֹם זֶה . . .

This is the day most blessed of all, this is the day of the Creator's rest. Six are
your days of labor, the seventh devote to your God; on Shabbat refrain
from work for gain: celebrate rather the work of creation. *This is the
day . . . .* The heavens declare His glory, earth is full of His love; See it all —
His handiwork, the Rock whose work is pure. *This is the day . . . .*

◆

38

YEDID NEFESH

ידיד נפש

Ye·did ne·fesh, av ha·ra·cha·man,

me·shoch av·de·cha el re·tso·ne·cha.

Ya·ruts av·de·cha ke·mo a·yal,

yish·ta·cha·veh el mul ha·da·re·cha.

יְדִיד נֶפֶשׁ, אָב הָרַחֲמָן,

מְשׁוֹךְ עַבְדְּךָ אֶל רְצוֹנֶךָ.

יָרוּץ עַבְדְּךָ כְּמוֹ אַיָּל,

יִשְׁתַּחֲוֶה אֶל מוּל הֲדָרֶךָ.

Heart's delight, Source of mercy, draw Your servant into Your arms: I leap
like a deer to stand in awe before You.

◆

VETAHEIR LIBEINU

וטהר לבנו

Ve·ta·heir li·bei·nu le·ov·de·cha
be·e·met.

Purify our hearts to serve You in truth.

וְטַהֵר לִבֵּנוּ לְעָבְדְּךָ בֶּאֱמֶת.

◆

BARUCH ELOHEINU

ברוך אלהינו

Ba·ruch E·lo·hei·nu

she·be·ra·a·nu li·che·vo·do,

ve·hiv·di·la·nu min ha·to·im,

ve·na·tan la·nu To·rat e·met

[ve·cha·yei o·lam na·ta be·to·chei·nu].

בָּרוּךְ אֱלֹהֵינוּ

שֶׁבְּרָאָנוּ לִכְבוֹדוֹ,

וְהִבְדִּילָנוּ מִן־הַתּוֹעִים,

וְנָתַן לָנוּ תּוֹרַת אֱמֶת

(וְחַיֵּי עוֹלָם נָטַע בְּתוֹכֵנוּ).

Blessed is our God, who has touched us with His glory, separated us from
error and given us a Torah of truth [implanting within us eternal life].

◆

AL SHELOSHA DEVARIM

על שלשה דברים

Al she·lo·sha de·va·rim

ha·o·lam o·meid:

al ha·torah,

ve·al ha·a·vo·da,

ve·al ge·mi·lut cha·sa·dim.

עַל־שְׁלֹשָׁה דְבָרִים

הָעוֹלָם עוֹמֵד:

עַל הַתּוֹרָה,

וְעַל הָעֲבוֹדָה,

וְעַל גְּמִילוּת חֲסָדִים.

The world depends on three things: on Torah, on worship, and on loving
deeds.

◆

DAVID MELECH

דוד מלך

Da·vid me·lech Yis·ra·eil

chai ve·ka·yam.

דָּוִד מֶלֶךְ יִשְׂרָאֵל

חַי וְקַיָּם.

David, king of Israel, lives and endures.

◆

RAD HALAILA

רד הלילה

Rad ha·lai·la rav shi·rei·nu,

רַד הַלַּיְלָה רַב שִׁירֵנוּ,

ha·bo·kei·a la·sha·ma·yim.

הַבּוֹקֵעַ לַשָּׁמָיִם.

Shu·vi shu·vi ho·ra·tei·nu

שׁוּבִי שׁוּבִי הוֹרָתֵנוּ

me·chu·de·shet shiv·a·ta·yim.

מְחוּדֶשֶׁת שִׁבְעָתָיִם.

Shu·vi shu·vi ve·na·sov

שׁוּבִי שׁוּבִי וְנָסוֹב

ki dar·kei·nu ein la sof,

כִּי דַרְכֵּנוּ אֵין לָהּ סוֹף,

ki od nim·she·chet ha·shal·she·let,

כִּי עוֹד נִמְשֶׁכֶת הַשַּׁלְשֶׁלֶת,

ki li·bei·nu leiv e·chad

כִּי לִבֵּנוּ לֵב אֶחָד

mi·ni az va·a·dei ad

מִינִי אָז וַעֲדֵי עַד

ki od nim·she·chet ha·shal·she·let.

כִּי עוֹד נִמְשֶׁכֶת הַשַּׁלְשֶׁלֶת.

La, la la, la la la la la la.....

ל, ל, ל, ל, ל, ל, ל...

Night descends, and great is our song which breaks through to the heavens. Again, again our Hora, renewed sevenfold. Again, again, and let us go around. For our path has no end; for the chain still continues. For our heart is one heart, now and always, for the chain still continues.

Welcoming Yom Tov

It is customary, before the beginning of Yom Tov, for each member of the household to contribute to some worthy cause.

"Happy are those who consider the poor."

Eternal God, we hereby vow to fulfill the Mitzvah of Tzedakah as we begin this day of holiness. We shall not forget the words of Your prophet, who called us to share our bread with the hungry, to clothe the naked, and never to hide ourselves from our own kin.

May we, together with the whole House of Israel, be mindful of the needs of others, sharing with them the fruits of our labor, helping to sustain them in body and soul. For all, may Your promise be fulfilled: "Then shall your light blaze forth like the dawn, and your wounds shall quickly heal; your right-eousness shall walk before you, the glory of the Lord shall follow you."

◆ ◆

הדלקת הנרות

We praise You, O God, the Source of light. Let Your light shine upon us. May our hearts and our homes be illumined by the assurance of Your love, and sanctified by the sense of Your presence.

◆ ◆

בָּרוּךְ אַתָּה, יְיָ אֱלֹהֵינוּ, מֶלֶךְ הָעוֹלָם, אֲשֶׁר קִדְּשָׁנוּ בְּמִצְוֹתָיו,
וְצִוָּנוּ לְהַדְלִיק נֵר שֶׁל (שַׁבָּת וְשֶׁל) יוֹם טוֹב.

Blessed is the Lord our God, Ruler of the universe, by whose Mitzvot we are hallowed, who commands us to kindle the lights of (Shabbat and) Yom Tov.

◆ ◆

We thank You, O God, for the joy of Yom Tov, and for the opportunity to celebrate it in the company of those we love. Blessed is the home in which the hearts of the children are turned to the parents, and the hearts of the parents to the children. Blessed is the home filled with light and gladness, the spirit of Yom Tov.

We give thanks, O God, for family and home. May it be warm with love and companionship. Here may we always find rest from the day's work, and refuge from cares; may our joys be deepened and our griefs softened by the love we give and receive.

◆ ◆

The parents bless the children

May God bless you and guide you. Be strong for the truth, charitable in your words, just and loving in your deeds. A noble heritage has been entrusted to you; guard it well.

For a boy	*For a girl*
יְשִׂמְךָ אֱלֹהִים כְּאֶפְרַיִם וְכִמְנַשֶּׁה.	יְשִׂמֵךְ אֱלֹהִים כְּשָׂרָה, רִבְקָה, רָחֵל, וְלֵאָה.
May God inspire you to live in the tradition of Ephraim and Menasheh, who carried forward the life of our people.	May God inspire you to live in the tradition of Sarah and Rebekah, Rachel and Leah, who carried forward the life of our people.

יְבָרֶכְךָ יְיָ וְיִשְׁמְרֶךָ,

יָאֵר יְיָ פָּנָיו אֵלֶיךָ וִיחֻנֶּךָ,

יִשָּׂא יְיָ פָּנָיו אֵלֶיךָ וְיָשֵׂם לְךָ שָׁלוֹם.

The Lord bless you and keep you;
The Lord look kindly upon you and be gracious to you;
The Lord bestow His favor upon you and give you peace. Amen.

There might now be a moment of silence, during which all present think of one another with blessing.

◆ ◆

42

Kiddush

ON PESACH

Pesach teaches us that all people must be free to serve God by ennobling themselves and by concern for others.

With wine, our symbol of joy, we celebrate this day and its holiness, and we give thanks for the liberating power that redeemed Israel from Egyptian bondage. May our worship make us aware of the blessing and responsibility of freedom. May it lead us to be loyal to our people and our faith, and to be unselfish toward all human beings.

Continue with Kiddush on page 45.

ON SHAVUOT

Shavuot teaches us that only by living under laws of truth and justice do we find happiness and hallow our lives.

With wine, our symbol of joy, we celebrate this day and its holiness, and we give thanks for the revelation of Torah and the first fruits of earth's goodness. May our worship help us to live in the light of Torah, and may we give of the first fruits of our strength for the well-being of our community and our people.

Continue with Kiddush on page 45.

ON SUKKOT

Sukkot teaches us to give thanks for the harvest of fruit and grain, and to share these and all our blessings with others.

With wine, our symbol of joy, we celebrate this day and its holiness, and give thanks to God, who has been with us in all our wanderings, and who sustains us from year to year by the fruitfulness of this world. Thankful for God's goodness, may we work to bring blessing to all the world.

Continue with Kiddush on page 45.

ON ATZERET-SIMCHAT TORAH

This festival teaches us that the study of Torah never ends, and that its influence can fill our lives with the beauty of holiness.

With wine, our symbol of joy, we celebrate this day and its holiness, giving thanks for the great teachers of every generation. May our worship make us eager to study our heritage and to use its knowledge in the service of humanity.

Continue with Kiddush on page 45.

For the Eve of Yom Tov

For transliteration, see page 58.

ON SHABBAT

וַיְכֻלּוּ הַשָּׁמַיִם וְהָאָרֶץ וְכָל־צְבָאָם. וַיְכַל אֱלֹהִים בַּיּוֹם
הַשְּׁבִיעִי מְלַאכְתּוֹ אֲשֶׁר עָשָׂה; וַיִּשְׁבֹּת בַּיּוֹם הַשְּׁבִיעִי מִכָּל־
מְלַאכְתּוֹ אֲשֶׁר עָשָׂה. וַיְבָרֶךְ אֱלֹהִים אֶת־יוֹם הַשְּׁבִיעִי וַיְקַדֵּשׁ
אֹתוֹ, כִּי בוֹ שָׁבַת מִכָּל־מְלַאכְתּוֹ אֲשֶׁר־בָּרָא אֱלֹהִים לַעֲשׂוֹת.

Now the whole universe — sky, earth, and all their array — was
completed. With the seventh day God ended His work of creation;
on the seventh day He rested, with all His work completed. Then
God blessed the seventh day and called it holy, for with this day He
had completed the work of creation.

◆

בָּרוּךְ אַתָּה, יְיָ אֱלֹהֵינוּ, מֶלֶךְ הָעוֹלָם, בּוֹרֵא פְּרִי הַגָּפֶן.

Blessed is the Lord our God, Ruler of the universe, Creator of the
fruit of the vine.

בָּרוּךְ אַתָּה, יְיָ אֱלֹהֵינוּ, מֶלֶךְ הָעוֹלָם, אֲשֶׁר בָּחַר בָּנוּ מִכָּל־
עָם, וְרוֹמְמָנוּ מִכָּל־לָשׁוֹן, וְקִדְּשָׁנוּ בְּמִצְוֹתָיו.

Blessed is the Lord our God, Ruler of the universe, who has chosen
us from all the peoples, exalting us by hallowing us with His Mitzvot.

וַתִּתֶּן־לָנוּ, יְיָ אֱלֹהֵינוּ, בְּאַהֲבָה, (שַׁבָּתוֹת לִמְנוּחָה וּ) מוֹעֲדִים
לְשִׂמְחָה, חַגִּים וּזְמַנִּים לְשָׂשׂוֹן, אֶת־יוֹם (הַשַּׁבָּת הַזֶּה וְאֶת־יוֹם)

In Your love, O Lord our God, You have given us (Sabbaths of
rest,) feasts of gladness and seasons of joy: this (Sabbath day
and this) festival of

Pesach—season of our freedom,	חַג הַמַּצּוֹת הַזֶּה — זְמַן חֵרוּתֵנוּ,
Shavuot—season of revelation,	חַג הַשָּׁבֻעוֹת הַזֶּה — זְמַן מַתַּן תּוֹרָתֵנוּ,
Sukkot—season of thanksgiving,	חַג הַסֻּכּוֹת הַזֶּה — זְמַן שִׂמְחָתֵנוּ,
Atzeret-Simchat Torah— season of our gladness,	הַשְּׁמִינִי חַג הָעֲצֶרֶת הַזֶּה — זְמַן שִׂמְחָתֵנוּ,

מִקְרָא קֹדֶשׁ, זֵכֶר לִיצִיאַת מִצְרָיִם.

to unite in worship and recall the Exodus from Egypt.

45

כִּי־בָנוּ בָחַרְתָּ וְאוֹתָנוּ קִדַּשְׁתָּ מִכָּל־הָעַמִּים, (וְשַׁבָּת) וּמוֹעֲדֵי
קָדְשֶׁךָ (בְּאַהֲבָה וּבְרָצוֹן) בְּשִׂמְחָה וּבְשָׂשׂוֹן הִנְחַלְתָּנוּ.
בָּרוּךְ אַתָּה, יְיָ, מְקַדֵּשׁ (הַשַּׁבָּת וְ) יִשְׂרָאֵל וְהַזְּמַנִּים.

For You have chosen us from all peoples, consecrating us to Your
service, and giving us (the Sabbath, a sign of Your love and favor,
and) the Festivals, a time of gladness and joy.

Blessed is the Lord, who hallows (the Sabbath,) the House of
Israel and the Festivals.

◆ ◆

This blessing is not recited on the last day of Pesach

בָּרוּךְ אַתָּה, יְיָ אֱלֹהֵינוּ, מֶלֶךְ הָעוֹלָם, שֶׁהֶחֱיָנוּ וְקִיְּמָנוּ וְהִגִּיעָנוּ
לַזְּמַן הַזֶּה.

Blessed is the Lord our God Ruler of the universe, for giving
us life, for sustaining us, and for enabling us to reach this
season.

◆ ◆

בָּרוּךְ אַתָּה, יְיָ אֱלֹהֵינוּ, מֶלֶךְ הָעוֹלָם, הַמּוֹצִיא לֶחֶם מִן
הָאָרֶץ.

Blessed is the Lord our God, Ruler of the universe, who causes
bread to come forth from the earth.

◆ ◆

IN THE SUKKAH

בָּרוּךְ אַתָּה, יְיָ אֱלֹהֵינוּ, מֶלֶךְ הָעוֹלָם, אֲשֶׁר קִדְּשָׁנוּ בְּמִצְוֹתָיו
וְצִוָּנוּ לֵישֵׁב בַּסֻּכָּה.

Blessed is the Lord our God, Ruler of the universe, by whose
Mitzvot we are hallowed, who commands us to celebrate in
the Sukkah.

46

For the Morning of Yom Tov

ON SHABBAT

Ve·sha·me·ru ve·nei Yis·ra·eil et ha·sha·bat,
la·a·sot et ha·sha·bat le·do·ro·tam, be·rit
o·lam. Bei·ni u·vein be·nei Yis·ra·eil ot
hi le·o·lam, ki shei·shet ya·mim a·sa A·do·nai
et ha·sha·ma·yim ve·et ha·a·rets, u·va·yom
ha·she·vi·i sha·vat va·yi·na·fash.

וְשָׁמְרוּ בְנֵי־יִשְׂרָאֵל אֶת־הַשַּׁבָּת,
לַעֲשׂוֹת אֶת־הַשַּׁבָּת לְדֹרֹתָם בְּרִית
עוֹלָם. בֵּינִי וּבֵין בְּנֵי יִשְׂרָאֵל אוֹת
הִיא לְעֹלָם, כִּי שֵׁשֶׁת יָמִים עָשָׂה יְיָ
אֶת־הַשָּׁמַיִם וְאֶת־הָאָרֶץ, וּבַיּוֹם
הַשְּׁבִיעִי שָׁבַת וַיִּנָּפַשׁ.

The people of Israel shall keep the Sabbath, observing the Sabbath
in every generation as a covenant for all time. It is a sign for ever
between Me and the people of Israel. For in six days the Eternal
God made heaven and earth, and on the seventh day He rested
from His labors.

עַל־כֵּן בֵּרַךְ יְיָ אֶת־יוֹם הַשַּׁבָּת וַיְקַדְּשֵׁהוּ.

Al kein bei·rach A·do·nai et yom ha·sha·bat va·ye·ka·de·shei·hu.
Therefore the Lord blessed the seventh day and called it holy.

❖ ❖

אֵלֶּה מוֹעֲדֵי יְיָ, מִקְרָאֵי קֹדֶשׁ, אֲשֶׁר תִּקְרְאוּ אֹתָם בְּמוֹעֲדָם.
וַיְדַבֵּר מֹשֶׁה אֶת־מוֹעֲדֵי יְיָ אֶל־בְּנֵי יִשְׂרָאֵל.

Ei·leh mo·a·dei A·do·nai, mik·ra·ei ko·desh, a·sher tik·re·u o·tam
be·mo·a·dam.
Va·ye·da·beir Mo·sheh et mo·a·dei A·do·nai el be·nei Yis·ra·eil.

These are the appointed seasons of the Lord, the sacred days,
that you shall proclaim at their appointed times.
And Moses declared the appointed seasons of the Lord to the
people of Israel.

בָּרוּךְ אַתָּה, יְיָ אֱלֹהֵינוּ, מֶלֶךְ הָעוֹלָם, בּוֹרֵא פְּרִי הַגָּפֶן.

Blessed is the Lord our God, Ruler of the universe, Creator of the
fruit of the vine.

❖ ❖

47

In the Sukkah

בָּרוּךְ אַתָּה, יְיָ אֱלֹהֵינוּ, מֶלֶךְ הָעוֹלָם, אֲשֶׁר קִדְּשָׁנוּ בְּמִצְוֹתָיו
וְצִוָּנוּ לֵישֵׁב בַּסֻּכָּה.

Ba·ruch a·ta, A·do·nai E·lo·hei·nu, me·lech ha·o·lam, a·sher
ki·de·sha·nu be·mits·vo·tav, ve·tsi·va·nu lei·sheiv ba·su·kah.

Blessed is the Lord our God, Ruler of the universe, by whose
Mitzvot we are hallowed, who commands us to celebrate in
the Sukkah.

◆ ◆

בָּרוּךְ אַתָּה, יְיָ אֱלֹהֵינוּ, מֶלֶךְ הָעוֹלָם, הַמּוֹצִיא לֶחֶם מִן
הָאָרֶץ.

Blessed is the Lord our God, Ruler of the universe, who causes
bread to come forth from the earth.

Welcoming Rosh Hashanah

It is customary, before the beginning of Rosh Hashanah, for each member of the household to contribute to some worthy cause.

"Happy are those who consider the poor."

Eternal God, we hereby vow to fulfill the Mitzvah of Tzedakah as we begin this day of holiness. We shall not forget the words of Your prophet, who called us to share our bread with the hungry, to clothe the naked, and never to hide ourselves from our own kin.

May we, together with the whole House of Israel, be mindful of the needs of others, sharing with them the fruits of our labor, helping to sustain them in body and soul. For all, may Your promise be fulfilled: "Then shall your light blaze forth like the dawn, and your wounds shall quickly heal; your righteousness shall walk before you, the glory of the Lord shall follow you."

♦ ♦

הדלקת הנרות

With the setting of this evening's sun, united with Jews of every place and time, we proclaim a new year of hope. Lord of the universe, let Your light and Your truth come forth to lead us. These flames we kindle are a symbol of Your eternal flame: may they open our eyes to the good we must do, moving us to work for harmony and peace, and so making the world bright with Your presence.

♦ ♦

בָּרוּךְ אַתָּה, יְיָ אֱלֹהֵינוּ, מֶלֶךְ הָעוֹלָם, אֲשֶׁר קִדְּשָׁנוּ בְּמִצְוֹתָיו וְצִוָּנוּ לְהַדְלִיק נֵר שֶׁל (שַׁבָּת וְשֶׁל) יוֹם טוֹב.

Blessed is the Lord our God, Ruler of the universe, by whose Mitzvot we are hallowed, who commands us to kindle the lights of (Shabbat and) Yom Tov.

♦ ♦

The parents bless the children

May God bless you and guide you. Be strong for the truth, charitable in your words, just and loving in your deeds. A noble heritage has been entrusted to you; guard it well.

For a boy   *For a girl*

יְשִׂמְךָ אֱלֹהִים כְּאֶפְרַיִם וְכִמְנַשֶּׁה.   יְשִׂמֵךְ אֱלֹהִים כְּשָׂרָה, רִבְקָה, רָחֵל, וְלֵאָה.

May God inspire you to live in the tradition of Ephraim and Menasheh, who carried forward the life of our people. | May God inspire you to live in the tradition of Sarah and Rebekah, Rachel and Leah, who carried forward the life of our people.

יְבָרֶכְךָ יְיָ וְיִשְׁמְרֶךָ,

יָאֵר יְיָ פָּנָיו אֵלֶיךָ וִיחֻנֶּךָּ,

יִשָּׂא יְיָ פָּנָיו אֵלֶיךָ וְיָשֵׂם לְךָ שָׁלוֹם.

The Lord bless you and keep you;
The Lord look kindly upon you and be gracious to you;
The Lord bestow His favor upon you and give you peace. Amen.

❖ ❖

There might now be a moment of silence, during which all present think of one another with blessing.

❖ ❖

Kiddush

The observance of Rosh Hashanah reminds us that all we say and do stands under judgment: our own and God's. It calls us to turn from old errors and failures, and to look ahead with fresh hope and determination.

Let us praise God with this symbol of joy, and give thanks for the goodness we have experienced during past year. May our worship on this day fill us with eagerness to embrace life and to hallow it. May the new year bring renewed strength to our people Israel, and peace to the world.

◆ ◆

For the Eve of Rosh Hashanah

For transliteration, see page 60.

ON SHABBAT

וַיְכֻלּוּ הַשָּׁמַיִם וְהָאָרֶץ וְכָל־צְבָאָם. וַיְכַל אֱלֹהִים בַּיּוֹם
הַשְּׁבִיעִי מְלַאכְתּוֹ אֲשֶׁר עָשָׂה; וַיִּשְׁבֹּת בַּיּוֹם הַשְּׁבִיעִי מִכָּל־
מְלַאכְתּוֹ אֲשֶׁר עָשָׂה. וַיְבָרֶךְ אֱלֹהִים אֶת־יוֹם הַשְּׁבִיעִי וַיְקַדֵּשׁ
אֹתוֹ, כִּי בוֹ שָׁבַת מִכָּל־מְלַאכְתּוֹ אֲשֶׁר־בָּרָא אֱלֹהִים לַעֲשׂוֹת.

Now the whole universe – sky, earth, and all their array – was completed. With the seventh day God ended His work of creation; on the seventh day He rested, with all His work completed. Then God blessed the seventh day and called it holy, for with this day He had completed the work of creation.

◆ ◆

51

בָּרוּךְ אַתָּה, יְיָ אֱלֹהֵינוּ, מֶלֶךְ הָעוֹלָם, בּוֹרֵא פְּרִי הַגָּפֶן.

Blessed is the Lord our God, Ruler of the universe, Creator of the fruit of the vine.

בָּרוּךְ אַתָּה, יְיָ אֱלֹהֵינוּ, מֶלֶךְ הָעוֹלָם, אֲשֶׁר בָּחַר בָּנוּ מִכָּל־
עָם, וְרוֹמְמָנוּ מִכָּל־לָשׁוֹן, וְקִדְּשָׁנוּ בְּמִצְוֹתָיו.

Blessed is the Lord our God, Ruler of the universe, who has chosen us from all the peoples, exalting us by hallowing us with the Mitzvot.

וַתִּתֶּן לָנוּ, יְיָ אֱלֹהֵינוּ, בְּאַהֲבָה אֶת־יוֹם (הַשַּׁבָּת הַזֶּה וְאֶת־יוֹם)
הַזִּכָּרוֹן הַזֶּה, יוֹם תְּרוּעָה, מִקְרָא קֹדֶשׁ, זֵכֶר לִיצִיאַת מִצְרָיִם.

In Your love, O Lord our God, You have given us this (Shabbat and this) Day of Remembrance, that we may hear the sound of the Shofar, unite in worship, and recall the Exodus from Egypt.

כִּי בָנוּ בָחַרְתָּ וְאוֹתָנוּ קִדַּשְׁתָּ מִכָּל־הָעַמִּים, וּדְבָרְךָ אֱמֶת
וְקַיָּם לָעַד.

בָּרוּךְ אַתָּה, יְיָ, מֶלֶךְ עַל כָּל־הָאָרֶץ, מְקַדֵּשׁ (הַשַּׁבָּת וְ) יִשְׂרָאֵל
וְיוֹם הַזִּכָּרוֹן.

For You have chosen us from all peoples, consecrating us to Your service, and Your word is truth eternal.

Blessed is the Sovereign God, Ruler of all the world, who hallows (the Sabbath,) the House of Israel and the Day of Remembrance.

◆

בָּרוּךְ אַתָּה, יְיָ אֱלֹהֵינוּ, מֶלֶךְ הָעוֹלָם, שֶׁהֶחֱיָנוּ וְקִיְּמָנוּ וְהִגִּיעָנוּ
לַזְּמַן הַזֶּה.

Blessed is the Lord our God, Ruler of the universe, for giving us life, for sustaining us, and for enabling us to reach this season.

Many eat a round Challah baked with raisins:

בָּרוּךְ אַתָּה, יְיָ אֱלֹהֵינוּ, מֶלֶךְ הָעוֹלָם, הַמּוֹצִיא לֶחֶם מִן
הָאָרֶץ.

Blessed is the Lord, our God, Ruler of the universe, who causes bread to come forth from the earth.

An apple dipped in honey is eaten after saying:

בָּרוּךְ אַתָּה, יְיָ אֱלֹהֵינוּ, מֶלֶךְ הָעוֹלָם, בּוֹרֵא פְּרִי הָעֵץ.

Blessed is the Lord our God, Ruler of the universe, Creator of the fruit of the tree.

Then it is customary to add:

יְהִי רָצוֹן מִלְפָנֶיךָ, יְיָ אֱלֹהֵינוּ וֵאלֹהֵי אֲבוֹתֵינוּ, שֶׁתְּחַדֵּשׁ עָלֵינוּ שָׁנָה טוֹבָה וּמְתוּקָה.

Lord our God and God of our people, may the new year be good for us, and sweet.

For the Morning of Rosh Hashanah

ON SHABBAT

Ve·sha·me·ru ve·nei Yis·ra·eil et ha·sha·bat,
la·a·sot et ha·sha·bat le·do·ro·tam, be·rit
o·lam. Bei·ni u·vein be·nei Yis·ra·eil ot

hi le·o·lam, ki shei·shet ya·mim a·sa A·do·nai
et ha·sha·ma·yim ve·et ha·a·rets, u·va·yom
ha·she·vi·i sha·vat va·yi·na·fash.

וְשָׁמְרוּ בְנֵי־יִשְׂרָאֵל אֶת־הַשַּׁבָּת,
לַעֲשׂוֹת אֶת־הַשַּׁבָּת לְדֹרֹתָם בְּרִית
עוֹלָם. בֵּינִי וּבֵין בְּנֵי יִשְׂרָאֵל אוֹת
הִיא לְעֹלָם, כִּי שֵׁשֶׁת יָמִים עָשָׂה יְיָ
אֶת־הַשָּׁמַיִם וְאֶת־הָאָרֶץ, וּבַיּוֹם
הַשְּׁבִיעִי שָׁבַת וַיִּנָּפַשׁ.

The people of Israel shall keep the Sabbath, observing the Sabbath
in every generation as a covenant for all time. It is a sign for ever
between Me and the people of Israel. For in six days the Eternal
God made heaven and earth, and on the seventh day He rested
from His labors.

✦ ✦

וּבְיוֹם שִׂמְחַתְכֶם וּבְמוֹעֲדֵיכֶם וּבְרָאשֵׁי חָדְשֵׁיכֶם, וּתְקַעְתֶּם
בַּחֲצֹצְרֹת... וְהָיוּ לָכֶם לְזִכָּרוֹן לִפְנֵי אֱלֹהֵיכֶם, אֲנִי, יְיָ,
אֱלֹהֵיכֶם.

U·ve·yom sim·cha·te·chem u·ve·mo·a·dei·chem u·ve·ra·shei
chod·shei·chem, u·te·ka·tem ba·cha·tso·tse·rot ... ve·ha·yu
la·chem le·zi·ka·ron li·fe·nei E·lo·hei·chem, a·ni, A·do·nai,
E·lo·hei·chem.

On your day of rejoicing, on your Festivals and New Moons,
you shall sound the trumpets ... as a remembrance before
your God; I, the Lord, am your God.

✦ ✦

54

תִּקְעוּ בַחְדֶשׁ שׁוֹפָר, בַּכֶּסֶה לְיוֹם חַגֵּנוּ. כִּי חֹק לְיִשְׂרָאֵל הוּא,
מִשְׁפָּט לֵאלֹהֵי יַעֲקֹב.

Ti·ke·u va·cho·desh sho·far, ba·ke·seh le·yom cha·gei·nu. Ki
chok le·yis·ra·eil hu, mish·pat lei·lo·hei Ya·a·kov

Sound the Shofar when the new moon appears, at the turning
of the year, at the returning of our solemn celebration. For this
is a statute binding on Israel, an ordinance of the God of Jacob.

◆ ◆

בָּרוּךְ אַתָּה, יְיָ אֱלֹהֵינוּ, מֶלֶךְ הָעוֹלָם, בּוֹרֵא פְּרִי הַגָּפֶן.

Blessed is the Lord our God, Ruler of the universe, Creator of the
fruit of the vine.

◆ ◆

בָּרוּךְ אַתָּה, יְיָ אֱלֹהֵינוּ, מֶלֶךְ הָעוֹלָם, הַמּוֹצִיא לֶחֶם מִן
הָאָרֶץ.

Blessed is the Lord our God, Ruler of the universe, who causes
bread to come forth from the earth.

55

Kindling the Yom Kippur Lights

It is customary, before the beginning of Yom Kippur, for each member of the household to contribute to some worthy cause.

"Happy are those who consider the poor."

Eternal God, we hereby vow to fulfill the Mitzvah of Tzedakah as we begin this day of holiness. We shall not forget the words of Your prophet, who called us to share our bread with the hungry, to clothe the naked, and never to hide ourselves from our own kin.

May we, together with the whole House of Israel, be mindful of the needs of others, sharing with them the fruits of our labor, helping to sustain them in body and soul. For all, may Your promise be fulfilled: "Then shall your light blaze forth like the dawn, and your wounds shall quickly heal; your righteousness shall walk before you, the glory of the Lord shall follow you."

♦ ♦

הדלקת הנרות

The holiest day of the year is about to begin. Let us use it well. May it be for each one of us a day of renewal. May it help us to overcome what is evil in us, and to strengthen what is good. May it bring us closer to one another, and make us more loyal to our community, our faith, and our God. ˙

בָּרוּךְ אַתָּה, יְיָ אֱלֹהֵינוּ, מֶלֶךְ הָעוֹלָם, אֲשֶׁר קִדְּשָׁנוּ בְּמִצְוֹתָיו, וְצִוָּנוּ לְהַדְלִיק נֵר שֶׁל (שַׁבָּת וְשֶׁל) יוֹם הַכִּפּוּרִים.

Blessed is the Lord our God, Ruler of the universe, by whose Mitzvot we are hallowed, who commands us to kindle the lights of (Shabbat and) the Day of Atonement.

בָּרוּךְ אַתָּה, יְיָ אֱלֹהֵינוּ, מֶלֶךְ הָעוֹלָם, שֶׁהֶחֱיָנוּ וְקִיְּמָנוּ וְהִגִּיעָנוּ לַזְּמַן הַזֶּה.

Blessed is the Lord our God, Ruler of the universe, for giving us life, for sustaining us, and for enabling us to reach this season.

♦ ♦

56

The parents bless the children

May God bless you and guide you. Be strong for the truth, charitable in your words, just and loving in your deeds. A noble heritage has been entrusted to you; guard it well.

For a boy	*For a girl*

יְשִׂמְךָ אֱלֹהִים כְּאֶפְרַיִם וְכִמְנַשֶּׁה.

יְשִׂמֵךְ אֱלֹהִים כְּשָׂרָה, רִבְקָה, רָחֵל, וְלֵאָה.

May God inspire you to live in the tradition of Ephraim and Menasheh, who carried forward the life of our people.

May God inspire you to live in the tradition of Sarah and Rebekah, Rachel and Leah, who carried forward the life of our people.

יְבָרֶכְךָ יְיָ וְיִשְׁמְרֶךָ,

יָאֵר יְיָ פָּנָיו אֵלֶיךָ וִיחֻנֶּךָּ,

יִשָּׂא יְיָ פָּנָיו אֵלֶיךָ וְיָשֵׂם לְךָ שָׁלוֹם.

The Lord bless you and keep you;
The Lord look kindly upon you and be gracious to you;
The Lord bestow His favor upon you and give you peace. Amen.

❖ ❖

There might now be a moment of silence, during which all present think of one another with blessing.

Transliteration of the Kiddush

KIDDUSH FOR THE EVE OF SHABBAT

Va·ye·hi e·rev, va·ye·hi vo·ker,

וַיְהִי עֶרֶב, וַיְהִי בֹקֶר,

yom ha·shi·shi. Va·ye·chu·lu ha·sha·ma·yim ve·ha·a·rets
ve·chol tse·va·am, va·ye·chal E·lo·him ba·yom
ha·she·vi·i me·lach·to a·sher a·sa;

יוֹם הַשִּׁשִּׁי. וַיְכֻלּוּ הַשָּׁמַיִם וְהָאָרֶץ
וְכָל צְבָאָם, וַיְכַל אֱלֹהִים בַּיּוֹם
הַשְּׁבִיעִי מְלַאכְתּוֹ אֲשֶׁר עָשָׂה;

va·yish·bot ba·yom ha·she·vi·i mi·kol

וַיִּשְׁבֹּת בַּיּוֹם הַשְּׁבִיעִי מִכָּל

me·lach·to a·sher a·sa. Va·ye·va·rech

מְלַאכְתּוֹ אֲשֶׁר עָשָׂה. וַיְבָרֶךְ

E·lo·him et yom ha·she·vi·i va·ye·ka·deish
o·to, ki vo sha·vat mi·kol me·lach·to

אֱלֹהִים אֶת־יוֹם הַשְּׁבִיעִי וַיְקַדֵּשׁ
אֹתוֹ, כִּי בוֹ שָׁבַת מִכָּל־מְלַאכְתּוֹ

a·sher ba·ra E·lo·him la·a·sot.

אֲשֶׁר בָּרָא אֱלֹהִים לַעֲשׂוֹת.

Ba·ruch a·ta, A·do·nai E·lo·hei·nu, me·lech
ha·o·lam, bo·rei pe·ri ha·ga·fen.

בָּרוּךְ אַתָּה, יְיָ אֱלֹהֵינוּ, מֶלֶךְ
הָעוֹלָם, בּוֹרֵא פְּרִי הַגָּפֶן.

Ba·ruch a·ta, A·do·nai E·lo·hei·nu, me·lech
ha·o·lam, a·sher ki·de·sha·nu be·mits·vo·tav
ve·ra·tsa va·nu, ve·sha·bat kod·sho be·a·ha·va
u·ve·ra·tson hin·chi·la·nu, zi·ka·ron le·ma·a·sei
ve·rei·shit. Ki hu yom te·chi·la

בָּרוּךְ אַתָּה, יְיָ אֱלֹהֵינוּ, מֶלֶךְ
הָעוֹלָם, אֲשֶׁר קִדְּשָׁנוּ בְּמִצְוֹתָיו
וְרָצָה בָנוּ, וְשַׁבַּת קָדְשׁוֹ בְּאַהֲבָה
וּבְרָצוֹן הִנְחִילָנוּ, זִכָּרוֹן לְמַעֲשֵׂה
בְרֵאשִׁית. כִּי הוּא יוֹם תְּחִלָּה

le·mik·ra·ei ko·desh, zei·cher li·tsi·at

לְמִקְרָאֵי קֹדֶשׁ, זֵכֶר לִיצִיאַת

Mits·ra·yim. Ki va·nu va·char·ta ve·o·ta·nu
ki·dash·ta mi·kol ha·a·mim, ve·sha·bat kod·she·cha
be·a·ha·va u·ve·ra·tson hin·chal·ta·nu. Ba·ruch
a·ta, A·do·nai, me·ka·deish ha·sha·bat.

מִצְרָיִם. כִּי בָנוּ־בָחַרְתָּ וְאוֹתָנוּ
קִדַּשְׁתָּ מִכָּל הָעַמִּים, וְשַׁבַּת קָדְשְׁךָ
בְּאַהֲבָה וּבְרָצוֹן הִנְחַלְתָּנוּ. בָּרוּךְ
אַתָּה, יְיָ, מְקַדֵּשׁ הַשַּׁבָּת.

KIDDUSH FOR THE EVE OF YOM TOV

On Shabbat begin here

Va·ye·hi e·rev, va·ye·hi vo·ker,

וַיְהִי עֶרֶב, וַיְהִי בֹקֶר,

yom ha·shi·shi. Va·ye·chu·lu ha·sha·ma·yim ve·ha·a·rets
ve·chol tse·va·am, va·ye·chal E·lo·him ba·yom

יוֹם הַשִּׁשִּׁי. וַיְכֻלּוּ הַשָּׁמַיִם וְהָאָרֶץ
וְכָל צְבָאָם, וַיְכַל אֱלֹהִים בַּיּוֹם

58

ha·she·vi·i me·lach·to a·sher a·sa;	הַשְּׁבִיעִי מְלַאכְתּוֹ אֲשֶׁר עָשָׂה;
va·yish·bot ba·yom ha·she·vi·i mi·kol	וַיִּשְׁבֹּת בַּיּוֹם הַשְּׁבִיעִי מִכָּל
me·lach·to a·sher a·sa. Va·ye·va·rech	מְלַאכְתּוֹ אֲשֶׁר עָשָׂה. וַיְבָרֶךְ
E·lo·him et yom ha·she·vi·i va·ye·ka·deish	אֱלֹהִים אֶת־יוֹם הַשְּׁבִיעִי וַיְקַדֵּשׁ
o·to, ki vo sha·vat mi·kol me·lach·to	אֹתוֹ, כִּי בוֹ שָׁבַת מִכָּל־מְלַאכְתּוֹ
a·sher ba·ra E·lo·him la·a·sot.	אֲשֶׁר בָּרָא אֱלֹהִים לַעֲשׂוֹת.

On weekdays begin here

Ba·ruch a·ta, A·do·nai E·lo·hei·nu,	בָּרוּךְ אַתָּה, יְיָ אֱלֹהֵינוּ,
me·lech ha·o·lam,	מֶלֶךְ הָעוֹלָם,
bo·rei pe·ri ha·ga·fen.	בּוֹרֵא פְּרִי הַגָּפֶן.

Ba·ruch a·ta, A·do·nai E·lo·hei·nu,	בָּרוּךְ אַתָּה, יְיָ אֱלֹהֵינוּ,
me·lech ha·o·lam, a·sher	מֶלֶךְ הָעוֹלָם, אֲשֶׁר
ba·char ba·nu mi·kol am,	בָּחַר בָּנוּ מִכָּל־עָם,
ve·ro·me·ma·nu mi·kol la·shon,	וְרוֹמְמָנוּ מִכָּל־לָשׁוֹן,
ve·ki·de·sha·nu be·mits·vo·tav.	וְקִדְּשָׁנוּ בְּמִצְוֹתָיו.

Va·ti·ten la·nu, A·do·nai E·lo·hei·nu,	וַתִּתֶּן־לָנוּ, יְיָ אֱלֹהֵינוּ,
be·a·ha·va (Sha·ba·tot li·me·nu·cha u·)	בְּאַהֲבָה (שַׁבָּתוֹת לִמְנוּחָה וּ)
mo·a·dim le·sim·cha, cha·gim u·ze·ma·nim	מוֹעֲדִים לְשִׂמְחָה, חַגִּים וּזְמַנִּים
le·sa·son, et yom (ha·sha·bat ha·zeh	לְשָׂשׂוֹן, אֶת־יוֹם (הַשַּׁבָּת הַזֶּה
ve·et yom)	וְאֶת־יוֹם)

On Pesach

chag ha·ma·tsot ha·zeh— ze·man chei·ru·tei·nu,	חַג הַמַּצּוֹת הַזֶּה – זְמַן חֵרוּתֵנוּ,

On Shavuot

chag ha·sha·vu·ot ha·zeh—	חַג הַשָּׁבֻעוֹת הַזֶּה –
ze·man ma·tan To·ra·tei·nu,	זְמַן מַתַּן תּוֹרָתֵנוּ,

On Sukkot

chag ha·su·kot ha·zeh— ze·man sim·cha·tei·nu,	חַג הַסֻּכּוֹת הַזֶּה – זְמַן שִׂמְחָתֵנוּ,

On Atzeret—Simchat Torah

ha·she·mi·ni chag ha·a·tse·ret ha·zeh—	הַשְּׁמִינִי חַג הָעֲצֶרֶת הַזֶּה –
ze·man sim·cha·tei·nu,	זְמַן שִׂמְחָתֵנוּ,

Continue here

mik·ra ko·desh, zei·cher li·tsi·at

Mits·ra·yim.

מִקְרָא קֹדֶשׁ, זֵכֶר לִיצִיאַת

מִצְרָיִם.

Ki va·nu va·char·ta ve·o·ta·nu
ki·dash·ta
mi·kol ha·a·mim, (ve·sha·bat)
u·mo·a·dei
kod·she·cha (be·a·ha·va u·ve·ra·tson,

be·sim·cha u·ve·sa·son hin·chal·ta·nu.

כִּי־בָנוּ בָחַרְתָּ וְאוֹתָנוּ קִדַּשְׁתָּ

מִכָּל־הָעַמִּים, (וְשַׁבָּת) וּמוֹעֲדֵי

קָדְשֶׁךָ (בְּאַהֲבָה וּבְרָצוֹן,)

בְּשִׂמְחָה וּבְשָׂשׂוֹן הִנְחַלְתָּנוּ.

Ba·ruch a·ta, A·do·nai,

me·ka·deish (ha·sha·bat ve·)

Yis·ra·eil ve·ha·ze·ma·nim.

בָּרוּךְ אַתָּה, יְיָ,

מְקַדֵּשׁ (הַשַׁבָּת וְ)

יִשְׂרָאֵל וְהַזְּמַנִּים.

Ba·ruch a·ta, A·do·nai

E·lo·hei·nu, me·lech ha·o·lam,

she·he·che·ya·nu ve·ki·ye·ma·nu

ve·hi·gi·a·nu la·ze·man ha·zeh.

בָּרוּךְ אַתָּה, יְיָ

אֱלֹהֵינוּ, מֶלֶךְ הָעוֹלָם,

שֶׁהֶחֱיָנוּ וְקִיְּמָנוּ

וְהִגִּיעָנוּ לַזְּמַן הַזֶּה.

KIDDUSH FOR THE EVE OF ROSH HASHANAH

On Shabbat begin here

Va·ye·hi e·rev, va·ye·hi vo·ker,

וַיְהִי עֶרֶב, וַיְהִי בֹקֶר,

yom ha·shi·shi. Va·ye·chu·lu
ha·sha·ma·yim ve·ha·a·rets
ve·chol tse·va·am, va·ye·chal E·lo·him
ba·yom
ha·she·vi·i me·lach·to a·sher a·sa;

va·yish·bot ba·yom ha·she·vi·i mi·kol

me·lach·to a·sher a·sa. Va·ye·va·rech

E·lo·him et yom ha·she·vi·i
va·ye·ka·deish
o·to, ki vo sha·vat mi·kol me·lach·to

a·sher ba·ra E·lo·him la·a·sot.

יוֹם הַשִׁשִׁי. וַיְכֻלוּ הַשָׁמַיִם וְהָאָרֶץ

וְכָל־צְבָאָם, וַיְכַל אֱלֹהִים בַּיּוֹם

הַשְׁבִיעִי מְלַאכְתּוֹ אֲשֶׁר עָשָׂה;

וַיִּשְׁבֹּת בַּיּוֹם הַשְׁבִיעִי מִכָּל

מְלַאכְתּוֹ אֲשֶׁר עָשָׂה. וַיְבָרֶךְ

אֱלֹהִים אֶת־יוֹם הַשְׁבִיעִי וַיְקַדֵּשׁ

אֹתוֹ, כִּי בוֹ שָׁבַת מִכָּל־מְלַאכְתּוֹ

אֲשֶׁר בָּרָא אֱלֹהִים לַעֲשׂוֹת.

On weekdays begin here

Ba·ruch a·ta, A·do·nai E·lo·hei·nu,

me·lech ha·o·lam,

bo·rei pe·ri ha·ga·fen.

בָּרוּךְ אַתָּה, יְיָ אֱלֹהֵינוּ,

מֶלֶךְ הָעוֹלָם,

בּוֹרֵא פְּרִי הַגָּפֶן.

Ba·ruch a·ta, A·do·nai E·lo·hei·nu,

me·lech ha·o·lam, a·sher

ba·char ba·nu mi·kol am,

ve·ro·me·ma·nu mi·kol la·shon,

ve·ki·de·sha·nu be·mits·vo·tav.

בָּרוּךְ אַתָּה, יְיָ אֱלֹהֵינוּ,
מֶלֶךְ הָעוֹלָם, אֲשֶׁר
בָּחַר בָּנוּ מִכָּל־עָם,
וְרוֹמְמָנוּ מִכָּל־לָשׁוֹן,
וְקִדְּשָׁנוּ בְּמִצְוֹתָיו.

Va·ti·ten la·nu, A·do·nai E·lo·hei·nu,

be·a·ha·va et yom

(ha·sha·bat ha·zeh, ve·et yom)

ha·zi·ka·ron ha·zeh, yom te·ru·a,

mik·ra ko·desh, zei·cher li·tsi·at

Mits·ra·yim.

וַתִּתֶּן־לָנוּ, יְיָ אֱלֹהֵינוּ,
בְּאַהֲבָה אֶת־יוֹם
(הַשַּׁבָּת הַזֶּה, וְאֶת־יוֹם)
הַזִּכָּרוֹן הַזֶּה, יוֹם תְּרוּעָה,
מִקְרָא קֹדֶשׁ, זֵכֶר לִיצִיאַת
מִצְרָיִם.

Ki va·nu va·char·ta ve·o·ta·nu
  ki·dash·ta
mi·kol ha·a·mim, u·de·va·re·cha e·met

ve·ka·yam la·ad.

כִּי־בָנוּ בָחַרְתָּ וְאוֹתָנוּ קִדַּשְׁתָּ
מִכָּל־הָעַמִּים, וּדְבָרְךָ אֱמֶת
וְקַיָּם לָעַד.

Ba·ruch a·ta, A·do·nai, me·lech al

kol ha·a·rets, me·ka·deish

(ha·sha·bat ve·) Yis·ra·eil ve·yom
  ha·zi·ka·ron.

בָּרוּךְ אַתָּה, יְיָ, מֶלֶךְ עַל
כָּל־הָאָרֶץ, מְקַדֵּשׁ
(הַשַּׁבָּת וְ)יִשְׂרָאֵל וְיוֹם הַזִּכָּרוֹן.

Ba·ruch a·ta, A·do·nai

E·lo·hei·nu, me·lech ha·o·lam,

she·he·che·ya·nu ve·ki·ye·ma·nu

ve·hi·gi·a·nu la·ze·man ha·zeh.

בָּרוּךְ אַתָּה, יְיָ
אֱלֹהֵינוּ, מֶלֶךְ הָעוֹלָם,
שֶׁהֶחֱיָנוּ וְקִיְּמָנוּ
וְהִגִּיעָנוּ לַזְּמַן הַזֶּה.

61

Havdalah I

The Leader lights the candle and hands it to the youngest person present

הִנֵּה אֵל יְשׁוּעָתִי, אֶבְטַח וְלֹא אֶפְחָד.
כִּי עָזִּי וְזִמְרָת יָהּ יְיָ, וַיְהִי־לִי לִישׁוּעָה.

Behold, God is my Deliverer; I trust in Him, I am not afraid.

For the Lord is my Strength and my Stronghold, the Source of my deliverance.

וּשְׁאַבְתֶּם מַיִם בְּשָׂשׂוֹן מִמַּעַיְנֵי הַיְשׁוּעָה.
לַיְיָ הַיְשׁוּעָה, עַל־עַמְּךָ בִרְכָתֶךָ, סֶּלָה.

With joy shall we draw water from the wells of salvation.

The Lord brings deliverance, His blessing to the people.

יְיָ צְבָאוֹת עִמָּנוּ, מִשְׂגַּב־לָנוּ אֱלֹהֵי יַעֲקֹב, סֶלָה.
יְיָ צְבָאוֹת, אַשְׁרֵי אָדָם בֹּטֵחַ בָּךְ!

The Lord of Hosts is with us; the God of Jacob is our stronghold.

O Lord of all the universe, happy is the one who trusts in You!

יְיָ, הוֹשִׁיעָה; הַמֶּלֶךְ יַעֲנֵנוּ בְיוֹם־קָרְאֵנוּ.
לַיְּהוּדִים הָיְתָה אוֹרָה וְשִׂמְחָה, וְשָׂשׂוֹן וִיקָר; כֵּן תִּהְיֶה לָנוּ.
כּוֹס יְשׁוּעוֹת אֶשָּׂא, וּבְשֵׁם יְיָ אֶקְרָא.

Save us, O Lord; answer us, O King, when we call upon You. Give us light and joy, gladness and honor, as in the happiest days of Israel's past.

Then we will lift up the cup to rejoice in Your saving power, and call out Your name in praise.

◆ ◆

The Leader raises the cup of wine

בָּרוּךְ אַתָּה, יְיָ אֱלֹהֵינוּ, מֶלֶךְ הָעוֹלָם, בּוֹרֵא פְּרִי הַגָּפֶן.

Blessed is the Lord our God, Ruler of the universe, Creator of the fruit of the vine.

The wine is circulated; the Leader holds up the spice-box

בָּרוּךְ אַתָּה, יְיָ אֱלֹהֵינוּ, מֶלֶךְ הָעוֹלָם, בּוֹרֵא מִינֵי בְשָׂמִים.

Blessed is the Lord our God, Ruler of the universe, Creator of all the spices.

The spice-box is circulated; the Leader holds up the candle

בָּרוּךְ אַתָּה, יְיָ אֱלֹהֵינוּ, מֶלֶךְ הָעוֹלָם, בּוֹרֵא מְאוֹרֵי הָאֵשׁ.

Blessed is the Lord our God, Ruler of the universe, Creator of the light of fire.

◆ ◆

We give thanks for the Sabbath day that now is ending. We are grateful for its many blessings: for peace and joy, rest for the body, and refreshment for the soul. May something of its meaning and message remain with us as we enter the new week, lifting all that we do to a higher plane of holiness, and inspiring us to work with new heart for the coming of the day when Elijah's spirit will herald our redemption from all sadness and every bondage.

◆ ◆

Ei·li·ya·hu ha·na·vi, Ei·li·ya·hu	אֵלִיָּהוּ הַנָּבִיא, אֵלִיָּהוּ
ha·tish·bi; Ei·li·ya·hu, Ei·li·ya·hu,	הַתִּשְׁבִּי; אֵלִיָּהוּ, אֵלִיָּהוּ,
Ei·li·ya·hu ha·gil·a·di.	אֵלִיָּהוּ הַגִּלְעָדִי.
Bi·me·hei·ra ve·ya·mei·nu, ya·vo	בִּמְהֵרָה בְיָמֵינוּ, יָבֹא
ei·lei·nu; im ma·shi·ach ben	אֵלֵינוּ; עִם מָשִׁיחַ בֶּן
Da·vid, im ma·shi·ach ben	דָוִד, עִם מָשִׁיחַ בֶּן
Da·vid. Ei·li·ya·hu	דָוִד. אֵלִיָּהוּ ....

◆ ◆

בָּרוּךְ אַתָּה, יְיָ אֱלֹהֵינוּ, מֶלֶךְ הָעוֹלָם, הַמַּבְדִּיל בֵּין קֹדֶשׁ
לְחוֹל, בֵּין אוֹר לְחְשֶׁךְ, בֵּין יוֹם הַשְּׁבִיעִי לְשֵׁשֶׁת יְמֵי הַמַּעֲשֶׂה.
בָּרוּךְ אַתָּה, יְיָ, הַמַּבְדִּיל בֵּין קֹדֶשׁ לְחוֹל.

Blessed is the Lord our God, Ruler of the universe, who separates sacred from profane, light from darkness, the seventh
day of rest from the six days of labor.

Blessed is the Lord, who separates the sacred from the profane.

The candle is extinguished

Ha·mav·dil bein ko·desh le·chol,	הַמַּבְדִּיל בֵּין קֹדֶשׁ לְחוֹל,
cha·to·tei·nu hu yim·chol,	חַטֹּאתֵינוּ הוּא יִמְחֹל,
zar·ei·nu ve·chas·pei·nu yar·beh ka·chol,	זַרְעֵנוּ וְכַסְפֵּנוּ יַרְבֶּה כַּחוֹל,
ve·cha·ko·cha·vim ba·lai·la.	וְכַכּוֹכָבִים בַּלֶּיְלָה.
Sha·vu·a tov ...	שָׁבוּעַ טוֹב ...

Yom pa·na ke·tseil to·mer,	יוֹם פָּנָה כְּצֵל תֹּמֶר,
Ek·ra la·eil, a·lai go·meir;	אֶקְרָא לָאֵל, עָלַי גֹּמֵר;
a·mar sho·meir, a·ta vo·ker,	אָמַר שׁוֹמֵר, אָתָא בֹקֶר,
ve·gam lai·la.	וְגַם־לָיְלָה.
Sha·vu·a tov ...	שָׁבוּעַ טוֹב ...

Tsid·ka·te·cha ke·har Ta·vor,	צִדְקָתְךָ כְּהַר תָּבוֹר,
al cha·ta·ai a·vor ta·a·vor,	עַל חֲטָאַי עָבוֹר תַּעֲבוֹר,
ke·yom et·mol ki ya·a·vor,	כְּיוֹם אֶתְמוֹל כִּי יַעֲבוֹר,
ve·ash·mu·ra va·lai·la.	וְאַשְׁמוּרָה בַלֶּיְלָה.
Sha·vu·a tov ...	שָׁבוּעַ טוֹב ...

64

Hei·a·teir, no·ra ve·a·yom,	הַעֲתֵר, נוֹרָא וְאָיוֹם,
a·sha·vei·a, te·na fid·yom,	אֲשַׁוֵּעַ, תְּנָה פִדְיוֹם,
be·ne·shef, be·e·rev yom,	בְּנֶשֶׁף, בְּעֶרֶב יוֹם,
be·i·shon lai·la.	בְּאִישׁוֹן לָיְלָה.
Sha·vu·a tov ...	שָׁבוּעַ טוֹב ...

You separate sacred from profane: separate us now from our sins! Let those who love You be as many as the sands, and as the stars of heaven.

Day has declined, the shadows are gone; we call to the One whose word is good. The sentry says: 'Morning will come, though it still be night.'

Your righteousness is a majestic mountain: forgive our sins. Let them be as yesterday when it is past, as a watch in the night.

Hear our prayer, O awesome God, and grant redemption! in the twilight, in the waning of the day, or in the blackness of the night!

Havdalah II

The Torah commands:

The Lord spoke to Aaron: "You shall distinguish between the sacred and the profane, the unclean and the clean."

Like Aaron, first of the priests, we who were called at Sinai to be a kingdom of priests are charged to make Havdalah:

We must distinguish between sacred and profane, between holy and common.

We must separate the holy and good from the unholy and evil, from all that stifles the image of God within us.

To this end has Shabbat been set aside.

◆ ◆

Shabbat, most precious of days. Shabbat, the day of holiness.

Shabbat is blessed rest from daily toil. More than rest, Shabbat is freedom:

To reach out to God, to family and friends.

To wash our souls clean, to search and hope to find goodness and beauty, holiness and truth.

Our fathers knew Shabbat as refuge from this world's compromises, from the brutalities and hurts of competition.

It was a refuge, haven, oasis for our mothers: a day of release from earthbound pursuits, from the relentless struggle for daily bread.

A foretaste of heaven which they called: 'Yom she-ku-lo Shabbat,' a time that is all Shabbat.

But our Shabbat is here on earth, this day's earth, and end it does.

With all reluctance we say farewell to this foretaste of heaven.

O let us carry into the coming week some Sabbath hope and joy, and bring them into our souls, our offices and shops, our hours of leisure.

And let the memory of Shabbat past and the anticipation of Shabbat to come lighten our burdens and make us more considerate and generous — determined to make our earthbound world more heavenly.

◆ ◆

VERSES OF THANKS

The ancients took words from Scripture to voice their thanks to God who saves and sustains us during the week as it passes. Within their words of praise was the hint of prayer for life and health in the week to come. May their tranquil faith be ours, as we make their praise our own.

The Leader lights the candle and hands it to the youngest person present

הִנֵּה אֵל יְשׁוּעָתִי, אֶבְטַח וְלֹא אֶפְחָד.

כִּי עָזִּי וְזִמְרָת יָהּ יְיָ, וַיְהִי־לִי לִישׁוּעָה.

Behold, God is my Deliverer; I trust in Him, I am not afraid.

For the Lord is my Strength and my Stronghold, the Source of my deliverance.

וּשְׁאַבְתֶּם מַיִם בְּשָׂשׂוֹן מִמַּעַיְנֵי הַיְשׁוּעָה.

לַיְיָ הַיְשׁוּעָה, עַל־עַמְּךָ בִרְכָתֶךָ, סֶלָה.

With joy shall we draw water from the wells of salvation.

The Lord brings deliverance, His blessing to the people.

יְיָ צְבָאוֹת עִמָּנוּ, מִשְׂגַּב־לָנוּ אֱלֹהֵי יַעֲקֹב, סֶלָה.

יְיָ צְבָאוֹת, אַשְׁרֵי אָדָם בֹּטֵחַ בָּךְ!

The Lord of Hosts is with us; the God of Jacob is our stronghold.

O Lord of all the universe, happy is the one who trusts in You!

יְיָ, הוֹשִׁיעָה; הַמֶּלֶךְ יַעֲנֵנוּ בְיוֹם־קָרְאֵנוּ.
לַיְהוּדִים הָיְתָה אוֹרָה וְשִׂמְחָה, וְשָׂשׂוֹן וִיקָר; כֵּן תִּהְיֶה לָּנוּ.
כּוֹס יְשׁוּעוֹת אֶשָּׂא, וּבְשֵׁם יְיָ אֶקְרָא.

Save us, O Lord; answer us, O King, when we call upon You.
Give us light and joy, gladness and honor, as in the happiest
days of Israel's past.

*Then we will lift up the cup to rejoice in Your saving power,
and call out Your name in praise.*

♦ ♦

THE WINE   פרי הגפן

The Leader raises the cup of wine

Wine gladdens the heart. In our gladness, we see beyond the
ugliness and misery which stain our world. Our eyes open to
unnoticed grace, blessings till now unseen, and the promise of
goodness we can bring to flower.

בָּרוּךְ אַתָּה, יְיָ אֱלֹהֵינוּ, מֶלֶךְ הָעוֹלָם, בּוֹרֵא פְּרִי הַגָּפֶן.

Blessed is the Lord our God, Ruler of the universe, Creator
of the fruit of the vine.

THE SPICES   בשמים

The Leader holds up the spice-box

The added soul Shabbat confers is leaving now, and these
spices will console us at the moment of its passing. They remind us that the six days will pass, and Shabbat return. And
their bouquet will make us yearn with thankful heart for the
sweetness of rest, and the fragrance of growing things; for the
clean smell of rainwashed earth and the sad innocence of child-
hood; and for the dream of a world healed of pain, pure and
wholesome as on that first Shabbat, when God, finding His
handiwork good, rested from the work of creation.

בָּרוּךְ אַתָּה, יְיָ אֱלֹהֵינוּ, מֶלֶךְ הָעוֹלָם, בּוֹרֵא מִינֵי בְשָׂמִים.

Blessed is the Lord our God, Ruler of the universe, Creator
of all the spices.

The spice-box is circulated

THE CANDLE מָאוֹרֵי הָאֵשׁ

The candle is raised

The Rabbis tell us: As night descended at the end of the world's first Sabbath, Adam feared and wept. Then God showed him how to make fire, and by its light and warmth to dispel the darkness and its terrors. Kindling flame is a symbol of our first labor upon the earth.

Shabbat departs and the workday begins as we kindle fire. And we, who dread the night no more, thank God for the flame by which we turn earth's raw stuff into things of use and beauty.

The candle's double wick reminds us that all qualities are paired. We have the power to create many different fires, some useful, others baneful. Let us be on guard never to let this gift of fire devour human life, sear cities and scorch fields, or foul the pure air of heaven, obscuring the very skies. Let the fire we kindle be holy; let it bring light and warmth to all humanity.

בָּרוּךְ אַתָּה, יְיָ אֱלֹהֵינוּ, מֶלֶךְ הָעוֹלָם, בּוֹרֵא מְאוֹרֵי הָאֵשׁ.

Blessed is the Lord our God, Ruler of the universe, Creator of the light of fire.

◆ ◆

SEPARATING OURSELVES הבדלה

Havdalah is not for the close of Shabbat alone; it is for all the days.

Havdalah means: separate yourself from the unholy; strive for holiness.

Havdalah means: separate yourself from fraud and exploitation; be fair and honest with all people.

Havdalah means: separate yourself from indifference to the poor and the deprived, the sick and the aged; work to ease their despair and their loneliness.

Havdalah means: separate yourself from hatred and violence; promote peace among people and nations.

May God give us understanding to reject the unholy and to choose the way of holiness.

May He who separates the holy from the profane inspire us to perform these acts of Havdalah.

בָּרוּךְ אַתָּה, יְיָ אֱלֹהֵינוּ, מֶלֶךְ הָעוֹלָם, הַמַּבְדִּיל בֵּין קֹדֶשׁ לְחוֹל, בֵּין אוֹר לְחֹשֶׁךְ, בֵּין יוֹם הַשְּׁבִיעִי לְשֵׁשֶׁת יְמֵי הַמַּעֲשֶׂה. בָּרוּךְ אַתָּה, יְיָ, הַמַּבְדִּיל בֵּין קֹדֶשׁ לְחוֹל.

Blessed is the Lord our God, Ruler of the universe, who separates sacred from profane, light from darkness, the seventh day of rest from the six days of labor.

Blessed is the Lord, who separates the sacred from the profane.

The candle is extinguished

The light is gone, and Shabbat with it, but hope illumines the night for us, who are called prisoners of hope. Amid the reality of a world shrouded in deep darkness, our hope is steadfast and our faith sure. There will come a Shabbat *without* Havdalah, when the glory of Shabbat, its peace and its love, will endure for ever. Herald of that wondrous Shabbat is Elijah, whom now, in hope and trust, we invoke in song:

Ei·li·ya·hu ha·na·vi, Ei·li·ya·hu	אֵלִיָּהוּ הַנָּבִיא, אֵלִיָּהוּ
ha·tish·bi; Ei·li·ya·hu, Ei·li·ya·hu,	הַתִּשְׁבִּי; אֵלִיָּהוּ, אֵלִיָּהוּ,
Ei·li·ya·hu ha·gil·a·di.	אֵלִיָּהוּ הַגִּלְעָדִי.
Bi·me·hei·ra ve·ya·mei·nu, ya·vo	בִּמְהֵרָה בְיָמֵינוּ, יָבֹא
ei·lei·nu; im ma·shi·ach ben	אֵלֵינוּ; עִם מָשִׁיחַ בֶּן
Da·vid, im ma·shi·ach ben	דָּוִד, עִם מָשִׁיחַ בֶּן
Da·vid. Ei·li·ya·hu	דָּוִד. אֵלִיָּהוּ ...

❖ ❖

A good week. A week of peace. May gladness reign and light increase . . .

Sha·vu·a tov . . .   שָׁבוּעַ טוֹב . . .

70

Havdalah for a Festival

Blessed is the Lord our God,

בָּרוּךְ אַתָּה, יְיָ אֱלֹהֵינוּ,

Ruler of the universe,

מֶלֶךְ הָעוֹלָם,

Creator of the fruit of the vine.

בּוֹרֵא פְּרִי הַגָּפֶן.

We thank You, O God, for the Festival we now conclude, and for all the blessings we have received from it. May its influence remain with us from this day until we celebrate it again. May its beauty and its joyful message never fade from our hearts.

Blessed is the Lord our God,

בָּרוּךְ אַתָּה, יְיָ אֱלֹהֵינוּ,

Ruler of the universe,

מֶלֶךְ הָעוֹלָם,

who separates the sacred from the profane.

הַמַּבְדִּיל בֵּין קֹדֶשׁ לְחוֹל.

Havdalah for Rosh Hashanah and Yom Kippur

The passages in small print are recited only when the conclusion of Rosh Ḥashanah or Yom Kippur coincides with the conclusion of Shabbat

הִנֵּה אֵל יְשׁוּעָתִי, אֶבְטַח וְלֹא אֶפְחָד.

כִּי עָזִּי וְזִמְרָת יָהּ יְיָ, וַיְהִי־לִי לִישׁוּעָה.

Behold, God is my Deliverer; I trust in Him, I am not afraid.

For the Lord is my Strength and my Stronghold, the Source of my deliverance.

וּשְׁאַבְתֶּם מַיִם בְּשָׂשׂוֹן מִמַּעַיְנֵי הַיְשׁוּעָה.

לַייָ הַיְשׁוּעָה, עַל־עַמְּךָ בִרְכָתֶךָ, סֶּלָה.

With joy shall we draw water from the wells of salvation.

The Lord brings deliverance, His blessing to the people.

יְיָ צְבָאוֹת עִמָּנוּ, מִשְׂגָּב־לָנוּ אֱלֹהֵי יַעֲקֹב, סֶלָה.

יְיָ צְבָאוֹת, אַשְׁרֵי אָדָם בֹּטֵחַ בָּךְ!

The Lord of Hosts is with us; the God of Jacob is our stronghold.

O Lord of all the universe, happy is the one who trusts in You!

יְיָ, הוֹשִׁיעָה; הַמֶּלֶךְ יַעֲנֵנוּ בְיוֹם־קָרְאֵנוּ.

לַיְּהוּדִים הָיְתָה אוֹרָה וְשִׂמְחָה, וְשָׂשׂוֹן וִיקָר; כֵּן תִּהְיֶה לָּנוּ.

כּוֹס יְשׁוּעוֹת אֶשָּׂא, וּבְשֵׁם יְיָ אֶקְרָא.

Save us, O Lord; answer us, O King, when we call upon You. Give us light and joy, gladness and honor, as in the happiest days of Israel's past.

Then we will lift up the cup to rejoice in Your saving power, and call out Your name in praise.

◆ ◆

The Leader raises the cup of wine

בָּרוּךְ אַתָּה, יְיָ אֱלֹהֵינוּ, מֶלֶךְ הָעוֹלָם, בּוֹרֵא פְּרִי הַגָּפֶן.

Blessed is the Lord our God, Ruler of the universe, Creator of the fruit of the vine.

72

The wine is circulated; the Leader holds up the spice box

בָּרוּךְ אַתָּה, יְיָ אֱלֹהֵינוּ, מֶלֶךְ הָעוֹלָם, בּוֹרֵא מִינֵי בְשָׂמִים.

Blessed is the Lord our God, Ruler of the universe, Creator of all
the spices.

The spice-box is circulated; the Leader holds up the candle

בָּרוּךְ אַתָּה, יְיָ אֱלֹהֵינוּ, מֶלֶךְ הָעוֹלָם, בּוֹרֵא מְאוֹרֵי הָאֵשׁ.

Blessed is the Lord our God, Ruler of the universe, Creator of
the light of fire.

✦ ◆

בָּרוּךְ אַתָּה, יְיָ אֱלֹהֵינוּ, מֶלֶךְ הָעוֹלָם, הַמַּבְדִּיל בֵּין קֹדֶשׁ
לְחוֹל, בֵּין אוֹר לְחֹשֶׁךְ, בֵּין יוֹם הַשְּׁבִיעִי לְשֵׁשֶׁת יְמֵי הַמַּעֲשֶׂה.
בָּרוּךְ אַתָּה, יְיָ, הַמַּבְדִּיל בֵּין קֹדֶשׁ לְחוֹל.

Blessed is the Lord our God, Ruler of the universe, who separates sacred from profane, light from darkness, the seventh
day of rest from the six days of labor.

Blessed is the Lord, who separates the sacred from the profane.

The candle is extinguished

Ha·mav·dil bein ko·desh le·chol,	הַמַּבְדִּיל בֵּין קֹדֶשׁ לְחוֹל,
cha·to·tei·nu hu yim·chol,	חַטֹּאתֵינוּ הוּא יִמְחֹל,
zar·ei·nu ve·chas·pei·nu yar·beh ka·chol,	זַרְעֵנוּ וְכַסְפֵּנוּ יַרְבֶּה כַחוֹל,
ve·cha·ko·cha·vim ba·lai·la.	וְכַכּוֹכָבִים בַּלָּיְלָה.
Sha·na tova . . .	שָׁנָה טוֹבָה . . .
Yom pa·na ke·tseil to·mer,	יוֹם פָּנָה כְּצֵל תֹּמֶר,
Ek·ra la·eil, a·lai go·meir;	אֶקְרָא לָאֵל, עָלַי גֹּמֵר;
a·mar sho·meir, a·ta vo·ker,	אָמַר שׁוֹמֵר, אָתָא בֹקֶר,
ve·gam lai·la.	וְגַם־לָיְלָה.
Sha·na tova . . .	שָׁנָה טוֹבָה . . .

Tsid·ka·te·cha ke·har Ta·vor,

al cha·ta·ai a·vor ta·a·vor,

ke·yom et·mol ki ya·a·vor,

ve·ash·mu·ra va·lai·la.

 Sha·na tova . . .

צִדְקָתְךָ כְּהַר תָּבוֹר,

עַל חֲטָאַי עָבוֹר תַּעֲבוֹר,

כְּיוֹם אֶתְמוֹל כִּי יַעֲבוֹר,

וְאַשְׁמוּרָה בַלָּיְלָה.

שָׁנָה טוֹבָה . . .

Hei·a·teir, no·ra ve·a·yom,

a·sha·vei·a, te·na fid·yom,

be·ne·shef, be·e·rev yom,

be·i·shon lai·la.

 Sha·na tova . . .

הֵעָתֵר, נוֹרָא וְאָיוֹם,

אֲשַׁוֵּעַ, תְּנָה פִדְיוֹם,

בְּנֶשֶׁף, בְּעֶרֶב יוֹם,

בְּאִישׁוֹן לָיְלָה.

שָׁנָה טוֹבָה . . .

You separate sacred from profane: separate us now from our sins! Let those who love You be as many as the sands, and as the stars of heaven.

Day has declined, the shadows are gone; we call to the One whose word is good. The sentry says: 'Morning will come, though it still be night.'

Your righteousness is a majestic mountain: forgive our sins. Let them be as yesterday when it is past, as a watch in the night.

Hear our prayer, O awesome God, and grant redemption! in the twilight, in the waning of the day, or in the blackness of the night!

The Sukkah

Psalm 15

יְיָ, מִי־יָגוּר בְּאָהֳלֶךָ, מִי־יִשְׁכֹּן בְּהַר קָדְשֶׁךָ?

הוֹלֵךְ תָּמִים וּפֹעֵל צֶדֶק וְדֹבֵר אֱמֶת בִּלְבָבוֹ.

Lord, who may abide in Your house? Who may dwell in
Your holy mountain?

*Those who are upright; who do justly; who speak the truth
within their hearts.*

לֹא־רָגַל עַל לְשֹׁנוֹ, לֹא־עָשָׂה לְרֵעֵהוּ רָעָה,
וְחֶרְפָּה לֹא נָשָׂא עַל־קְרֹבוֹ.

נִבְזֶה בְּעֵינָיו נִמְאָס, וְאֶת־יִרְאֵי יְיָ יְכַבֵּד.

Who do not slander others, or wrong them, or bring shame
upon them.

Who scorn the lawless, but honor those who revere the Lord.

נִשְׁבַּע לְהָרַע וְלֹא יָמִיר.

כַּסְפּוֹ לֹא־נָתַן בְּנֶשֶׁךְ וְשֹׁחַד עַל־נָקִי לֹא לָקָח.

Who give their word, and, come what may, do not retract.

Who do not exploit others, who never take bribes.

עֹשֵׂה אֵלֶּה לֹא יִמּוֹט לְעוֹלָם.

Those who live in this way shall never be shaken.

❖ ❖

Eternal Lord, God of our people, let Your presence dwell among us. Spread over us the tabernacle of Your peace. Be with us on this Festival, as with love and awe we celebrate Your greatness and Your infinite goodness to all the living. We build this Sukkah with joy and gratitude for the gift of life and for all that sustains our bodies and enriches our spirits.

בָּרוּךְ אַתָּה, יְיָ אֱלֹהֵינוּ, מֶלֶךְ הָעוֹלָם, אֲשֶׁר קִדְּשָׁנוּ בְּמִצְוֹתָיו וְצִוָּנוּ עַל מִצְוַת סֻכָּה.

Ba·ruch a·ta, A·do·nai E·lo·hei·nu, me·lech ha·o·lam, a·sher ki·de·sha·nu be·mits·vo·tav ve·tsi·va·nu al mits·vat su·ka.

Blessed is the Lord our God, Ruler of the universe, by whose Mitzvot we are hallowed, who teaches us concerning the Mitzvah of the Sukkah.

◆ ◆

Kiddush is said on the eve of the first day of Sukkot.
The Ritual begins on page 41.

בָּרוּךְ אַתָּה, יְיָ אֱלֹהֵינוּ, מֶלֶךְ הָעוֹלָם, שֶׁהֶחֱיָנוּ וְקִיְּמָנוּ וְהִגִּיעָנוּ לַזְּמַן הַזֶּה.

Blessed is the Lord our God, Ruler of the universe, for giving us life, for sustaining us, and for enabling us to reach this season.

Ushpizin—Welcoming Guests into the Sukkah

According to the Zohar, the Ancients are our invisible companions in the Sukkah, and we are urged to invite the poor to share our meals with us, in gratitude for the gift of spirit that comes to us from entering into the Sukkah with the great ones of our past.

Lord our God and God of our mothers and fathers, be present here among us, spread over us the shelter of Your peace, and surround us with Your radiance, Your pure and holy glory. Let there be food and drink for all who hunger and thirst. Blessed is the Lord for ever. Amen and Amen.

To this meal we summon sublime guests:
Abraham, Isaac, and Jacob; Joseph, Moses, Aaron, and David. Sarah and Rebekah, Rachel and Leah; Miriam, Hannah, and Deborah.

The following passages are said on the appropriate day:

בְּמָטוּ מִנָּךְ, אַבְרָהָם ‹יִצְחָק, יַעֲקֹב, יוֹסֵף, מֹשֶׁה, אַהֲרֹן, דָּוִד›, אֲשְׁפִּיזִי עִלָּאִי, דְּיֵתְבוּ עִמִּי וְעִמָּךְ כָּל אֲשְׁפִּיזֵי עִלָּאֵי: ‹אַבְרָהָם,› יִצְחָק, יַעֲקֹב, יוֹסֵף, מֹשֶׁה, אַהֲרֹן, וְדָוִד.

בְּמָטוּ מִינִיךְ, שָׂרָה ‹רִבְקָה, רָחֵל, לֵאָה, מִרְיָם, חַנָּה, דְּבוֹרָה› אֲשְׁפִּיזָתִי עִלָּיתָא, דְּיֵתְבָן עִמִּי וְעִמָּךְ כָּל אֲשְׁפִּיזָתָא עִלָּהָתָא: ‹שָׂרָה,› רִבְקָה, רָחֵל, לֵאָה, מִרְיָם, חַנָּה, וּדְבוֹרָה.

1. Abraham, exalted guest, you are welcome here, along with Isaac, Jacob, Joseph, Moses, Aaron, and David.

   Sarah, exalted guest, you are welcome here, along with Rebekah, Rachel, Leah, Miriam, Hannah, and Deborah.

2. Isaac, exalted guest, you are welcome here, along with Abraham, Jacob, Joseph, Moses, Aaron, and David.

   Rebekah, exalted guest, you are welcome here, along with Sarah, Rachel, Leah, Miriam, Hannah, and Deborah.

3. Jacob, exalted guest, you are welcome here, along with Abraham, Isaac, Joseph, Moses, Aaron, and David.

   Rachel, exalted guest, you are welcome here, along with Sarah, Rebekah, Leah, Miriam, Hannah, and Deborah.

4. Joseph, exalted guest, you are welcome here, along with Abraham, Isaac, Jacob, Moses, Aaron, and David.

Leah, exalted guest, you are welcome here, along with Sarah, Rebekah, Rachel, Miriam, Hannah, and Deborah.

5. Moses, exalted guest, you are welcome here, along with Abraham, Isaac, Jacob, Joseph, Aaron, and David.

Miriam, exalted guest, you are welcome here, along with Sarah, Rebekah, Rachel, Leah, Hannah, and Deborah.

6. Aaron, exalted guest, you are welcome here, along with Abraham, Isaac, Jacob, Joseph, Moses, and David.

Hannah, exalted guest, you are welcome here, along with Sarah, Rebekah, Rachel, Leah, Miriam, and Deborah.

7. David, exalted guest, you are welcome here, along with Abraham, Isaac, Jacob, Joseph, Moses, and Aaron.

Deborah, exalted guest, you are welcome here, along with Sarah, Rebekah, Rachel, Leah, Miriam, and Hannah.

The Lulav and Etrog may be taken up, and the following meditation recited silently or aloud:

I take Lulav and Etrog, in remembrance of these words of Torah: "On the first day, take for yourselves the fruit of a goodly tree, branches of palms, leaves of the myrtle and willows of the brook." Holy be my thoughts, in token of the abundance of blessing that is mine from heaven and earth. With these four species I reach out to the Source of all life, God Supreme and Lord Supreme, whose kingdom extends to all creation. Let the beauty of our Eternal God be with us, and may our work have lasting value.

✦ ✦

בָּרוּךְ אַתָּה, יְיָ אֱלֹהֵינוּ, מֶלֶךְ הָעוֹלָם,
אֲשֶׁר קִדְּשָׁנוּ בְּמִצְוֹתָיו וְצִוָּנוּ עַל-נְטִילַת לוּלָב.

Blessed is the Lord our God, Ruler of the universe, by whose Mitzvot we are hallowed, who gives us the Mitzvah of the Lulav.

78

Thanksgiving Day

Lord of the universe, creative Source of all being, from You come our blessings from day to day and from year to year. How great are Your love and kindness, O God! The towering mountains and the shaded forests, the abundant streams and the fruitful earth tell of Your endless bounty.

For this land so richly blessed, we raise our voice in joyous thanks. To these shores Your children have come from many lands to seek liberty and new hope. All have been pilgrims to this western world. Though they did not always practice the justice they sought, here they found renewed purpose, increased strength, and the opportunity to outgrow old fears and superstitions. For our country, for its freedom promised and attained, the richness of its natural blessing, and the growing harmony of its citizens, we give humble thanks.

O God of justice and right, inspire all who dwell in our beloved land with loyalty to the ideals of its founders. Give us wisdom and strength to labor for its well-being, on the firm foundation of justice and truth. Fill us with the spirit of kindness, generosity, and peace, that this land may be a beacon-light to many peoples.

Ha·mo·tsi le·chem min ha·a·rets,

הַמּוֹצִיא לֶחֶם מִן הָאָרֶץ

We give thanks to God for bread.
Our voices rise in song together,
As our joyful prayer is said:

בָּרוּךְ אַתָּה, יְיָ אֱלֹהֵינוּ, מֶלֶךְ הָעוֹלָם, הַמּוֹצִיא לֶחֶם מִן הָאָרֶץ.

Ba·ruch a·ta, A·do·nai E·lo·hei·nu, me·lech ha·o·lam, ha·mo·tsi le·chem min ha·a·rets.

Blessed is the Lord our God, Ruler of the universe, who causes bread to come forth from the earth.

Chanukah

The lights of Chanukah are a symbol of our joy. In time of
darkness, our ancestors had the courage to struggle for freedom: freedom to be themselves, freedom to worship in their
own way. Theirs was a victory of the weak over the strong,
the few over the many, and the righteous over the arrogant.
It was a victory for all ages and all peoples.

◆ ◆

אַשְׁרֵי הַגַּפְרוּר שֶׁנִּשְׂרַף וְהִצִּית לְהָבוֹת.
אַשְׁרֵי הַלֶּהָבָה שֶׁבָּעֲרָה בְּסִתְרֵי לְבָבוֹת.
אַשְׁרֵי הַלְּבָבוֹת שֶׁיָּדְעוּ לַחֲדוֹל בְּכָבוֹד.
אַשְׁרֵי הַגַּפְרוּר שֶׁנִּשְׂרַף וְהִצִּית לְהָבוֹת.

Blessed is the match consumed in kindling flame.
Blessed is the flame that burns in the heart's secret places.
Blessed is the heart with strength to stop its beating for
     honor's sake.
Blessed is the match consumed in kindling flame.

◆ ◆

Zion hears and is glad;   שָׁמְעָה וַתִּשְׂמַח צִיּוֹן;

the cities of Judah rejoice, O Lord,   וַתָּגֵלְנָה בְּנוֹת יְהוּדָה,

because of Your judgments.   לְמַעַן מִשְׁפָּטֶיךָ, יְיָ.

◆ ◆

Within living memory, our people was plunged into deepest
darkness. But we endured; the light of faith still burns brightly,
and once again we see kindled the flame of freedom. Our people Israel has survived all who sought to destroy us. Now,
through love and self-sacrifice, we labor to renew our life.

*Let the lights we kindle shine forth for the world. May they
illumine our lives even as they fill us with gratitude that our
faith has been saved from extinction time and again.*

◆ ◆

CHANUKAH

*The candles are placed in the Menorah from right to left,
and kindled from left to right*

בָּרוּךְ אַתָּה, יְיָ אֱלֹהֵינוּ, מֶלֶךְ הָעוֹלָם, אֲשֶׁר קִדְּשָׁנוּ
בְּמִצְוֹתָיו, וְצִוָּנוּ לְהַדְלִיק נֵר שֶׁל חֲנֻכָּה.

Blessed is the Lord our God, Ruler of the universe, by whose Mitzvot
we are hallowed, who commands us to kindle the Chanukah lights.

◆

בָּרוּךְ אַתָּה, יְיָ אֱלֹהֵינוּ, מֶלֶךְ הָעוֹלָם, שֶׁעָשָׂה נִסִּים לַאֲבוֹתֵינוּ
בַּיָּמִים הָהֵם בַּזְּמַן הַזֶּה.

Blessed is the Lord our God, Ruler of the universe, who performed
wondrous deeds for our ancestors in days of old, at this season.

◆

On the first night only

בָּרוּךְ אַתָּה, יְיָ אֱלֹהֵינוּ, מֶלֶךְ הָעוֹלָם, שֶׁהֶחֱיָנוּ וְקִיְּמָנוּ וְהִגִּיעָנוּ
לַזְּמַן הַזֶּה.

Blessed is the Lord our God, Ruler of the universe, for giving us
life, for sustaining us, and for enabling us to reach this season.

◆ ◆

The following verses might be recited after the lights are kindled

1. הָעָם הַהֹלְכִים בַּחֹשֶׁךְ רָאוּ אוֹר גָּדוֹל.

The people who walked in darkness have seen a great light.

2. כִּי נָפַלְתִּי, קָמְתִּי; כִּי־אֵשֵׁב בַּחֹשֶׁךְ, יְיָ אוֹר לִי.

Though I fall, I shall rise; though I sit in darkness, the Lord
shall be a light to me.

3. כִּי־אַתָּה תָּאִיר נֵרִי; יְיָ אֱלֹהַי יַגִּיהַּ חָשְׁכִּי.

For You light my lamp; the Lord God makes bright my
darkness.

4. זָרַח בַּחֹשֶׁךְ אוֹר לַיְשָׁרִים; חַנּוּן, וְרַחוּם, וְצַדִּיק.

Light dawns in the darkness for the upright; for the one who
is gracious, compassionate, and just.

81

5. יְיָ אוֹרִי וְיִשְׁעִי; מִמִּי אִירָא?

The Lord is my light and my help; whom shall I fear?

6. כִּי נֵר מִצְוָה, וְתוֹרָה אוֹר.

For the Mitzvah is a lamp, and the Torah is light.

7. קוּמִי, אוֹרִי, כִּי בָא אוֹרֵךְ, וּכְבוֹד יְיָ עָלַיִךְ זָרָח.

Arise, shine, for your light has come, and the splendor of the
Lord shall dawn upon you.

8. לֹא־יִהְיֶה־לָּךְ עוֹד הַשֶּׁמֶשׁ לְאוֹר יוֹמָם, וּלְנֹגַהּ הַיָּרֵחַ לֹא־
יָאִיר לָךְ; וְהָיָה־לָךְ יְיָ לְאוֹר עוֹלָם, וֵאלֹהַיִךְ לְתִפְאַרְתֵּךְ.

No more shall the sun be your light by day, nor shall the
moon give light to you by night; but the Lord will be your
everlasting light, and your God your glory.

❖ ❖

הַנֵּרוֹת הַלָּלוּ אֲנַחְנוּ מַדְלִיקִין עַל הַנִּסִּים וְעַל הַנִּפְלָאוֹת וְעַל
הַתְּשׁוּעוֹת וְעַל הַמִּלְחָמוֹת, שֶׁעָשִׂיתָ לַאֲבוֹתֵינוּ בַּיָּמִים הָהֵם
בַּזְּמַן הַזֶּה.

וְכָל שְׁמוֹנַת יְמֵי חֲנֻכָּה הַנֵּרוֹת הַלָּלוּ קֹדֶשׁ הֵם, וְאֵין לָנוּ רְשׁוּת
לְהִשְׁתַּמֵּשׁ בָּהֶם אֶלָּא לִרְאוֹתָם בִּלְבָד, כְּדֵי לְהוֹדוֹת וּלְהַלֵּל
לְשִׁמְךָ הַגָּדוֹל עַל נִסֶּיךָ וְעַל נִפְלְאוֹתֶיךָ וְעַל יְשׁוּעָתֶךָ.

We kindle these lights because of the wondrous deliverance
You performed for our ancestors.

During these eight days of Chanukah these lights are sacred;
we are not to use them but only to behold them, so that their
glow may rouse us to give thanks for Your wondrous acts of
deliverance.

Chanukah Songs

MI YEMALEIL

Mi ye·ma·leil ge·vu·rot Yis·ra·eil,
o·tan mi yim·neh?
Hein be·chol dor ya·kum ha·gi·bor,
go·eil ha·am.

מִי יְמַלֵל

מִי יְמַלֵל גְּבוּרוֹת יִשְׂרָאֵל,
אוֹתָן מִי יִמְנֶה?
הֵן בְּכָל דּוֹר יָקוּם הַגִּבּוֹר,
גּוֹאֵל הָעָם.

She·ma! Ba·ya·mim ha·heim
ba·ze·man ha·zeh,
Ma·ka·bi mo·shi·a u·fo·deh.

U·ve·ya·mei·nu kol am Yis·ra·eil
yit·a·cheid, ya·kum le·hi·ga·eil!

שְׁמַע! בַּיָּמִים הָהֵם בַּזְּמַן הַזֶּה
מַכַּבִּי מוֹשִׁיעַ וּפוֹדֶה.

וּבְיָמֵינוּ כָּל עַם יִשְׂרָאֵל
יִתְאַחֵד יָקוּם לְהִגָּאֵל!

Who can retell the things that befell us,
Who can count them?
In every age a hero or sage
Came to our aid.

Hark! In days of yore, in Israel's ancient land,
Brave Maccabeus led his faithful band.
And now all Israel must as one arise,
Redeem itself through deed and sacrifice!

MA·OZ TSUR

Ma·oz tsur ye·shu·a·ti,
le·cha na·eh le·sha·bei·ach;
ti·kon beit te·fi·la·ti,
ve·sham to·da ne·za·bei·ach.
Le·eit ta·chin mat·bei·ach,
mi·tsar ha·me·na·bei·ach,
az eg·mor, be·shir miz·mor,
cha·nu·kat ha·miz·bei·ach.

מָעוֹז צוּר

מָעוֹז צוּר יְשׁוּעָתִי,
לְךָ נָאֶה לְשַׁבֵּחַ;
תִּכּוֹן בֵּית תְּפִלָּתִי,
וְשָׁם תּוֹדָה נְזַבֵּחַ.
לְעֵת תָּכִין מַטְבֵּחַ,
מִצָּר הַמְנַבֵּחַ,
אָז אֶגְמוֹר, בְּשִׁיר מִזְמוֹר,
חֲנֻכַּת הַמִּזְבֵּחַ.

ROCK OF AGES

Rock of ages, let our song
Praise Your saving power;
You, amid the raging foes,
Were our sheltering tower.
Furious, they assailed us,
But Your arm availed us,
     And Your word
     Broke their sword,
When our own strength failed us.

Kindling new the holy lamps,
Priests approved in suffering,
Purified the nation's shrines,
Brought to God their offering.
And His courts surrounding
Hear, in joy abounding,
     Happy throngs,
     Singing songs,
With a mighty sounding.

Children of the Maccabees,
Whether free or fettered,
Wake the echoes of the songs,
Where you may be scattered.
Yours the message cheering,
That the time is nearing,
     Which will see
     All men free,
Tyrants disappearing.

AL HANISIM

עַל הנסים

Al ha·ni·sim ve·al ha·pur·kan,

עַל הַנִּסִּים, וְעַל הַפֻּרְקָן,

ve·al ha·ge·vu·rot, ve·al ha·te·shu·ot,

וְעַל הַגְּבוּרוֹת, וְעַל הַתְּשׁוּעוֹת,

ve·al ha·mil·cha·mot,

וְעַל הַמִּלְחָמוֹת,

she·a·si·ta la·a·vo·tei·nu,

שֶׁעָשִׂיתָ לַאֲבוֹתֵינוּ

ba·ya·mim ha·heim, ba·ze·man ha·zeh.

בַּיָּמִים הָהֵם, בַּזְּמַן הַזֶּה.

84

Bi·mei Ma·tit·ya·hu ben Yo·cha·nan

ko·hein ga·dol, Chash·mo·na·i
  u·va·nav,
ke·she·a·me·da mal·chut Ya·van

al a·me·cha Yis·ra·eil,

le·hash·ki·cham To·ra·te·cha,

u·le·ha·a·vi·ram mei·chu·kei
  re·tso·ne·cha.

Ve·a·ta be·ra·cha·me·cha ha·ra·bim,

a·mad·ta la·hem be·eit tsa·ra·tam.

בִּימֵי מַתִּתְיָהוּ בֶּן־יוֹחָנָן

כֹּהֵן גָּדוֹל, חַשְׁמוֹנָאִי וּבָנָיו,

כְּשֶׁעָמְדָה מַלְכוּת יָוָן

עַל עַמְּךָ יִשְׂרָאֵל,

לְהַשְׁכִּיחָם תּוֹרָתֶךָ,

וּלְהַעֲבִירָם מֵחֻקֵּי רְצוֹנֶךָ.

וְאַתָּה בְּרַחֲמֶיךָ הָרַבִּים,

עָמַדְתָּ לָהֶם בְּעֵת צָרָתָם.

We give thanks for the redeeming wonders and the mighty deeds by which, at this season, our people was saved in days of old.

In the days of the Hasmoneans, a tyrant arose against our ancestors, determined to make them forget Your Torah, and to turn them away from obedience to Your will. But You were at their side in time of trouble.

Purim

We come before You, O God, with words of praise and thanksgiving for the care and guidance under which Your people Israel has ever lived, and for the manifold blessings You have showered upon us and all humanity.

This day brings to mind the darkness and gloom we have experienced in many generations. Painful trials and bitter struggles, torment of body and agony of mind have been our portion too many times. But sustained by the undying hope that in the end right will triumph over wrong, good over evil, and love over hate, we have held aloft the banner of Your truth.

Loyal to the memory of our heroic ancestors, we have come to affirm the living hope born in the prophetic soul of Israel, our people. Before the mighty onrush of Your light and love, we shall yet see the forces of darkness, cruel Amalek and vindictive Haman, succumb and vanish. And although many a bitter experience may await us before prejudice and hate shall have vanished, still we trust that in the end all humanity will unite in love.

Grant us, Lord, the vision to see and the courage to do Your will. Imbue our hearts with the fidelity of Mordecai and the devotion of Esther, that we may never swerve from the path of duty and loyalty to our heritage. Endow us with patience and strength, with purity of heart and unity of purpose, that we may continue to proclaim Your law of love and truth to the peoples of the earth, until all have learned that they are one, the children of the Eternal God. Amen.

THE PATH OF LIFE

Psalms for Reflection

From Psalm 3

Lord, how many are my foes,
how many rise up against me!
How many say of me
that You, O God, will not help me.
Oh, but Lord, You are the Shield that covers me,
my Glory who keeps my head erect!
Lord, I cry out to You,
and from Your holy mountain's summit
Your answer comes.
I lie down and sleep,
and then I am awake,
safe in Your hand,
and unafraid . . .
Lord, rise up;
help me, O my God,
for You, Lord, are the One
from whom help comes,
and Your blessing rests upon Your people.

From Psalm 4

When I call, be my Answer,
O God, my Champion.
In my times of trouble You set me free:
be gracious now, and hear my prayer.
Great ones of the world,
how long will you disdain me?
How long will you love illusions
and run after lies?
See how the Lord shows me marvellous love;
the Lord hears my every prayer.
Tremble, then, and sin no more;
commune with your own heart upon your bed,
and hold your peace.
Let your offering be justice,

and trust in the Lord.
How many say, 'Oh, that we could see some good,
but the light of Your presence has fled from us, Lord!'
Yet you have put joy in my heart,
more than some have
from a rich yield of grain and wine.
Now I will lie down in peace, and sleep;
for You alone, Lord, make me live unafraid.

From Psalm 5

Lord, give ear to my words,
and hear the whisper of my soul;
heed my cry for help,
my Sovereign God
to whom my prayer goes forth.
Hear my voice at daybreak, Lord;
at daybreak I plead with You,
and wait.
For You are not a God who welcomes wickedness;
evil cannot be Your guest.
No arrogance can look You in the face.
You hate those who do evil,
You make an end to all who lie;
Lord, You detest the murderer and the traitor.
As for me, in Your abundant lovingkindness
let me enter Your house,
reverently to worship in Your holy temple.
Lead me, Lord, as You are just,
safe from those who lie in wait for me;
make Your way straight for me.
For they are not sincere,
they are empty inside,
their throat a gaping tomb,
their talk so very smooth.
Judge them, O God:
their own devices make them fall;
their many crimes drive them out,
for they defy You.
But for all who trust in You

there is joy and everlasting song;
You will give them shelter;
and all who love Your name
shall exult in You.
For You give Your benediction to the just;
Lord, You throw Your favor about them like a shield.

From Psalm 11

In the Lord I have found refuge;
why then say to me:
'Flee to the hills like a bird;
see how the wicked have bent the bow,
fitting the arrow to the string,
to shoot in the dark at the upright.
When the foundations are destroyed,
what can the righteous do?'
Lord, You are in Your holy temple;
Lord, the skies are Your throne;
Your eyes look down upon the world,
You take our measure in a glance.
Lord, You weigh just and unjust,
You detest the lover of violence.
As for the wicked,
red-hot coals shall rain upon them,
fire and brimstone and scorching winds
shall be the cup they drink.
For You are righteous, Lord;
You love righteous deeds;
the upright shall behold Your face.

From Psalm 12

Help, Lord, for the loyal have vanished;
good faith among Your children is gone.
Empty forms of speech pass among neighbors,
they speak with smooth lips and double hearts.
Make an end, Lord, of such smooth lips,
such high-sounding words,
of those who say: 'Our tongue can win the day;

words are our friends; none can master us.'
'Now,' says the Lord,
'I will bestir Myself
for the poor who are oppressed,
for the needy who groan.
I will grant them the help for which they plead.'
The words of the Lord are pure words,
silver from a furnace,
seven times refined.
Though the wicked walk about,
stepping high as though they owned the earth,
You will keep us, Lord,
preserving us always from this base breed.

From Psalm 13

Lord, must I still go unremembered?
How long will You turn Your face from me?
Each day my soul is torn,
my heart filled with grief: how long?
How long shall my enemy have the upper hand?
Look at me and answer, O Lord my God;
give light to these eyes lest I sleep the sleep of death;
lest my enemy say: 'I have prevailed';
lest my foes rejoice to see my fall.
As for me, I trust in Your unfailing love;
my heart shall rejoice in Your deliverance.
I will sing to the Lord,
who has shown me such good!

From Psalm 36

Sin speaks to the wicked
deep in their hearts.
There is no fear of God
before their eyes.
They flatter themselves
that their hateful guilt
will never come to light.
Their words are cruel and false.

All wisdom and good is gone.
They lie awake plotting mischief.
The course they choose is not good,
they never tire of evil.
But Your love, O Lord,
is high as heaven,
Your faithfulness reaches to the skies.
Your righteousness is like the mighty mountains,
Your justice is like the great deep;
Lord, You help every human, every beast.
How precious is Your faithful love, O God!
Your children take refuge in the shadow of Your wings.
We feast on the riches of Your house;
we drink from the stream of Your delights.
For with You is the fountain of life;
and by Your light do we see light.
O continue to show Your love
to those who would know You,
Your justice to the upright in heart.
Let the foot of pride not crush me,
nor the hand of the wicked cast me out.
See how those who do evil have fallen;
they are hurled down, never to rise.

Beginning a New Enterprise

"Unless the Lord builds the house, its builders toil in vain."

Creator of the universe, by whose will the world is renewed day by day, You have implanted in us a spark of Your creative will. You have made us Your partners in the building of the world, and we are grateful.

Often we cannot know the outcome of our work. At times, in our ignorance or our greed, we mar the landscape of Your creation. Enlighten me with Your wisdom, therefore, that I do not impoverish the very world that sustains my life. Let me gain my livelihood honorably; and, as I strive for myself, let nothing I do be built upon another's ruin or result in misery and pain. Rather, let me add to the contentment of others, through my devotion to justice, goodness, and truth.

In this enterprise I need strength. I need a clear vision and a wise judgment. But more than all this I need the wisdom not to become so immersed in my task that I neglect my dear ones, or injure my health, or become remote from You, Divine Spirit of the world, the Well of living waters. May I walk with those I love in the light of Your presence, O God, and use all my powers for blessing. Amen.

At a Time of Success

You are the strength of my hands, O God, and the light of my life. All that I am and all that I may yet be, I owe to the creative power that You have implanted within me. Give me, therefore, a wise and constant spirit, a mind cleansed of arrogance and vanity. Make me conscious of my limitations, my weaknesses and imperfections. Above all, fill me with an awareness of my debt to others for what I have achieved.

Even as I exult in the success of my labors, so may I glory to be kind in thought, gentle in word, and generous in deed, that others may have cause to rejoice in my accomplishments. O give me a grateful heart and a loving disposition, that I may be Your messenger of blessing for the poor, the helpless, and the sick. Thus would I give thanks for the blessings that have come to me! Amen.

At a Time of Disappointment

O God of love, as You renew the work of creation day by day, so, now, help me find renewal in my time of sadness and disappointment. Let Your presence be a light within to dispel the darkness. Open my eyes to see that Your nearness, Your silent speech within the heart, is a shield to me.

I pray for the courage to carry on despite defeat, for the wisdom to learn from adversity and to build a new and stronger life. Your strength can transform affliction into salvation; enlighten me, therefore, that I may look to the dawn of a new day with confidence and trust, and give me hope that will rise up above the moment's loss. For You, O God of hope, are my sustaining power, even when I have fallen. Though I look upon the ground where lie so many frustrated expectations, I shall yet prevail. You are with me, and I am at peace. Amen.

On Life with Others

O God, when I am estranged from others, when walls of misunderstanding rise between us, I fade and wither like a leaf separated from its stem. How much I need the balm of friendship, the warmth of understanding! How greatly I need to be needed and cherished! I pray therefore that my soul may know the joy of love given and received, and that no unworthiness diminish me, as I reach out to family and friends.

Open my eyes to the beauty that shines within all who walk the earth. Keep me from imagined hurts, from seeing foes where only friends are to be found. And give me insight into my own heart, that I may uproot all that weakens me. Help me to be patient when others misunderstand me, open to the thoughts of those who are near to me, and quick to forgive all who wound me. When I feel lonely and forsaken, may I find strength to bear the ache of my loneliness in the faith that You are with me, and in the confidence that friends will find me once again. Help me to walk with integrity, and to face the world with an open and trusting mind. Let me not judge others in arrogant haste, nor follow them in self-abasement. Rather may we go hand in hand, all conflicts abated, all resentments forgotten. As we walk through life together, let me and my dear ones go with that righteousness which leads to peace, that love which will bring us harmony and joy, that regard whose fruit is enduring friendship. Amen.

On Reaching the Age of Retirement

As I look back over the years that have gone, I humbly acknowledge the errors that cast a shadow over my days, the times when I fell short of the noble ideals and pure motives by which I meant to guide my life. For the occasions when I failed to make use of the divine powers implanted within me, I am deeply sorry.

But in the years of work and struggle, there were also many times when I did my best. I gave of myself; the day's work was well and faithfully done; I brought benefit to those who depended on me, and help to those who needed me. For all the goodness I wrought, all my honest striving and achievement, I look back with pride, and give thanks. Your strength, O God, upheld me these many long years.

Now I ask to see life as a whole from youth to age; sustain me with faith that the best is yet to be. Many are the opportunities that now await me. There are blessings that only the maturity of age can bring; there is a ripeness that experience alone can yield. May I find the sweetness of that joy which is reserved for those who serve others through the counsel and guidance learned in the school of life. Out of the lessons drawn from disappointment and success alike, may I be able to help them discover value in life's struggles, find joys and triumphs that endure.

Now I have precious time to give to those I love, to family and friends. I pray for insight and a warm heart: let me be with them when they need me, let me respond when they call to me. And let me use my leisure to explore new worlds of thought and feeling. Now I can study my heritage of Torah, savor the beauties of nature and of art, find new meaning and inspiration in my religion. Let the passage of time continually deepen within me the spirit of wisdom and understanding, the spirit of knowledge and reverence for life.

And let me hold fast to the spirit of youth, never losing that sense of wonder which stirs within me in the presence of Your creation and which beckons me to greet each day with zest and eager welcome. Thus will my life be renewed and blessed; and thus will I bring blessing to many in the years to come. Amen.

Marriage Prayers

FOR BRIDE AND GROOM

I

I am about to enter into marriage with the one whom I love, and who loves me. We have committed ourselves to one another with joy and in hope. May I be worthy of my beloved's trust; may we be faithful friends, each a help and support to the other in all that befalls us. May we be blessed with children, a new generation which will grow in health and beauty of spirit.

May there be tenderness between us; let us be gentle and understanding, and quick to forgive each other's faults. Lord, help us create a union of hands for honest labor and fruitful effort. In joy and sorrow we shall work together to achieve the happiness for which we yearn. And give us, Lord, wisdom to look beyond ourselves, to see that we are part of the greater family of the House of Israel, a people bound to Your service. Then we shall abide in faithfulness, truth, and peace. Amen.

II

In mercy You have touched me again and again, O God, and in compassion You guide me on the path of life. Now, in hope and need, I come before You on the eve of my marriage. Let the life I am about to enter be good and true, and filled with devotion. In the darkest moments as in the lightest, may my beloved and I lean upon each other with perfect confidence.

O God, give us Your blessing! Let us each come to understand the other, and gain insight into our own hearts. Keep us loyal to the ideals with which we begin this union, and help us to honor and sustain one another. Smile upon us and teach us to give and receive love with open hearts.

For all the lessons that life has taught me, for the good I have known, and the happiness that is yet to come, I give thanks and praise. Amen.

ON THE MARRIAGE OF A SON OR DAUGHTER

How can I give thanks enough for this blessed day? How can I express what I feel for my beloved child? My heart is full to overflowing.

Many have been my anxious moments: times of accident and sickness, periods of uncertainty and trepidation. I did not always know how best to convey my love and understanding. I did not always know the right path to pursue during the years of my child's growth.

And yet I remember joys that far exceeded our trials and pains. We shared so much goodness, so much joyous laughter. Hand in hand we walked towards the new day, bound in ties of love that cannot break. And through it all we taught each other precious truths of life and its beauty.

Now my beloved child joins hands with another at the threshold of a new life. Grant, O God, that the home they establish will be built on firm foundations. Let the ideals with which they begin remain with them to ennoble their lives. May their love never fade, but grow brighter through the years. May their union mature through shared tasks and constant effort to bring blessing to us all.

May they be blessed with children, a new generation which will grow in health and beauty of spirit. And may the family they establish be a strong and helpful part of our larger family, united in affection for ever. O let the Divine Presence illumine their home and their lives always, blessing them with unfailing love and good. Amen.

FOR A WEDDING ANNIVERSARY

"I am my beloved's, and my beloved is mine." God of all generations, be a blessing to us, as we look back upon the day of our union, and forward to the years ahead. Let Your spirit glow within us, that we may each see Your image in the other. Let our way of life be loving and good, that we may help to bear each other's burdens and share our joys: then will we find grace in the eyes of all who behold us.

May we continue to know the joy of maintaining a home that honors the House of Israel, a peaceful habitation, where contentment, love, and felicity find their dwelling-place. May we grow old together in health, and live in gratitude for our marriage. Amen.

SILVER OR GOLDEN WEDDING ANNIVERSARY

In the fullness of this day's joy, we turn in thanksgiving to the Eternal Source of blessing. We give thanks for the strength that has preserved and sustained us and permitted us to reach this hour. In the midst of family and loved ones, we look back in reverent and grateful reminiscence upon the years that have passed since first we pledged our hearts to one another. Many and varied have been our experiences since that hour; many have been the mingled occasions of victory and defeat, of fulfillment and disappointment. We recall the joys which sweetened our lives; we remember the storms which shook us to the very roots. In bliss and trial alike, O God, You have been with us and in us; so may You continue to bless us with Your presence in the years to come.

Let these be years of health and contentment; of unclouded bliss in the circle of our family and loved ones; of unbroken service of righteousness, love, and peace to those who are far and to those who are near. Amen.

בָּרוּךְ אַתָּה, יְיָ אֱלֹהֵינוּ, מֶלֶךְ הָעוֹלָם, שֶׁהֶחֱיָנוּ וְקִיְּמָנוּ וְהִגִּיעָנוּ לַזְּמַן הַזֶּה.

Consecration of a House

In the spirit of our Jewish faith, we consecrate this house with
prayers of thanksgiving and invoke upon it the blessing of God.

❖ ❖

שְׁמַע יִשְׂרָאֵל: יְיָ אֱלֹהֵינוּ, יְיָ אֶחָד!

Hear, O Israel: the Lord is our God, the Lord is One!

בָּרוּךְ שֵׁם כְּבוֹד מַלְכוּתוֹ לְעוֹלָם וָעֶד!

Blessed is His glorious kingdom for ever and ever!

וְאָהַבְתָּ אֵת יְיָ אֱלֹהֶיךָ בְּכָל־לְבָבְךָ וּבְכָל־נַפְשְׁךָ וּבְכָל־מְאֹדֶךָ.
וְהָיוּ הַדְּבָרִים הָאֵלֶּה, אֲשֶׁר אָנֹכִי מְצַוְּךָ הַיּוֹם, עַל־לְבָבֶךָ.
וְשִׁנַּנְתָּם לְבָנֶיךָ, וְדִבַּרְתָּ בָּם בְּשִׁבְתְּךָ בְּבֵיתֶךָ, וּבְלֶכְתְּךָ
בַדֶּרֶךְ, וּבְשָׁכְבְּךָ וּבְקוּמֶךָ.

*You shall love the Lord your God with all your mind, with all
your strength, with all your being. Set these words, which I
command you this day, upon your heart. Teach them faithfully
to your children; speak of them in your home and on your way,
when you lie down and when you rise up.*

וּקְשַׁרְתָּם לְאוֹת עַל־יָדֶךָ, וְהָיוּ לְטֹטָפֹת בֵּין עֵינֶיךָ, וּכְתַבְתָּם
עַל־מְזֻזוֹת בֵּיתֶךָ, וּבִשְׁעָרֶיךָ.

*Bind them as a sign upon your hand; let them be a symbol
before your eyes; inscribe them on the doorposts of your house,
and on your gates.*

103

לְמַעַן תִּזְכְּרוּ וַעֲשִׂיתֶם אֶת־כָּל־מִצְוֹתָי, וִהְיִיתֶם קְדֹשִׁים
לֵאלֹהֵיכֶם. אֲנִי יְיָ אֱלֹהֵיכֶם, אֲשֶׁר הוֹצֵאתִי אֶתְכֶם מֵאֶרֶץ
מִצְרַיִם לִהְיוֹת לָכֶם לֵאלֹהִים. אֲנִי יְיָ אֱלֹהֵיכֶם.

Be mindful of all My mitzvot, and do them: so shall you
consecrate yourselves to your God. I, the Lord, am your God
who led you out of Egypt to be your God; I, the Lord, am
your God.

◆ ◆

Our homes have always been the dwelling place of the Jewish
spirit. Our tables have been altars of faith and love. "When
words of Torah pass between us, the Divine Presence is in our
midst." Our doors have been open to the stranger and the
needy. May this home we now consecrate keep alive the
beauty of our noble heritage.

Challah is dipped in salt and distributed

בָּרוּךְ אַתָּה, יְיָ אֱלֹהֵינוּ, מֶלֶךְ הָעוֹלָם, הַמּוֹצִיא לֶחֶם מִן
הָאָרֶץ.

Blessed is the Lord our God, Ruler of the universe, who causes
bread to come forth from the earth.

Wine is given to each guest

Wine is a symbol of joy. May all who dwell within these walls,
and all who enter here, know contentment, happiness, and
peace.

בָּרוּךְ אַתָּה, יְיָ אֱלֹהֵינוּ, מֶלֶךְ הָעוֹלָם, בּוֹרֵא פְּרִי הַגָּפֶן.

Blessed is the Lord our God, Ruler of the universe, Creator
of the fruit of the vine.

The open Bible is raised

The Torah has been our life; it has taught us how to live. May
this home be a place for learning and doing. May the hearts
of all who dwell here be filled with a love of the Torah and
its teachings.

104

בָּרוּךְ אַתָּה, יְיָ אֱלֹהֵינוּ, מֶלֶךְ הָעוֹלָם, אֲשֶׁר קִדְּשָׁנוּ בְּמִצְוֹתָיו
וְצִוָּנוּ לַעֲסוֹק בְּדִבְרֵי תוֹרָה.

Ba·ruch a·ta, A·do·nai E·lo·hei·nu, me·lech ha·o·lam, a·sher
ki·de·sha·nu be·mits·vo·tav ve·tsi·va·nu la·a·sok be·di·ve·rei
To·rah.

Blessed is the Lord our God, Ruler of the universe, by whose
Mitzvot we are hallowed, who commands us to engage in the
study of Torah.

❖ ❖

Psalm 15

יְיָ, מִי־יָגוּר בְּאָהֳלֶךָ, מִי־יִשְׁכֹּן בְּהַר קָדְשֶׁךָ?
הוֹלֵךְ תָּמִים וּפֹעֵל צֶדֶק וְדֹבֵר אֱמֶת בִּלְבָבוֹ.

Lord, who may abide in Your house? Who may dwell in Your
holy mountain?

*Those who are upright; who do justly; who speak the truth
within their hearts.*

לֹא־רָגַל עַל־לְשֹׁנוֹ, לֹא־עָשָׂה לְרֵעֵהוּ רָעָה,
וְחֶרְפָּה לֹא־נָשָׂא עַל־קְרֹבוֹ.
נִבְזֶה בְּעֵינָיו נִמְאָס, וְאֶת־יִרְאֵי יְיָ יְכַבֵּד.

Who do not slander others, or wrong them, or bring shame
upon them.

Who scorn the lawless, but honor those who revere the Lord.

נִשְׁבַּע לְהָרַע וְלֹא יָמִיר,
כַּסְפּוֹ לֹא־נָתַן בְּנֶשֶׁךְ וְשֹׁחַד עַל־נָקִי לֹא־לָקָח.

Who give their word, and, come what may, do not retract.

Who do not exploit others, who never take bribes.

עֹשֵׂה אֵלֶּה לֹא יִמּוֹט לְעוֹלָם.

Those who live in this way shall never be shaken.

❖ ❖

*An additional Scriptural passage, such as First Kings 8.54–61,
might be read here.*

❖ ❖

The Mezuzah is raised

This ancient symbol speaks to us of our need to love God and to live by the words of the Eternal One. We affix the Mezuzah to the doorposts of this house with the hope that it will always remind us of our duties to God and to one another. May the divine spirit fill this house — the spirit of love and kindness and consideration for all people.

בָּרוּךְ אַתָּה, יְיָ אֱלֹהֵינוּ, מֶלֶךְ הָעוֹלָם, אֲשֶׁר קִדְּשָׁנוּ בְּמִצְוֹתָיו
וְצִוָּנוּ לִקְבְּוֹעַ מְזוּזָה.

Ba·ruch a·ta, A·do·nai E·lo·hei·nu, me·lech ha·o·lam, a·sher
ki·de·sha·nu be·mits·vo·tav ve·tsi·va·nu lik·bo·a me·zu·zah.

Blessed is the Lord our God, Ruler of the universe, by whose Mitzvot we are hallowed, who commands us to affix the Mezuzah.

The Mezuzah, its top inclining inward, is affixed to the upper part of the doorpost on the right, as one enters the house. If desired, a Mezuzah may be affixed to the right doorpost of the principal rooms.

✦

בָּרוּךְ אַתָּה, יְיָ אֱלֹהֵינוּ, מֶלֶךְ הָעוֹלָם, שֶׁהֶחֱיָנוּ וְקִיְּמָנוּ
וְהִגִּיעָנוּ לַזְּמַן הַזֶּה.

Blessed is the Lord our God, Ruler of the universe, for giving us life, for sustaining us, and for enabling us to reach this happy day.

✦ ✦

אִם־יְיָ לֹא יִבְנֶה בַיִת, שָׁוְא עָמְלוּ בוֹנָיו בּוֹ.

"Unless the Lord builds the house, its builders toil in vain."

In this awareness we pray that our home be blessed by the sense of God's presence.

Accept, O God, our offering of thanksgiving for the promise of security and happiness this home represents, and fortify our resolve to make it, now and always, a temple dedicated to You. Let it be filled with the beauty of holiness and the warmth of love. May the guest and stranger find within it welcome and friendship. So will it ever merit the praise: "How lovely are your tents, O Jacob, your dwelling-places, O Israel!"

For all who are assembled here, and for all who will enter these doors, we invoke Your blessing:

יְיָ יִשְׁמָר־צֵאתְךָ וּבוֹאֶךָ, מֵעַתָּה וְעַד־עוֹלָם.

May the Lord watch over you when you go out and when you come in, now and always. Amen.

On Behalf of a Woman in Childbirth

Lord of all generations, You have blessed our life with comradeship and mutual love. For all Your past gifts I am thankful; now my heart is full, in this time of expectant hope.

My beloved awaits the birth of a new life and You are with her. As a parent holds the hand of an anxious child, so now make her spirit serene. Let her wait in confidence and calm, her body strong, her heart unafraid. Let our little one be born to health and happiness, my wife restored to strength. Help us then to be parents worthy of our trust, and bless us with long life together in family love. Amen.

On the Birth or Adoption of a Child

בָּרוּךְ אַתָּה, יְיָ אֱלֹהֵינוּ, מֶלֶךְ הָעוֹלָם, שֶׁהֶחֱיָנוּ וְקִיְּמָנוּ וְהִגִּיעָנוּ לַזְּמַן הַזֶּה.

We give thanks to You, O Lord our God, Ruler of the universe, for giving us life, for sustaining us, and for enabling us to reach this day of joy. Amen.

Source of all life, our hearts are filled with joy for the new life which has been entrusted to us. Not with words alone shall we voice our thanks, but with our striving to rear our child with love and understanding and tender care.

Bestow Your blessing on our child, that he (she) may grow in strength of body, mind, and spirit. May he (she) learn to love all that is good and beautiful and true, to be a blessing to society and a joy to himself (herself).

May our child find his (her) way in the paths of Torah and good deeds as a loyal member of his (her) people, always faithful to the Covenant. Give us, O God, the wisdom, courage, and faith that we as parents shall need to raise our child to be a human and humane being, a strong and happy and loving person. Amen.

On the Birth or Adoption of a Grandchild

בָּרוּךְ אַתָּה, יְיָ אֱלֹהֵינוּ, מֶלֶךְ הָעוֹלָם, שֶׁהֶחֱיָנוּ וְקִיְּמָנוּ וְהִגִּיעָנוּ לַזְּמַן הַזֶּה.

Blessed is the Lord our God, Ruler of the universe, for giving us life, for sustaining us, and for enabling us to reach this happy day.

We are thankful for the many joys with which our life has been blessed. Now this great goodness has come to us: a new life, a new child to love, the opening of a new chapter in the chronicle of our family's existence. O may this child grow up in health and happiness, to become a blessing to family, friends, and neighbors.

May her (his) dear parents find much joy in the years that lie before them. Grant, O God, that they rear their child with wisdom and understanding, teaching her (him) the ways of righteousness, leading her (him) to the study of Torah and the practice of love and kindness.

And may we, too, be granted the joy of seeing her (him) develop all her (his) faculties, and the gratification of helping her (him) to fulfill the best that is in her (him). Then our humble prayer shall have found its answer: the days and years to come shall be for us times of peace and wondrous fulfillment. Amen.

The Covenant of Milah

This ritual is conducted on the eighth day

May he who comes be blessed.   בָּרוּךְ הַבָּא.

The rite of circumcision has been enjoined upon us as a sign of our covenant with God, as it is written: And God said to Abraham: You shall keep My covenant, you and your children after you. He who is eight days old shall be circumcised, every male throughout your generations.

We recall the prophetic promise that one day the sign of our covenant with God will be imprinted upon our hearts and the hearts of our children, as well as upon our flesh, so that we may rise to the selfless love of God, and therein find life.

May we, like our father Abraham, obey the commandment of God: Walk before Me, and reach for perfection.

A Parent

Joyfully do we present our son for the covenant of circumcision.

וַיָּקֶם עֵדוּת בְּיַעֲקֹב, וְתוֹרָה שָׂם בְּיִשְׂרָאֵל, אֲשֶׁר צִוָּה אֶת־
אֲבוֹתֵינוּ לְהוֹדִיעָם לִבְנֵיהֶם; לְמַעַן יֵדְעוּ דוֹר אַחֲרוֹן בָּנִים
יִוָּלֵדוּ.

Lord, You established a testimony in Jacob, You set a Teaching in Israel, commanding our ancestors to make them known to their children; that the generations to come — children yet unborn — might know them.

זָכַר לְעוֹלָם בְּרִיתוֹ, דָּבָר צִוָּה לְאֶלֶף דּוֹר: אֲשֶׁר כָּרַת
אֶת־אַבְרָהָם, וּשְׁבוּעָתוֹ לְיִשְׂחָק, וַיַּעֲמִידֶהָ לְיַעֲקֹב לְחֹק,
לְיִשְׂרָאֵל בְּרִית עוֹלָם.

You are for ever mindful of Your covenant, the word You commanded for a thousand generations: the covenant You made with Abraham; Your sworn promise to Isaac; the commitment You made to Jacob, Your everlasting covenant with Israel.

הוֹדוּ לַיָי כִּי־טוֹב, כִּי לְעוֹלָם חַסְדוֹ.

O give thanks to the Lord, who is good, whose love is ever-lasting.

⋆ ⋆

Mohel or a Parent

בָּרוּךְ אַתָּה, יְיָ אֱלֹהֵינוּ, מֶלֶךְ הָעוֹלָם, אֲשֶׁר קִדְּשָׁנוּ בְּמִצְוֹתָיו וְצִוָּנוּ עַל הַמִּילָה.

Blessed is the Lord our God, Ruler of the universe, by whose Mitzvot we are hallowed, who has given us the Mitzvah of circumcision.

The Circumcision is performed

A Parent

בָּרוּךְ אַתָּה, יְיָ אֱלֹהֵינוּ, מֶלֶךְ הָעוֹלָם, אֲשֶׁר קִדְּשָׁנוּ בְּמִצְוֹתָיו וְצִוָּנוּ לְהַכְנִיסוֹ בִּבְרִיתוֹ שֶׁל אַבְרָהָם אָבִינוּ.

Ba·ruch a·ta, A·do·nai E·lo·hei·nu, me·lech ha·o·lam, a·sher ki·de·sha·nu be·mits·vo·tav ve·tsi·va·nu le·hach·ni·so bi·ve·ri·to shel Av·ra·ham a·vi·nu.

Blessed is the Lord our God, Ruler of the universe, by whose Mitzvot we are hallowed, who commands us to bring our sons into the covenant of Abraham.

Mohel or Leader

בָּרוּךְ אַתָּה, יְיָ אֱלֹהֵינוּ, מֶלֶךְ הָעוֹלָם, בּוֹרֵא פְּרִי הַגָּפֶן.

Blessed is the Lord our God, Ruler of the universe, Creator of the fruit of the vine.

אֱלֹהֵינוּ וֵאלֹהֵי אֲבוֹתֵינוּ, קַיֵּם אֶת־הַיֶּלֶד הַזֶּה לְאָבִיו וּלְאִמּוֹ, וְיִקָּרֵא שְׁמוֹ בְּיִשְׂרָאֵל . . . יִשְׂמַח הָאָב בְּיוֹצֵא חֲלָצָיו וְתָגֵל אִמּוֹ בִּפְרִי בִטְנָהּ. זֶה הַקָּטָן גָּדוֹל יִהְיֶה. כְּשֵׁם שֶׁנִּכְנַס לַבְּרִית כֵּן יִכָּנֵס לְתוֹרָה, לְחֻפָּה, וּלְמַעֲשִׂים טוֹבִים.

Our God and God of our people, sustain this child, and let him be known in the House of Israel as . . . . May he bring much joy to his parents in the months and years to come. As he has entered into the covenant of Abraham, so may he enter into the study of Torah, the blessing of marriage, and the practice of goodness.

מִי שֶׁבֵּרַךְ אֲבוֹתֵינוּ אַבְרָהָם, יִצְחָק, וְיַעֲקֹב, הוּא יְבָרֵךְ אֶת־
הַיֶּלֶד הָרַךְ הַנִּמּוֹל וִירַפֵּא אוֹתוֹ רְפוּאָה שְׁלֵמָה. וְיִזְכּוּ אֲבוֹתָיו
לְגַדְּלוֹ לְחַנְּכוֹ וּלְחַכְּמוֹ. וְיִהְיוּ יָדָיו וְלִבּוֹ לְאֵל אֱמוּנָה,
וְנֹאמַר: אָמֵן.

May the One who blessed our fathers, Abraham, Isaac, and Jacob, bless this child and keep him from all harm. May his parents rear him to dedicate his life in faithfulness to God, his heart receptive always to Torah and Mitzvot. Then shall he bring blessing to his parents, his people, and all the world.

יְבָרֶכְךָ יְיָ וְיִשְׁמְרֶךָ,
יָאֵר יְיָ פָּנָיו אֵלֶיךָ וִיחֻנֶּךָּ,
יִשָּׂא יְיָ פָּנָיו אֵלֶיךָ וְיָשֵׂם לְךָ שָׁלוֹם.

The Lord bless you and keep you;
The Lord look kindly upon you and be gracious to you;
The Lord bestow favor upon you and give you peace. Amen.

The service might conclude with a reading in the form of an alphabetical acrostic of the child's name, selected from Psalm 119 or other Scriptural verses.

❖ ❖

If the mother is not present, this prayer may be offered when the child is taken to her.

O God, we give thanks to You for the gift of our child, who has entered into the covenant of Abraham. Keep him from all harm, and grant that he may be a source of joy to us and all his dear ones. Be with us, and give us health and length of days. Teach us to rear our child with care and affection, with wisdom and understanding, that he may be a faithful child of our people, and a blessing to the world. We give thanks to You, O Lord, the Source of life. Amen.

The Covenant of Life

This ritual is conducted on the eighth day

May she who comes be blessed.　　　　　בְּרוּכָה הַבָּאָה.

Reverence for life has been enjoined upon us as a fulfillment of our covenant with God, as it is written: And God said to Israel: Choose life, that you and your descendants may live.

The birth of a daughter brings us joy and hope, and the courage to reaffirm our enduring covenant with life and its Creator.

The mother kindles a light and takes her daughter:

Joyfully I bring my daughter into the covenant of Israel: a covenant with God, with Torah, and with life.

בָּרוּךְ אַתָּה, יְיָ אֱלֹהֵינוּ, מֶלֶךְ הָעוֹלָם, אֲשֶׁר קִדְּשָׁנוּ בְּמִצְוֹתָיו
וְצִוָּנוּ עַל קִדּוּשׁ הַחַיִּים.

Ba·ruch a·ta, A·do·nai E·lo·hei·nu, me·lech ha·o·lam, a·sher ki·de·sha·nu be·mits·vo·tav ve·tsi·va·nu al ki·dush ha·cha·yim.

Blessed is the Lord our God, Ruler of the universe, by whose Mitzvot we are hallowed, who commands us to sanctify life.

The father kindles a light and takes his daughter:

אֲנִי יְיָ, וְאֶתֶּנְךָ לִבְרִית עָם, לְאוֹר גּוֹיִם.

I, the Lord, have made you a covenant people, a light to the nations.

כִּי נֵר מִצְוָה וְתוֹרָה אוֹר.

For the Mitzvah is a lamp and the Torah a light.

בָּרוּךְ אַתָּה, יְיָ, הַמֵּאִיר לָעוֹלָם כֻּלּוֹ בִּכְבוֹדוֹ.

Blessed is the Lord, whose presence gives light to all the world.

Both parents say:

בָּרוּךְ אַתָּה, יְיָ אֱלֹהֵינוּ, מֶלֶךְ הָעוֹלָם, שֶׁהֶחֱיָנוּ וְקִיְּמָנוּ וְהִגִּיעָנוּ
לַזְּמַן הַזֶּה.

Blessed is the Lord our God, Ruler of the universe, for giving us
life, for sustaining us, and for enabling us to reach this day
of joy.

זֶה הַיּוֹם עָשָׂה יְיָ; נָגִילָה וְנִשְׂמְחָה בוֹ!

This is the day the Lord has made; let us rejoice and be glad
in it.

◆ ◆

וַיָּקֶם עֵדוּת בְּיַעֲקֹב, וְתוֹרָה שָׂם בְּיִשְׂרָאֵל, אֲשֶׁר צִוָּה אֶת־
אֲבוֹתֵינוּ לְהוֹדִיעָם לִבְנֵיהֶם; לְמַעַן יֵדְעוּ דוֹר אַחֲרוֹן בָּנִים
יִוָּלֵדוּ.

Lord, You established a testimony among us, You set a Teaching in Israel, commanding our ancestors to make them known
to their children; that the generations to come — children yet
unborn — might know them.

זָכַר לְעוֹלָם בְּרִיתוֹ, דָּבָר צִוָּה לְאֶלֶף דּוֹר: אֲשֶׁר כָּרַת אֶת־
אַבְרָהָם, וּשְׁבוּעָתוֹ לְיִשְׂחָק, וַיַּעֲמִידֶהָ לְיַעֲקֹב לְחֹק, לְיִשְׂרָאֵל
בְּרִית עוֹלָם.

You are for ever mindful of Your covenant, the word You
commanded for a thousand generations: the covenant You
made with the founders, Your sworn promise to their descendants, the commitment You made to our people, Your
everlasting covenant with Israel.

הוֹדוּ לַיְיָ כִּי־טוֹב, כִּי לְעוֹלָם חַסְדּוֹ.

O give thanks to the Lord, who is good, whose love is everlasting.

◆ ◆

115

בָּרוּךְ אַתָּה, יְיָ אֱלֹהֵינוּ, מֶלֶךְ הָעוֹלָם, בּוֹרֵא פְּרִי הַגָּפֶן.

Blessed is the Lord our God, Ruler of the universe, Creator of
the fruit of the vine.

אֱלֹהֵינוּ וֵאלֹהֵי אִמּוֹתֵינוּ, קַיֵּם אֶת־הַיַּלְדָּה הַזֹּאת לְאָבִיהָ
וּלְאִמָּהּ, וְיִקָּרֵא שְׁמָהּ בְּיִשְׂרָאֵל ... יִשְׂמַח הָאָב בְּיוֹצֵאת
חֲלָצָיו וְתָגֵל אִמָּהּ בִּפְרִי בִטְנָהּ. זֹאת הַקְּטַנָּה גְּדוֹלָה תִּהְיֶה.
כְּשֵׁם שֶׁנִּכְנְסָה לַבְּרִית כֵּן תִּכָּנֵס לְתוֹרָה, לְחֻפָּה, וּלְמַעֲשִׂים
טוֹבִים.

Our God, God of all generations, sustain this child, and let her
be known in the House of Israel as........ May she bring
much joy to her parents in the months and years to come. As
she has entered into the covenant of life, so may she enter into
the study of Torah, the blessing of marriage, and the practice
of goodness.

מִי שֶׁבֵּרַךְ אִמּוֹתֵינוּ שָׂרָה, רִבְקָה, רָחֵל, וְלֵאָה, הוּא יְבָרֵךְ
אֶת־הַיַּלְדָּה הָרַכָּה וְיִשְׁמְרֶהָ מִכָּל־צָרָה וְצוּקָה. וְיִזְכּוּ הוֹרֶיהָ
לְגַדְּלָהּ לַחֲנָכָה וּלְחָכְמָה. וְיִהְיוּ יָדֶיהָ וְלִבָּהּ לְאֵל אֱמוּנָה,
וְנֹאמַר: אָמֵן.

May the One who blessed our mothers, Sarah, Rebekah, Leah
and Rachel, bless this child and keep her from all harm. May
her parents rear her to dedicate her life in faithfulness to God,
her heart receptive always to Torah and Mitzvot. Then shall
she bring blessing to her parents, her people, and all the world.

יְבָרֶכְךָ יְיָ וְיִשְׁמְרֶךָ,

יָאֵר יְיָ פָּנָיו אֵלֶיךָ וִיחֻנֶּךָּ,

יִשָּׂא יְיָ פָּנָיו אֵלֶיךָ וְיָשֵׂם לְךָ שָׁלוֹם.

The Lord bless you and keep you;
The Lord look kindly upon you and be gracious to you;
The Lord bestow favor upon you and give you peace. Amen.

❖ ❖

The service might conclude with a reading in the form of an alphabetical acrostic of the child's name, selected from Psalm 119 or other scriptural verses.

◆ ◆

In the event that one of the parents is not present at the ceremony, this prayer may be offered later.

O God, we give thanks to You for the gift of our child, who has entered into the covenant of life. Keep her from all harm, and grant that she may be a source of joy to us and all her dear ones. Be with us, and give us health and length of days. Teach us to rear our child with care and affection, with wisdom and understanding, that she may be a faithful child of our people, and a blessing to the world. We give thanks to You, O Lord, the Source of life.

For the Naming of a Child

This ceremony may be performed in the Synagogue or at home.

Rabbi

God and Creator, happy parents have come into Your presence
to voice the longings of their hearts in prayer. Give them the
wisdom to teach their child to be faithful to the heritage of the
Household of Israel, that he (she) may grow up with the
knowledge that You are always near to him (her), guiding and
sustaining him (her). Keep open the eyes of his (her) spirit,
that he (she) may ever be conscious of the beauty and wonder
of Your world. And let him (her) learn to love the goodness
that is in man and woman, that he (she) may ever nourish the
goodness that has been implanted within him (her). Though
none can escape sorrow and pain, we humbly ask for him (her)
the courage to face evil, the faith to transcend it, and the
strength to subdue it. Grant him (her) health of mind and
strength of body, that he (she) may enjoy fullness of years and
live to do Your will in faithfulness. Amen.

◆ ◆

בָּרוּךְ אַתָּה, יְיָ אֱלֹהֵינוּ, מֶלֶךְ הָעוֹלָם, גּוֹמֵל חֲסָדִים טוֹבִים.

Blessed is the Lord our God, Ruler of the universe, whose love
and kindness extend to all the world.

◆ ◆

Parents

בָּרוּךְ אַתָּה, יְיָ אֱלֹהֵינוּ, מֶלֶךְ הָעוֹלָם, שֶׁהֶחֱיָנוּ וְקִיְּמָנוּ
וְהִגִּיעָנוּ לַזְּמַן הַזֶּה.

Blessed is the Lord our God, Ruler of the universe, for giving
us life, for sustaining us, and for enabling us to reach this
happy day.

O God, for the gift of this child we give thanks, praying that we
will be worthy of the blessing and responsibility of parenthood.

For a boy

May we show our gratitude to You by leading our son in the way of righteousness. Teach us so to guide and instruct him, that he may grow up to be loyal to Judaism and a worthy member of the Jewish community.

For a girl

May we show our gratitude to You by leading our daughter in the way of righteousness. Teach us so to guide and instruct her, that she may grow up to be loyal to Judaism and a worthy member of the Jewish community.

◆ ◆

Rabbi

מִי שֶׁבֵּרַךְ אֲבוֹתֵינוּ, אַבְרָהָם, יִצְחָק, וְיַעֲקֹב, וְאִמּוֹתֵינוּ, שָׂרָה, רִבְקָה, רָחֵל וְלֵאָה, הוּא יְבָרֵךְ אֶת־הַיֶּלֶד הַזֶּה (אֶת־הַיַּלְדָּה הַזֹּאת). הַקָּדוֹשׁ בָּרוּךְ הוּא יִשְׁמְרֵהוּ (יִשְׁמְרֶהָ) וְיַטֶּה אֶת־לֵב הַיֶּלֶד (הַיַּלְדָּה) לָלֶכֶת בְּדַרְכֵי יֹשֶׁר וִיהִי יְיָ עִמּוֹ (עִמָּהּ) וְיִתֶּן לוֹ (לָהּ) דֵּעָה, בִּינָה, וְהַשְׂכֵּל, חַיִּים וָחֶסֶד, בְּרָכָה וְשָׁלוֹם, וְיִזְכּוּ אֲבוֹתָיו (אֲבוֹתֶיהָ) לְגַדְּלוֹ (לְגַדְּלָהּ) וּלְחַנְּכוֹ (וּלְחַנְּכָהּ) לְתוֹרָה, לְחֻפָּה, וּלְמַעֲשִׂים טוֹבִים, וְנֹאמַר: אָמֵן.

May the One who blessed our fathers, Abraham, Isaac, and Jacob, bless this child with life and health. May he be a joy to his parents. May he live to bring honor to the House of Israel, blessing to humanity, and glory to the name of God.

May the One who blessed our mothers, Sarah, Rebekah, Leah and Rachel, bless this child with life and health. May she be a joy to her parents. May she live to bring honor to the House of Israel, blessing to humanity, and glory to the name of God.

◆

Now, in the presence of loved ones, we give to this child the name.... Let it become a name honored and respected for wisdom and good deeds. May God's blessing rest upon this child now and always.

יְבָרֶכְךָ יְיָ וְיִשְׁמְרֶךָ,

יָאֵר יְיָ פָּנָיו אֵלֶיךָ וִיחֻנֶּךָ,

יִשָּׂא יְיָ פָּנָיו אֵלֶיךָ וְיָשֵׂם לְךָ שָׁלוֹם.

The Lord bless you and keep you;
The Lord look kindly upon you and be gracious to you;
The Lord bestow favor upon you and give you peace. Amen.

◆ ◆

בָּרוּךְ אַתָּה, יְיָ אֱלֹהֵינוּ, מֶלֶךְ הָעוֹלָם, בּוֹרֵא פְּרִי הַגָּפֶן.

Blessed is the Lord our God, Ruler of the universe, Creator
of the fruit of the vine.

A few drops are given to the child.

The cup may be shared by parents and loved ones.

At a Birthday Celebration

God of days and years, Author of life, our times are in Your hand. We thank You day by day for Your abounding blessings and, as year follows year, we are grateful for all Your gifts.

We gather today in special thankfulness to share in the happiness of our dear . . . . Be with him (her) always as the joy of his (her) life. May he (she) be blessed with health and happiness, and the strength to overcome sickness and sorrow.

We pray that our lives may be filled with good and abundance of blessing; and may we have the joy of coming together for many more years, as a family united by mutual reverence and love.

בָּרוּךְ אַתָּה, יְיָ אֱלֹהֵינוּ, מֶלֶךְ הָעוֹלָם, שֶׁהֶחֱיָנוּ וְקִיְּמָנוּ וְהִגִּיעָנוּ לַזְּמַן הַזֶּה.

Blessed is the Lord our God, Ruler of the universe, for giving us life, for sustaining us, and for enabling us to reach this day.

בָּרוּךְ אַתָּה, יְיָ אֱלֹהֵינוּ, מֶלֶךְ הָעוֹלָם, בּוֹרֵא מִינֵי מְזוֹנוֹת.

Ba·ruch a·ta, A·do·nai E·lo·hei·nu, me·lech ha·o·lam, bo·rei mi·nei me·zo·not.

Blessed is the Lord our God, Ruler of the universe, Creator of many kinds of food.

On the Beginning of a Child's Religious Education

"Set these words, which I command you this day, upon your heart. . . . Teach them faithfully to your children."

Source of all knowledge, Teacher of Israel and all the world, You reveal Yourself to us in the order and beauty of nature, in the call of conscience, in the greatness of sacred tradition. The hearts and minds of children sense Your Presence: "Out of the mouths of babes You have established Your strength." This intuition we would foster through education, that through knowledge it may gain strength, through worship take root in the soul, and through deeds of mercy and justice ennoble the life of all Your children.

Therefore, as our mothers and fathers have done in every age, as our own parents did with us, we bring our child to Your house to study Your Law, to be among those who seek to know Your ways and to follow the path of Your Mitzvot.

We pray that this child will grow in heart and mind. May the story of our people inspire him (her). May the truths of Torah guide him (her). And may the grandeur of the prophetic word of truth and righteousness enter his (her) spirit and be for him (her) a lasting benediction. Amen.

At Bar Mitzvah, Bat Mitzvah, or Confirmation

"And all your children shall be taught of the Lord, and great shall be the peace of your children."

Humbly do we give thanks for this day, and for the years of growth and learning that have preceded it. Now as our child steps forward to affirm her (his) commitment to the ideals and Mitzvot of our faith, our soul is joyful, our mind is at peace.

בָּרוּךְ אַתָּה, יְיָ אֱלֹהֵינוּ, מֶלֶךְ הָעוֹלָם, שֶׁהֶחֱיָנוּ וְקִיְּמָנוּ וְהִגִּיעָנוּ לַזְּמַן הַזֶּה.

Blessed is the Lord our God, Ruler of the universe, for giving us life, for sustaining us, and for enabling us to reach this great day.

We pray that this day's service may long echo in our child's memory. May it engrave on the tablet of her (his) heart the understanding that this day initiates a life more firmly dedicated to the study of Torah and the fulfillment of Mitzvot, to deeds of justice and kindness, to faithful membership in the household of Israel.

O God, make each of us a worthy example to our children. Let nothing estrange us from them and from You, the Source of all goodness and compassion. Help us, too, again and again to renew our attachment to the Covenant of Israel, to walk hand in hand with our child in the ways of righteousness and truth. Amen.

On Entering College

"You favor us with knowledge and teach mortals understanding. May You continue to favor us with knowledge, understanding, and insight. Blessed is the Lord, gracious Giver of knowledge."

As I begin my studies anew, I pray for wisdom to hold all truth sacred, whether it comes from the Torah and its interpreters of old, or from the scholars of our own age. Help me, Lord, to see beyond the surface of things, to understand that their beauty is but a dim reflection of Your wondrous creative power at work in me and in all the universe. Give me, also, a discerning mind, that I may recognize what is good, and reject what is false and harmful. And grant me a heart of wisdom, that I may learn to use my knowledge for righteous purpose, that I may be Your partner in the work of creation all the days of my life.

Wherever I go, and whatever I do, let me be a true child of my people Israel, faithful to justice and truth, eager for knowledge and insight. And may the study of Torah be sweet to me as honey to my lips. Amen.

In Illness and on Recovery

One of the following

1

In sickness I turn to You, O God, as a child turns to a parent for comfort and help. Strengthen within me the wondrous power of healing that You have implanted in Your children. Guide my doctors and nurses that they may speed my recovery. Let the knowledge of Your love comfort my dear ones, lighten their burdens, and renew their faith.

May my sickness not weaken my faith in You, nor diminish my love for other human beings. From my illness may I gain a truer appreciation of life's gifts, a deeper awareness of life's blessings, and a fuller sympathy for all who are in pain.

בָּרוּךְ אַתָּה, יְיָ, רוֹפֵא הַחוֹלִים.

Ba·ruch a·ta, A·do·nai, ro·fei ha·cho·lim.

Blessed is the Lord, the Source of healing.

2

My God and God of all generations, in my great need I pour out my heart to You. The long days and weeks of suffering are hard to endure. In my struggle, I reach out for the help that only You can give. Let me feel that You are near, and that Your care enfolds me. Rouse in me the strength to overcome my weakness, and brighten my spirit with the assurance of Your love. Make me grateful for the care and concern that are expended on my behalf. Help me to sustain the hopes of my dear ones, as they strive to strengthen and encourage me. May the healing power You have placed within me give me strength to recover, so that I may proclaim with all my being: I shall not die, but live and declare the works of the Lord.

בָּרוּךְ אַתָּה, יְיָ, רוֹפֵא הַחוֹלִים.

Ba·ruch a·ta, A·do·nai, ro·fei ha·cho·lim.

Blessed is the Lord, the Source of healing.

✦ ✦

On convalescence

Loving God, Your healing power has saved me. You have sustained me in my weakness, supported me in my suffering, and set me on the road to recovery. By Your grace, I have found the strength to endure the hours of distress and pain. Lord, now give me patience and peace of mind. Help me, after I have recovered, to express gratitude for all Your mercies by greater devotion to Your service.

בָּרוּךְ אַתָּה, יְיָ, רוֹפֵא הַחוֹלִים.

Ba·ruch a·ta, A·do·nai, ro·fei ha·cho·lim.

Blessed is the Lord, the Source of healing.

✦ ✦

On recovery

For health of body and of spirit, I thank You, Lord. I was broken and now am whole; weary, but now am rested; anxious, but now am reassured.

I thank You for those who helped me in my need, who heartened me in my fear, and who visited me in my loneliness. For the strength You gave me, O God, I give thanks to You.

בָּרוּךְ אַתָּה, יְיָ, רוֹפֵא הַחוֹלִים.

Ba·ruch a·ta, A·do·nai, ro·fei ha·cho·lim.

Blessed is the Lord, the Source of healing.

✦ ✦

By a sick child

O God, help me to become well. Teach me to do whatever my parents, the doctor, and all who love and care for me ask. Make me brave when I feel pain. I know that You are with me, now and always.

בָּרוּךְ אַתָּה, יְיָ, רוֹפֵא הַחוֹלִים.

Ba·ruch a·ta, A·do·nai, ro·fei ha·cho·lim.
Thank You, Lord, for the healing power that You have made a part of me.

◆ ◆

By a child on recovery

O God, I thank You for life and health. I thank You for all who have helped me become well and strong again.

בָּרוּךְ אַתָּה, יְיָ, רוֹפֵא הַחוֹלִים.

Ba·ruch a·ta, A·do·nai, ro·fei ha·cho·lim.
Thank You, Lord, for the healing power that You have made a part of me.

◆ ◆

On behalf of the sick

Lord, we thank You for the gift of life and the strength of faith. Sustain . . ., our loved one, through these days of illness with the courage to endure weakness and pain. We thank You for the healing powers at work within him (her). Be with all who suffer illness of body or mind. May they recover speedily from their afflictions and return in health to family and friends.

בָּרוּךְ אַתָּה, יְיָ, רוֹפֵא הַחוֹלִים.

Ba·ruch a·ta, A·do·nai, ro·fei ha·cho·lim.
Blessed is the Lord, the Source of healing.

In Contemplation of Death

Lord my God and God of the universe, Creator of all that lives: although I pray for healing and continued life, still I know that I am mortal. Give me courage to accept whatever befalls me.

If only my hands were clean and my heart pure! But, alas, I have committed many wrongs and left so much undone! And yet I also know the good I did or tried to do. May that goodness impart an eternal meaning to my life.

Protector of the helpless, watch over my loved ones in whose souls my own is knit. You are my Rock and my Redeemer, the divine Source of mercy and truth.

בְּיָדוֹ אַפְקִיד רוּחִי בְּעֵת אִישַׁן וְאָעִירָה.
וְעִם־רוּחִי גְּוִיָּתִי; יְיָ לִי, וְלֹא אִירָא.

Into Your hands I commend my spirit, both when I sleep and when I wake. Body and soul are Yours, and in Your presence, Lord, I cast off fear and am at rest.

יְיָ מֶלֶךְ, יְיָ מָלָךְ, יְיָ יִמְלֹךְ לְעוֹלָם וָעֶד.

The Lord reigns, the Lord will reign for ever and ever.

בָּרוּךְ שֵׁם כְּבוֹד מַלְכוּתוֹ לְעוֹלָם וָעֶד.

Blessed is His glorious kingdom for ever and ever.

יְיָ הוּא הָאֱלֹהִים.

The Eternal Lord is God.

שְׁמַע יִשְׂרָאֵל: יְיָ אֱלֹהֵינוּ, יְיָ אֶחָד!

Hear, O Israel: the Lord is our God, the Lord is One!

After Death

בָּרוּךְ אַתָּה, יְיָ אֱלֹהֵינוּ, מֶלֶךְ הָעוֹלָם, דַּיַּן הָאֱמֶת.

Ba·ruch a·ta, A·do·nai E·lo·hei·nu, me·lech ha·o·lam, da·yan ha·e·met.

Blessed is the Lord our God, Ruler of the universe, the right-eous Judge.

On Returning Home After a Funeral

Out of the depths I cry unto You, Lord; hear my supplication. A heavy burden has fallen upon me and sorrow has bowed my head. Days of anguish have been my lot; days and nights of weeping. And now I turn to You, the Source of good, for comfort and help. Give me the eyes to see that pain is not Your will, that somewhere there weeps with me One who feels my trouble and knows the suffering of my soul! O divine Spirit in whose image my own spirit is cast, I seek the Light that will dispel the darkness that has overtaken me. Let me find You in the love of family and friends, in the sources of healing that are implanted within all the living, in the mind that conquers all infirmity and trouble. Grant me the strength to endure what cannot be escaped, and the courage to go on without bitterness or despair, basing my life on the abiding foundations of Your law. Amen.

נֵר־לְרַגְלִי דְבָרֶךָ, וְאוֹר לִנְתִיבָתִי.

Neir le·rag·li de·va·re·cha, ve·or li·ne·ti·va·ti.

Your word, Lord, is a lamp to my feet, a light to my path.

The memorial light is kindled

נֵר יְיָ נִשְׁמַת אָדָם.

בָּרוּךְ אַתָּה, יְיָ, נוֹטֵעַ בְּתוֹכֵנוּ חַיֵּי עוֹלָם.

Neir A·do·nai nish·mat a·dam.

Ba·ruch a·ta, A·do·nai, no·tei·a be·to·chei·nu cha·yei o·lam.

The human spirit is the lamp of God.

Blessed is the Eternal One, who has implanted within us eternal life.

WEEKDAY SERVICES

Weekday Evening Service ערבית לחול

Lord, You give meaning to our hopes, to our struggles and our strivings. Without You we are lost, our lives empty. And so when all else fails us, we turn to You! In the stillness of night, when the outer darkness enters the soul; in the press of the crowd, when we walk alone though yearning for companionship; and when in agony we are bystanders to our own confusion, we look to You for hope and peace.

Lord, we do not ask for a life of ease, for happiness without alloy. Instead we ask You to teach us to be uncomplaining and unafraid. In our darkness help us to find Your light, and in our loneliness to discover the many spirits akin to our own. Give us strength to face life with hope and courage, that even from its discords and conflicts we may draw blessing. Make us understand that life calls us not merely to enjoy the richness of the earth, but to exult in heights attained after the toil of climbing.

Let our darkness be dispelled by Your love, that we may rise above fear and failure, our steps sustained by faith.

Lord, You give meaning to our lives; You are our support and our trust.

◆ ◆

All rise

שמע וברכותיה

בָּרְכוּ אֶת־יְיָ הַמְבֹרָךְ!

Praise the Lord, to whom our praise is due!

בָּרוּךְ יְיָ הַמְבֹרָךְ לְעוֹלָם וָעֶד!

Praised be the Lord, to whom our praise is due,
now and for ever!

◆ ◆

מעריב ערבים

בָּרוּךְ אַתָּה, יְיָ אֱלֹהֵינוּ, מֶלֶךְ הָעוֹלָם, אֲשֶׁר בִּדְבָרוֹ מַעֲרִיב עֲרָבִים. בְּחָכְמָה פּוֹתֵחַ שְׁעָרִים, וּבִתְבוּנָה מְשַׁנֶּה עִתִּים, וּמַחֲלִיף אֶת־הַזְּמַנִּים, וּמְסַדֵּר אֶת־הַכּוֹכָבִים בְּמִשְׁמְרוֹתֵיהֶם בָּרָקִיעַ כִּרְצוֹנוֹ.

Praised be the Lord our God, Ruler of the universe, whose word brings on the evening. His wisdom opens heaven's gates; His understanding makes the ages pass and the seasons alternate; and His will controls the stars as they travel through the skies.

בּוֹרֵא יוֹם וָלָיְלָה, גּוֹלֵל אוֹר מִפְּנֵי חֹשֶׁךְ וְחֹשֶׁךְ מִפְּנֵי אוֹר, וּמַעֲבִיר יוֹם וּמֵבִיא לָיְלָה, וּמַבְדִּיל בֵּין יוֹם וּבֵין לָיְלָה, יְיָ צְבָאוֹת שְׁמוֹ.

He is Creator of day and night, rolling light away from darkness, and darkness from light; He causes day to pass and brings on the night; He sets day and night apart: He is the Lord of Hosts.

אֵל חַי וְקַיָּם, תָּמִיד יִמְלוֹךְ עָלֵינוּ, לְעוֹלָם וָעֶד. בָּרוּךְ אַתָּה, יְיָ, הַמַּעֲרִיב עֲרָבִים.

May the living and eternal God rule us always, to the end of time! Blessed is the Lord, whose word makes evening fall.

✦ ✦

אהבת עולם

אַהֲבַת עוֹלָם בֵּית יִשְׂרָאֵל עַמְּךָ אָהָבְתָּ: תּוֹרָה וּמִצְוֹת, חֻקִּים וּמִשְׁפָּטִים אוֹתָנוּ לִמַּדְתָּ.

Unending is Your love for Your people, the House of Israel: Torah and Mitzvot, laws and precepts have You taught us.

עַל־כֵּן, יְיָ אֱלֹהֵינוּ, בְּשָׁכְבֵּנוּ וּבְקוּמֵנוּ נָשִׂיחַ בְּחֻקֶּיךָ, וְנִשְׂמַח בְּדִבְרֵי תוֹרָתְךָ וּבְמִצְוֹתֶיךָ לְעוֹלָם וָעֶד.

Therefore, O Lord our God, when we lie down and when we rise up, we will meditate on Your laws and rejoice in Your Torah and Mitzvot for ever.

כִּי הֵם חַיֵּינוּ וְאֹרֶךְ יָמֵינוּ, וּבָהֶם נֶהְגֶּה יוֹמָם וָלָיְלָה. וְאַהֲבָתְךָ
אַל־תָּסִיר מִמֶּנּוּ לְעוֹלָמִים! בָּרוּךְ אַתָּה, יְיָ, אוֹהֵב עַמּוֹ יִשְׂרָאֵל.

*Day and night we will reflect on them, for they are our life
and the length of our days. Then Your love shall never depart
from our hearts! Blessed is the Lord, who loves His people Israel.*

✦ ✦

שְׁמַע יִשְׂרָאֵל: יְיָ אֱלֹהֵינוּ, יְיָ אֶחָד!

Hear, O Israel: the Lord is our God, the Lord is One!

בָּרוּךְ שֵׁם כְּבוֹד מַלְכוּתוֹ לְעוֹלָם וָעֶד!

Blessed is His glorious kingdom for ever and ever!

All are seated

וְאָהַבְתָּ אֵת יְיָ אֱלֹהֶיךָ בְּכָל־לְבָבְךָ וּבְכָל־נַפְשְׁךָ וּבְכָל־מְאֹדֶךָ.
וְהָיוּ הַדְּבָרִים הָאֵלֶּה, אֲשֶׁר אָנֹכִי מְצַוְּךָ הַיּוֹם, עַל־לְבָבֶךָ.
וְשִׁנַּנְתָּם לְבָנֶיךָ, וְדִבַּרְתָּ בָּם בְּשִׁבְתְּךָ בְּבֵיתֶךָ, וּבְלֶכְתְּךָ
בַדֶּרֶךְ, וּבְשָׁכְבְּךָ וּבְקוּמֶךָ.

*You shall love the Lord your God with all your mind, with
all your strength, with all your being.
Set these words, which I command you this day, upon your
heart. Teach them faithfully to your children; speak of them
in your home and on your way, when you lie down and when
you rise up.*

וּקְשַׁרְתָּם לְאוֹת עַל־יָדֶךָ, וְהָיוּ לְטֹטָפֹת בֵּין עֵינֶיךָ, וּכְתַבְתָּם
עַל־מְזֻזוֹת בֵּיתֶךָ, וּבִשְׁעָרֶיךָ.

*Bind them as a sign upon your hand; let them be a symbol
before your eyes; inscribe them on the doorposts of your
house, and on your gates.*

לְמַעַן תִּזְכְּרוּ וַעֲשִׂיתֶם אֶת־כָּל־מִצְוֹתָי, וִהְיִיתֶם קְדֹשִׁים
לֵאלֹהֵיכֶם. אֲנִי יְיָ אֱלֹהֵיכֶם, אֲשֶׁר הוֹצֵאתִי אֶתְכֶם מֵאֶרֶץ
מִצְרַיִם לִהְיוֹת לָכֶם לֵאלֹהִים. אֲנִי יְיָ אֱלֹהֵיכֶם.

*Be mindful of all My mitzvot, and do them: so shall you
consecrate yourselves to your God. I, the Lord, am your God*

who led you out of Egypt to be your God; I, the Lord, am
your God.

◆ ◆

גְּאוּלָה

אֱמֶת וֶאֱמוּנָה כָּל־זֹאת, וְקַיָּם עָלֵינוּ כִּי הוּא יְיָ אֱלֹהֵינוּ וְאֵין
זוּלָתוֹ, וַאֲנַחְנוּ יִשְׂרָאֵל עַמּוֹ.
הַפּוֹדֵנוּ מִיַּד מְלָכִים, מַלְכֵּנוּ הַגּוֹאֲלֵנוּ מִכַּף כָּל־הֶעָרִיצִים.

All this we hold to be true and sure: He alone is our God;
there is none else, and we are Israel His people.
He is our King: He delivers us from the hand of oppressors,
and saves us from the fist of tyrants.

הָעֹשֶׂה גְדֹלוֹת עַד אֵין חֵקֶר, וְנִפְלָאוֹת עַד־אֵין מִסְפָּר.
הַשָּׂם נַפְשֵׁנוּ בַּחַיִּים, וְלֹא־נָתַן לַמּוֹט רַגְלֵנוּ.

He does wonders without number, marvels that pass our
understanding.
He gives us our life; by His help we survive all who seek our
destruction.

הָעֹשֶׂה לָּנוּ נִסִּים בְּפַרְעֹה, אוֹתוֹת וּמוֹפְתִים בְּאַדְמַת בְּנֵי חָם.
וַיּוֹצֵא אֶת־עַמּוֹ יִשְׂרָאֵל מִתּוֹכָם לְחֵרוּת עוֹלָם.

He did wonders for us in the land of Egypt, miracles and marvels in the land of Pharaoh.
He led His people Israel out, for ever to serve Him in freedom.

וְרָאוּ בָנָיו גְּבוּרָתוֹ; שִׁבְּחוּ וְהוֹדוּ לִשְׁמוֹ. וּמַלְכוּתוֹ בְּרָצוֹן קִבְּלוּ
עֲלֵיהֶם. מֹשֶׁה וּבְנֵי יִשְׂרָאֵל לְךָ עָנוּ שִׁירָה בְּשִׂמְחָה רַבָּה,
וְאָמְרוּ כֻלָּם:

When His children witnessed His power, they extolled Him
and gave Him thanks; freely they acclaimed Him King; and
full of joy, Moses and all Israel sang this song:

Who is like You, Eternal One, among
the gods that are worshipped?   מִי־כָמֹכָה בָּאֵלִם, יְיָ?

Who is like You, majestic in holiness,   מִי כָּמֹכָה, נֶאְדָּר בַּקֹּדֶשׁ,

awesome in splendor, doing wonders?   נוֹרָא תְהִלֹּת, עֹשֵׂה פֶלֶא?

מַלְכוּתְךָ רָאוּ בָנֶיךָ, בּוֹקֵעַ יָם לִפְנֵי מֹשֶׁה; "זֶה אֵלִי!" עָנוּ
וְאָמְרוּ: "יְיָ יִמְלֹךְ לְעֹלָם וָעֶד!"

In their escape from the sea, Your children saw Your sovereign
might displayed. "This is my God!" they cried. "The Eternal will
reign for ever and ever!"

וְנֶאֱמַר: "כִּי־פָדָה יְיָ אֶת־יַעֲקֹב, וּגְאָלוֹ מִיַּד חָזָק מִמֶּנּוּ." בָּרוּךְ
אַתָּה, יְיָ, גָּאַל יִשְׂרָאֵל.

And it has been said: "The Eternal delivered Jacob, and redeemed
him from the hand of one stronger than himself." Blessed is the
Lord, the Redeemer of Israel.

◆ ◆

DIVINE PROVIDENCE   הַשְׁכִּיבֵנוּ

הַשְׁכִּיבֵנוּ, יְיָ אֱלֹהֵינוּ, לְשָׁלוֹם וְהַעֲמִידֵנוּ, מַלְכֵּנוּ, לְחַיִּים.
וּפְרוֹשׂ עָלֵינוּ סֻכַּת שְׁלוֹמֶךָ, וְתַקְּנֵנוּ בְּעֵצָה טוֹבָה מִלְּפָנֶיךָ,
וְהוֹשִׁיעֵנוּ לְמַעַן שְׁמֶךָ, וְהָגֵן בַּעֲדֵנוּ. וְהָסֵר מֵעָלֵינוּ אוֹיֵב,
דֶּבֶר וְחֶרֶב וְרָעָב וְיָגוֹן; וְהָסֵר שָׂטָן מִלְּפָנֵינוּ וּמֵאַחֲרֵינוּ;
וּבְצֵל כְּנָפֶיךָ תַּסְתִּירֵנוּ, כִּי אֵל שׁוֹמְרֵנוּ וּמַצִּילֵנוּ אָתָּה, כִּי
אֵל מֶלֶךְ חַנּוּן וְרַחוּם אָתָּה. וּשְׁמוֹר צֵאתֵנוּ וּבוֹאֵנוּ לְחַיִּים
וּלְשָׁלוֹם, מֵעַתָּה וְעַד עוֹלָם. בָּרוּךְ אַתָּה, יְיָ, שׁוֹמֵר עַמּוֹ
יִשְׂרָאֵל לָעַד.

Grant, O Eternal God, that we may lie down in peace, and
raise us up, O Sovereign, to life renewed. Spread over us the
shelter of Your peace; guide us with Your good counsel; and
for Your name's sake, be our Help.

*Shield us from hatred and plague; keep us from war and
famine and anguish; subdue our inclination to evil. O God
our Guardian and Helper, our gracious and merciful Ruler,
give us refuge in the shadow of Your wings. O guard our
coming and our going, that now and always we have life and
peace.*

Blessed is the Lord, Guardian of His people Israel for ever.

READER'S KADDISH   חצי קדיש

יִתְגַּדַּל וְיִתְקַדַּשׁ שְׁמֵהּ רַבָּא בְּעָלְמָא דִּי־בְרָא כִרְעוּתֵהּ,
וְיַמְלִיךְ מַלְכוּתֵהּ בְּחַיֵּיכוֹן וּבְיוֹמֵיכוֹן וּבְחַיֵּי דְכָל־בֵּית
יִשְׂרָאֵל, בַּעֲגָלָא וּבִזְמַן קָרִיב, וְאִמְרוּ: אָמֵן.

יְהֵא שְׁמֵהּ רַבָּא מְבָרַךְ לְעָלַם וּלְעָלְמֵי עָלְמַיָּא.

יִתְבָּרַךְ וְיִשְׁתַּבַּח, וְיִתְפָּאַר וְיִתְרוֹמַם וְיִתְנַשֵּׂא, וְיִתְהַדָּר
וְיִתְעַלֶּה וְיִתְהַלָּל שְׁמֵהּ דְּקוּדְשָׁא, בְּרִיךְ הוּא, לְעֵלָּא מִן
כָּל־בִּרְכָתָא וְשִׁירָתָא, תֻּשְׁבְּחָתָא וְנֶחֱמָתָא דַּאֲמִירָן בְּעָלְמָא,
וְאִמְרוּ: אָמֵן.

Let the glory of God be extolled, let His great name be
hallowed in the world whose creation He willed. May His
kingdom soon prevail, in our own day, our own lives, and
the life of all Israel, and let us say: Amen.

Let His great name be blessed for ever and ever.

Let the name of the Holy One, blessed is He, be glorified,
exalted and honored, though He is beyond all the praises,
songs, and adorations that we can utter, and let us say:
Amen.

◆ ◆

All rise

תפלה

אֲדֹנָי, שְׂפָתַי תִּפְתָּח, וּפִי יַגִּיד תְּהִלָּתֶךָ.

Eternal God, open my lips, that my mouth may declare Your glory.

GOD OF ALL GENERATIONS   אבות

בָּרוּךְ אַתָּה, יְיָ אֱלֹהֵינוּ וֵאלֹהֵי אֲבוֹתֵינוּ, אֱלֹהֵי אַבְרָהָם, אֱלֹהֵי
יִצְחָק, וֵאלֹהֵי יַעֲקֹב: הָאֵל הַגָּדוֹל, הַגִּבּוֹר וְהַנּוֹרָא, אֵל עֶלְיוֹן.

We praise You, Lord our God and God of all generations: God
of Abraham, God of Isaac, God of Jacob; great, mighty, and
awesome God, God supreme.

גּוֹמֵל חֲסָדִים טוֹבִים, וְקוֹנֵה הַכֹּל, וְזוֹכֵר חַסְדֵי אָבוֹת, וּמֵבִיא
גְאֻלָּה לִבְנֵי בְנֵיהֶם, לְמַעַן שְׁמוֹ, בְּאַהֲבָה.*

Master of all the living, Your ways are ways of love. You remember the faithfulness of our ancestors, and in love bring
redemption to their children's children for the sake of Your
name.*

מֶלֶךְ עוֹזֵר וּמוֹשִׁיעַ וּמָגֵן. בָּרוּךְ אַתָּה, יְיָ, מָגֵן אַבְרָהָם.

You are our King and our Help, our Savior and our Shield.
Blessed is the Lord, the Shield of Abraham.

* *On the Ten Days of Repentance insert:*

זָכְרֵנוּ לְחַיִּים, מֶלֶךְ חָפֵץ בַּחַיִּים,
וְכָתְבֵנוּ בְּסֵפֶר הַחַיִּים, לְמַעַנְךָ אֱלֹהִים חַיִּים.

Remember us unto life, for You are the King who delights in life, and
inscribe us in the Book of Life, that Your will may prevail, O God of
life.

◆ ◆

GOD'S POWER

גבורות

אַתָּה גִבּוֹר לְעוֹלָם, אֲדֹנָי, מְחַיֵּה הַכֹּל אַתָּה, רַב לְהוֹשִׁיעַ.

Eternal is Your might, O Lord; all life is Your gift; great is Your power to save!

מְכַלְכֵּל חַיִּים בְּחֶסֶד, מְחַיֵּה הַכֹּל בְּרַחֲמִים רַבִּים. סוֹמֵךְ נוֹפְלִים, וְרוֹפֵא חוֹלִים, וּמַתִּיר אֲסוּרִים, וּמְקַיֵּם אֱמוּנָתוֹ לִישֵׁנֵי עָפָר.

With love You sustain the living, with great compassion give life to all. You send help to the falling and healing to the sick; You bring freedom to the captive and keep faith with those who sleep in the dust.

מִי כָמוֹךָ, בַּעַל גְּבוּרוֹת, וּמִי דוֹמֶה לָּךְ, מֶלֶךְ מֵמִית וּמְחַיֶּה וּמַצְמִיחַ יְשׁוּעָה?*

וְנֶאֱמָן אַתָּה לְהַחֲיוֹת הַכֹּל. בָּרוּךְ אַתָּה, יְיָ, מְחַיֵּה הַכֹּל.

Who is like You, Master of Might? Who is Your equal, O Lord of life and death, Source of salvation?* Blessed is the Lord, the Source of life.

* *On the Ten Days of Repentance insert:*

מִי כָמוֹךָ, אַב הָרַחֲמִים, זוֹכֵר יְצוּרָיו לְחַיִּים בְּרַחֲמִים?

Who is like You, Source of mercy, who in compassion sustains the life of His children?

• •

GOD'S HOLINESS

קדושת השם

אַתָּה קָדוֹשׁ וְשִׁמְךָ קָדוֹשׁ, וּקְדוֹשִׁים בְּכָל־יוֹם יְהַלְלוּךָ סֶּלָה.*

בָּרוּךְ אַתָּה, יְיָ, הָאֵל הַקָּדוֹשׁ.

You are holy, Your name is holy, and those who strive to be holy declare Your glory day by day.* Blessed is the Lord, the holy God.

* *On the Ten Days of Repentance conclude:*

Blessed is the Lord, the holy King. בָּרוּךְ אַתָּה, יְיָ, הַמֶּלֶךְ הַקָּדוֹשׁ.

All are seated

• •

FOR UNDERSTANDING

בִּינָה

אַתָּה חוֹנֵן לְאָדָם דַּעַת וּמְלַמֵּד לָאֱנוֹשׁ בִּינָה. חָנֵּנוּ מֵאִתְּךָ
דֵּעָה, בִּינָה וְהַשְׂכֵּל.
בָּרוּךְ אַתָּה, יְיָ, חוֹנֵן הַדָּעַת.

You favor us with knowledge and teach mortals understanding.
May You continue to favor us with knowledge, understanding,
and insight.

Blessed is the Lord, gracious Giver of knowledge.

◆ ◆

FOR REPENTANCE

תְּשׁוּבָה

הֲשִׁיבֵנוּ אָבִינוּ לְתוֹרָתֶךָ, וְקָרְבֵנוּ מַלְכֵּנוּ לַעֲבוֹדָתֶךָ,
וְהַחֲזִירֵנוּ בִּתְשׁוּבָה שְׁלֵמָה לְפָנֶיךָ.
בָּרוּךְ אַתָּה, יְיָ, הָרוֹצֶה בִּתְשׁוּבָה.

Help us to return, our Maker, to Your Torah; draw us near,
O Sovereign God, to Your service; and bring us back into Your
presence in perfect repentance.

Blessed is the Lord, who calls for repentance.

◆ ◆

FOR FORGIVENESS

סְלִיחָה

סְלַח־לָנוּ אָבִינוּ כִּי חָטָאנוּ, מְחַל־לָנוּ מַלְכֵּנוּ כִּי פָשָׁעְנוּ, כִּי
מוֹחֵל וְסוֹלֵחַ אָתָּה.
בָּרוּךְ אַתָּה, יְיָ, חַנּוּן הַמַּרְבֶּה לִסְלוֹחַ.

Forgive us, our Creator, when we have sinned; pardon us, our
King, when we transgress; for You are a forgiving God.

*Blessed is the Lord, the gracious God, whose forgiveness is
abundant.*

◆ ◆

FOR REDEMPTION גאולה

רְאֵה בְעָנְיֵנוּ וְרִיבָה רִיבֵנוּ, וּגְאָלֵנוּ מְהֵרָה לְמַעַן שְׁמֶךָ, כִּי גוֹאֵל חָזָק אֶתָּה.

בָּרוּךְ אַתָּה, יְיָ, גּוֹאֵל יִשְׂרָאֵל.

Look upon our affliction and help us in our need; O mighty Redeemer, redeem us speedily for Your name's sake.

Blessed is the Lord, the Redeemer of Israel.

◆ ◆

FOR HEALTH רפואה

רְפָאֵנוּ יְיָ וְנֵרָפֵא, הוֹשִׁיעֵנוּ וְנִוָּשֵׁעָה, וְהַעֲלֵה רְפוּאָה שְׁלֵמָה לְכָל־מַכּוֹתֵינוּ.

בָּרוּךְ אַתָּה, יְיָ, רוֹפֵא הַחוֹלִים.

Heal us, O Lord, and we shall be healed; save us, and we shall be saved; grant us a perfect healing from all our wounds.

Blessed is the Lord, Healer of the sick.

◆ ◆

FOR ABUNDANCE ברכת השנים

בָּרֵךְ עָלֵינוּ, יְיָ אֱלֹהֵינוּ, אֶת־הַשָּׁנָה הַזֹּאת וְאֶת־כָּל־מִינֵי תְבוּאָתָהּ לְטוֹבָה. וְתֵן בְּרָכָה עַל־פְּנֵי הָאֲדָמָה, וְשַׂבְּעֵנוּ מִטּוּבֶךָ.

בָּרוּךְ אַתָּה, יְיָ, מְבָרֵךְ הַשָּׁנִים.

Bless this year, O Lord our God, and let its produce bring us well-being. Bestow Your blessing on the earth and satisfy us with Your goodness.

Blessed is the Lord, from whom all blessings flow.

◆ ◆

FOR FREEDOM חרות

תְּקַע בְּשׁוֹפָר גָּדוֹל לְחֵרוּתֵנוּ, וְשָׂא נֵס לִפְדּוֹת עֲשׁוּקֵינוּ, וְקוֹל
דְּרוֹר יִשָּׁמַע בְּאַרְבַּע כַּנְפוֹת הָאָרֶץ.
בָּרוּךְ אַתָּה, יְיָ, פּוֹדֶה עֲשׁוּקִים.

Sound the great horn to proclaim freedom, inspire us to strive
for the liberation of the oppressed, and let the song of liberty
be heard in the four corners of the earth.

Blessed is the Lord, Redeemer of the oppressed.

◆ ◆

FOR JUSTICE משפט

עַל שׁוֹפְטֵי אֶרֶץ שְׁפוֹךְ רוּחֶךָ, וְהַדְרִיכֵם בְּמִשְׁפְּטֵי צִדְקֶךָ,
וּמְלוֹךְ עָלֵינוּ אַתָּה לְבַדֶּךָ, בְּחֶסֶד וּבְרַחֲמִים!
בָּרוּךְ אַתָּה, יְיָ, מֶלֶךְ אוֹהֵב צְדָקָה וּמִשְׁפָּט.

Pour Your spirit upon the rulers of all lands; guide them, that
they may govern justly. O may You alone reign over us in
steadfast love and compassion!

*Blessed is the Sovereign Lord, who loves righteousness and
justice.*

◆ ◆

FOR RIGHTEOUSNESS צדיקים

עַל־הַצַּדִּיקִים וְעַל־הַחֲסִידִים וְעָלֵינוּ יֶהֱמוּ רַחֲמֶיךָ, יְיָ אֱלֹהֵינוּ,
וְתֵן שָׂכָר טוֹב לְכָל הַבּוֹטְחִים בְּשִׁמְךָ בֶּאֱמֶת, וְשִׂים חֶלְקֵנוּ
עִמָּהֶם לְעוֹלָם.
בָּרוּךְ אַתָּה, יְיָ, מִשְׁעָן וּמִבְטָח לַצַּדִּיקִים.

Have mercy, O Lord our God, upon the righteous and faithful
of all peoples, and upon all of us. Uphold all who faithfully
put their trust in You, and grant that we may always be num-
bered among them.

Blessed is the Lord, the Staff and Support of the righteous.

◆ ◆

FOR JERUSALEM   שלום ירושלים

וְלִירוּשָׁלַיִם עִירְךָ בְּרַחֲמִים תִּפְנֶה, וִיהִי שָׁלוֹם בִּשְׁעָרֶיהָ,
וְשַׁלְוָה בְּלֵב יוֹשְׁבֶיהָ, וְתוֹרָתְךָ מִצִּיּוֹן תֵּצֵא וּדְבָרְךָ
מִירוּשָׁלָיִם.

בָּרוּךְ אַתָּה, יְיָ, נוֹתֵן שָׁלוֹם בִּירוּשָׁלָיִם.

And turn in compassion to Jerusalem, Your city. Let there be
peace in her gates, quietness in the hearts of her inhabitants.
Let Your Torah go forth from Zion and Your word from
Jerusalem.

Blessed is the Lord, who gives peace to Jerusalem.

✦ ✦

FOR DELIVERANCE   ישועה

אֶת־צֶמַח צְדָקָה מְהֵרָה תַצְמִיחַ, וְקֶרֶן יְשׁוּעָה תָּרוּם כִּנְאֻמֶךָ,
כִּי לִישׁוּעָתְךָ קִוִּינוּ כָּל־הַיּוֹם.

בָּרוּךְ אַתָּה, יְיָ, מַצְמִיחַ קֶרֶן יְשׁוּעָה.

Cause the plant of justice to spring up soon. Let the light of
deliverance shine forth according to Your word, for we await
Your deliverance all the day.

*Blessed is the Lord, who will cause the light of deliverance to
dawn for all the world.*

✦ ✦

FOR ACCEPTANCE OF PRAYER   שומע תפלה

שְׁמַע קוֹלֵנוּ, יְיָ אֱלֹהֵינוּ, חוּס וְרַחֵם עָלֵינוּ, וְקַבֵּל בְּרַחֲמִים
וּבְרָצוֹן אֶת תְּפִלָּתֵנוּ, כִּי אֵל שׁוֹמֵעַ תְּפִלּוֹת וְתַחֲנוּנִים אָתָּה.

בָּרוּךְ אַתָּה, יְיָ, שׁוֹמֵעַ תְּפִלָּה.

Hear our voice, O Lord our God; have compassion upon us,
and accept our prayer with favor and mercy, for You are a
God who hears prayer and supplication.

Blessed is the Lord, who hearkens to prayer.

✦ ✦

עֲבוֹדָה

רְצֵה, יְיָ אֱלֹהֵינוּ, בְּעַמְּךָ יִשְׂרָאֵל, וּתְפִלָּתָם בְּאַהֲבָה תְקַבֵּל, וּתְהִי לְרָצוֹן תָּמִיד עֲבוֹדַת יִשְׂרָאֵל עַמֶּךָ. אֵל קָרוֹב לְכָל־קֹרְאָיו, פְּנֵה אֶל עֲבָדֶיךָ וְחָנֵּנוּ; שְׁפוֹךְ רוּחֲךָ עָלֵינוּ, וְתֶחֱזֶינָה עֵינֵינוּ בְּשׁוּבְךָ לְצִיּוֹן בְּרַחֲמִים. בָּרוּךְ אַתָּה, יְיָ, הַמַּחֲזִיר שְׁכִינָתוֹ לְצִיּוֹן.

Be gracious, O Lord our God, to Your people Israel, and receive our prayers with love. O may our worship always be
acceptable to You.

Fill us with the knowledge that You are near to all who seek
You in truth. Let our eyes behold Your presence in our
midst and in the midst of our people in Zion.

*Blessed is the Lord, whose presence gives life to Zion and all
Israel.*

◆ ◆

ON ROSH CHODESH AND CHOL HAMO-EID

אֱלֹהֵינוּ וֵאלֹהֵי אֲבוֹתֵינוּ, יַעֲלֶה וְיָבֹא וְיַגִּיעַ וְיֵרָאֶה וְיִזָּכֵר זִכְרוֹנֵנוּ וְזִכְרוֹן כָּל־עַמְּךָ בֵּית יִשְׂרָאֵל לְפָנֶיךָ, לְטוֹבָה לְחֵן לְחֶסֶד וּלְרַחֲמִים, לְחַיִּים וּלְשָׁלוֹם בְּיוֹם

Our God and God of all ages, be mindful of Your people Israel on this

first day of the new month,	רֹאשׁ הַחֹדֶשׁ הַזֶּה.
day of Pesach,	חַג הַמַּצּוֹת הַזֶּה.
day of Sukkot,	חַג הַסֻּכּוֹת הַזֶּה.

and renew in us love and compassion, goodness, life and peace.

This day remember us for well-being. *Amen.*	זָכְרֵנוּ, יְיָ אֱלֹהֵינוּ, בּוֹ לְטוֹבָה. אָמֵן.
This day bless us with Your nearness. *Amen.*	וּפָקְדֵנוּ בוֹ לִבְרָכָה. אָמֵן.
This day help us to a fuller life. *Amen.*	וְהוֹשִׁיעֵנוּ בוֹ לְחַיִּים. אָמֵן.

◆ ◆

הודאה

מוֹדִים אֲנַחְנוּ לָךְ, שָׁאַתָּה הוּא יְיָ אֱלֹהֵינוּ וֵאלֹהֵי אֲבוֹתֵינוּ
לְעוֹלָם וָעֶד. צוּר חַיֵּינוּ, מָגֵן יִשְׁעֵנוּ, אַתָּה הוּא לְדוֹר וָדוֹר.
נוֹדֶה לְךָ וּנְסַפֵּר תְּהִלָּתֶךָ, עַל־חַיֵּינוּ הַמְּסוּרִים בְּיָדֶךָ, וְעַל־
נִשְׁמוֹתֵינוּ הַפְּקוּדוֹת לָךְ, וְעַל־נִסֶּיךָ שֶׁבְּכָל־יוֹם עִמָּנוּ, וְעַל־
נִפְלְאוֹתֶיךָ וְטוֹבוֹתֶיךָ שֶׁבְּכָל־עֵת, עֶרֶב וָבֹקֶר וְצָהֳרָיִם.הַטּוֹב:
כִּי לֹא־כָלוּ רַחֲמֶיךָ, וְהַמְרַחֵם: כִּי־לֹא תַמּוּ חֲסָדֶיךָ, מֵעוֹלָם
קִוִּינוּ לָךְ.

*We gratefully acknowledge that You are the Lord our God
and God of our people, the God of all generations. You are
the Rock of our life, the Power that shields us in every age.
We thank You and sing Your praises: for our lives, which are
in Your hand; for our souls, which are in Your keeping; for
the signs of Your presence we encounter every day; and for
Your wondrous gifts at all times, morning, noon, and night.
You are Goodness: Your mercies never end; You are Compassion: Your love will never fail. You have always been our hope.*

וְעַל כֻּלָּם יִתְבָּרַךְ וְיִתְרוֹמַם שִׁמְךָ, מַלְכֵּנוּ, תָּמִיד לְעוֹלָם וָעֶד.

For all these things, O Sovereign God, let Your name be for
ever exalted and blessed.

On the Ten Days of Repentance insert:

וּכְתוֹב לְחַיִּים טוֹבִים כָּל־בְּנֵי בְרִיתֶךָ.

Let life abundant be the heritage of all Your children.

וְכֹל הַחַיִּים יוֹדוּךָ סֶּלָה, וִיהַלְלוּ אֶת שִׁמְךָ בֶּאֱמֶת, הָאֵל
יְשׁוּעָתֵנוּ וְעֶזְרָתֵנוּ סֶלָה. בָּרוּךְ אַתָּה, יְיָ, הַטּוֹב שִׁמְךָ וּלְךָ נָאֶה
לְהוֹדוֹת.

O God our Redeemer and Helper, let all who live affirm You
and praise Your name in truth. Lord, whose nature is Goodness, we give You thanks and praise.

✦ ✦

ON CHANUKAH

עַל הַנִּסִּים וְעַל הַפֻּרְקָן, וְעַל הַגְּבוּרוֹת וְעַל הַתְּשׁוּעוֹת, וְעַל הַמִּלְחָמוֹת, שֶׁעָשִׂיתָ לַאֲבוֹתֵינוּ בַּיָּמִים הָהֵם בַּזְּמַן הַזֶּה.

בִּימֵי מַתִּתְיָהוּ בֶּן־יוֹחָנָן כֹּהֵן גָּדוֹל, חַשְׁמוֹנַי וּבָנָיו, כְּשֶׁעָמְדָה מַלְכוּת יָוָן הָרְשָׁעָה עַל־עַמְּךָ יִשְׂרָאֵל לְהַשְׁכִּיחָם תּוֹרָתֶךָ, וּלְהַעֲבִירָם מֵחֻקֵּי רְצוֹנֶךָ.

וְאַתָּה בְּרַחֲמֶיךָ הָרַבִּים עָמַדְתָּ לָהֶם בְּעֵת צָרָתָם. רַבְתָּ אֶת־רִיבָם, דַּנְתָּ אֶת־דִּינָם, מָסַרְתָּ גִּבּוֹרִים בְּיַד חַלָּשִׁים, וְרַבִּים בְּיַד מְעַטִּים, וּטְמֵאִים בְּיַד טְהוֹרִים, וּרְשָׁעִים בְּיַד צַדִּיקִים, וְזֵדִים בְּיַד עוֹסְקֵי תוֹרָתֶךָ.

וּלְךָ עָשִׂיתָ שֵׁם גָּדוֹל וְקָדוֹשׁ בְּעוֹלָמֶךָ, וּלְעַמְּךָ יִשְׂרָאֵל עָשִׂיתָ תְּשׁוּעָה גְדוֹלָה וּפֻרְקָן כְּהַיּוֹם הַזֶּה.

וְאַחַר כֵּן בָּאוּ בָנֶיךָ לִדְבִיר בֵּיתֶךָ, וּפִנּוּ אֶת־הֵיכָלֶךָ, וְטִהֲרוּ אֶת־מִקְדָּשֶׁךָ, וְהִדְלִיקוּ נֵרוֹת בְּחַצְרוֹת קָדְשֶׁךָ, וְקָבְעוּ שְׁמוֹנַת יְמֵי חֲנֻכָּה אֵלּוּ לְהוֹדוֹת וּלְהַלֵּל לְשִׁמְךָ הַגָּדוֹל.

We give thanks for the redeeming wonders and the mighty deeds by which, at this season, our people was saved in days of old.

In the days of the Hasmoneans, a tyrant arose against our ancestors, determined to make them forget Your Torah, and to turn them away from obedience to Your will. But You were at their side in time of trouble. You gave them strength to struggle and to triumph, that they might serve You in freedom.

Through the power of Your spirit the weak defeated the strong, the few prevailed over the many, and the righteous were triumphant. Then Your children returned to Your house, to purify the sanctuary and kindle its lights. And they dedicated these days to give thanks and praise to Your great name.

◆ ◆

ON PURIM

עַל הַנִּסִּים וְעַל הַפֻּרְקָן, וְעַל הַגְּבוּרוֹת וְעַל הַתְּשׁוּעוֹת, וְעַל
הַמִּלְחָמוֹת, שֶׁעָשִׂיתָ לַאֲבוֹתֵינוּ בַּיָּמִים הָהֵם בַּזְּמַן הַזֶּה.

בִּימֵי מָרְדְּכַי וְאֶסְתֵּר בְּשׁוּשַׁן הַבִּירָה, כְּשֶׁעָמַד עֲלֵיהֶם הָמָן הָרָשָׁע,
בִּקֵּשׁ לְהַשְׁמִיד לַהֲרוֹג וּלְאַבֵּד אֶת־כָּל־הַיְּהוּדִים, מִנַּעַר וְעַד־זָקֵן, טַף
וְנָשִׁים, בְּיוֹם אֶחָד, בִּשְׁלוֹשָׁה עָשָׂר לְחֹדֶשׁ שְׁנֵים־עָשָׂר, הוּא־חֹדֶשׁ אֲדָר,
וּשְׁלָלָם לָבוֹז.

וְאַתָּה בְּרַחֲמֶיךָ הָרַבִּים הֵפַרְתָּ אֶת־עֲצָתוֹ, וְקִלְקַלְתָּ אֶת־מַחֲשַׁבְתּוֹ.

We give thanks for the redeeming wonders and the mighty deeds by
which, at this season, our people was saved in days of old.
In the days of Mordecai and Esther, the wicked Haman arose in
Persia, plotting the destruction of all the Jews. He planned to destroy
them in a single day, the thirteenth of Adar, and to permit the plunder
of their possessions.
But through Your great mercy his plan was thwarted, his scheme
frustrated. We therefore thank and bless You, O great and gracious
God!

◆ ◆

PEACE   ברכת שלום

שָׁלוֹם רָב עַל־יִשְׂרָאֵל עַמְּךָ תָּשִׂים לְעוֹלָם, כִּי אַתָּה הוּא
מֶלֶךְ אָדוֹן לְכָל־הַשָּׁלוֹם. וְטוֹב בְּעֵינֶיךָ לְבָרֵךְ אֶת־עַמְּךָ
יִשְׂרָאֵל בְּכָל־עֵת וּבְכָל־שָׁעָה בִּשְׁלוֹמֶךָ.*

בָּרוּךְ אַתָּה, יְיָ, הַמְבָרֵךְ אֶת־עַמּוֹ יִשְׂרָאֵל בַּשָּׁלוֹם.

O Sovereign Lord of peace, let Israel Your people know enduring peace, for it is good in Your sight continually to bless
Israel with Your peace.* Praised be the Lord, who blesses His
people Israel with peace.

*On the Ten Days of Repentance conclude:

בְּסֵפֶר חַיִּים וּבְרָכָה נִכָּתֵב לְחַיִּים טוֹבִים וּלְשָׁלוֹם.
בָּרוּךְ אַתָּה, יְיָ, עוֹשֵׂה הַשָּׁלוֹם.

Teach us then to find our happiness in the search for righteousness and peace.
Blessed is the Lord, the Source of peace.

◆ ◆

SILENT PRAYER

אֱלֹהַי, נְצֹר לְשׁוֹנִי מֵרָע, וּשְׂפָתַי מִדַּבֵּר מִרְמָה, וְלִמְקַלְלַי
נַפְשִׁי תִדּוֹם, וְנַפְשִׁי כֶּעָפָר לַכֹּל תִּהְיֶה. פְּתַח לִבִּי בְּתוֹרָתֶךָ,
וּבְמִצְוֹתֶיךָ תִּרְדּוֹף נַפְשִׁי, וְכֹל הַחוֹשְׁבִים עָלַי רָעָה, מְהֵרָה
הָפֵר עֲצָתָם וְקַלְקֵל מַחֲשַׁבְתָּם. עֲשֵׂה לְמַעַן שְׁמֶךָ, עֲשֵׂה לְמַעַן
יְמִינֶךָ, עֲשֵׂה לְמַעַן קְדֻשָּׁתֶךָ, עֲשֵׂה לְמַעַן תּוֹרָתֶךָ. לְמַעַן
יֵחָלְצוּן יְדִידֶיךָ, הוֹשִׁיעָה יְמִינְךָ וַעֲנֵנִי.

O God, keep my tongue from evil and my lips from deceit.
Help me to be silent in the face of derision, humble in the presence of all. Open my heart to Your Torah, and I will hasten
to do Your Mitzvot. Save me with Your power; in time of
trouble be my answer, that those who love You may rejoice.

◆ ◆

יִהְיוּ לְרָצוֹן אִמְרֵי־פִי וְהֶגְיוֹן לִבִּי לְפָנֶיךָ, יְיָ, צוּרִי וְגוֹאֲלִי.

May the words of my mouth, and the meditations of my heart, be
acceptable to You, O Lord, my Rock and my Redeemer.

or

עֹשֶׂה שָׁלוֹם בִּמְרוֹמָיו, הוּא יַעֲשֶׂה שָׁלוֹם עָלֵינוּ וְעַל כָּל־
יִשְׂרָאֵל, וְאִמְרוּ אָמֵן.

May He who causes peace to reign in the high heavens let peace
descend on us, on all Israel, and all the world.

◆ ◆

Prayers at a House of Mourning begin on page 183.

Concluding Prayers begin on page 187.

Havdalah for the conclusion of Shabbat is on page 62.

149

For Weekday Mornings

Praise the Lord, O my soul!   בָּרְכִי נַפְשִׁי אֶת יְיָ!

O Lord my God, You are very great!   יְיָ אֱלֹהַי, גָּדַלְתָּ מְאֹד!

Arrayed in glory and majesty,   הוֹד וְהָדָר לָבָשְׁתָּ,

You wrap Yourself in light as with a garment,   עֹטֶה אוֹר כַּשַּׂלְמָה,

You stretch out the heavens like a curtain.   נוֹטֶה שָׁמַיִם כַּיְרִיעָה.

בָּרוּךְ אַתָּה, יְיָ אֱלֹהֵינוּ, מֶלֶךְ הָעוֹלָם,
אֲשֶׁר קִדְּשָׁנוּ בְּמִצְוֹתָיו וְצִוָּנוּ לְהִתְעַטֵּף בַּצִּיצִת.

Blessed is the Lord our God, Ruler of the universe, by whose Mitzvot
we are hallowed, who teaches us to wrap ourselves in the fringed
Tallit.

◆ ◆

For those who wear Tefillin

הִנְנִי מְכַוֵּן בַּהֲנָחַת תְּפִלִּין לְקַיֵּם מִצְוַת בּוֹרְאִי שֶׁצִּוָּנוּ לְהָנִיחַ תְּפִלִּין,
כַּכָּתוּב בַּתּוֹרָה: וּקְשַׁרְתָּם לְאוֹת עַל יָדֶךָ, וְהָיוּ לְטֹטָפֹת בֵּין עֵינֶיךָ.

In the Torah it is written: "Bind them as a sign upon your hand; let
them be a symbol before your eyes."

וְהֵם אַרְבַּע פָּרָשִׁיוֹת אֵלוּ: שְׁמַע, וְהָיָה אִם שָׁמֹעַ, קַדֶּשׁ, וְהָיָה כִּי
יְבִיאֲךָ, שֶׁיֵּשׁ בָּהֶם יִחוּדוֹ וְאַחְדוּתוֹ יִתְבָּרַךְ שְׁמוֹ.
וְצִוָּנוּ לְהָנִיחַ עַל הַיָּד לְזִכָּרוֹן זְרוֹעוֹ הַנְּטוּיָה; וְשֶׁהִיא נֶגֶד הַלֵּב, לְשַׁעְבֵּד
בָּזֶה תַּאֲוֹת וּמַחְשְׁבוֹת לִבֵּנוּ לַעֲבוֹדָתוֹ, יִתְבָּרַךְ שְׁמוֹ; וְעַל הָרֹאשׁ נֶגֶד
הַמֹּחַ, שֶׁהַנְּשָׁמָה שֶׁבְּמֹחִי עִם שְׁאָר חוּשַׁי וְכֹחוֹתַי כֻּלָּם יִהְיוּ מְשֻׁעְבָּדִים
לַעֲבוֹדָתוֹ, יִתְבָּרַךְ שְׁמוֹ.

By this we proclaim the unity and uniqueness of the Blessed One;
we recall the wonder of the Exodus; and we acclaim His power in all
the universe.

By this symbol we bind hand, heart, and mind to the service of the
Blessed One.

FOR THE HAND

בָּרוּךְ אַתָּה, יְיָ אֱלֹהֵינוּ, מֶלֶךְ הָעוֹלָם,
אֲשֶׁר קִדְּשָׁנוּ בְּמִצְוֹתָיו וְצִוָּנוּ לְהָנִיחַ תְּפִלִּין.

Blessed is the Lord our God, Ruler of the universe, by whose Mitzvot
we are hallowed, who teaches us to wear Tefillin.

FOR THE HEAD

בָּרוּךְ אַתָּה, יְיָ אֱלֹהֵינוּ, מֶלֶךְ הָעוֹלָם,
אֲשֶׁר קִדְּשָׁנוּ בְּמִצְוֹתָיו וְצִוָּנוּ עַל־מִצְוַת תְּפִלִּין.
בָּרוּךְ שֵׁם כְּבוֹד מַלְכוּתוֹ לְעוֹלָם וָעֶד!

Blessed is the Lord our God, Ruler of the universe, by whose Mitzvot
we are hallowed, who teaches us concerning the Mitzvah of Tefillin.

Blessed is His glorious kingdom for ever and ever!

UPON WINDING THE RETSUAH ON THE FINGER

וְאֵרַשְׂתִּיךְ לִי לְעוֹלָם,
וְאֵרַשְׂתִּיךְ לִי בְּצֶדֶק וּבְמִשְׁפָּט וּבְחֶסֶד וּבְרַחֲמִים.
וְאֵרַשְׂתִּיךְ לִי בֶּאֱמוּנָה, וְיָדַעַתְּ אֶת־יְיָ.

"I will betroth you to Me for ever; I will betroth you to Me in righteousness and justice, in love and compassion; I will betroth you to
Me in faithfulness, and you shall know the Lord."

ברכות השחר

FOR THE BLESSING OF WORSHIP   מה טבו

מַה־טֹּבוּ אֹהָלֶיךָ, יַעֲקֹב, מִשְׁכְּנֹתֶיךָ, יִשְׂרָאֵל!

How lovely are Your tents, O Jacob, your dwelling-places, O Israel!

וַאֲנִי, בְּרֹב חַסְדְּךָ אָבֹא בֵיתֶךָ,
אֶשְׁתַּחֲוֶה אֶל־הֵיכַל קָדְשְׁךָ בְּיִרְאָתֶךָ.

In Your abundant lovingkindness, O God, let me enter Your house,
reverently to worship in Your holy temple.

יְיָ, אָהַבְתִּי מְעוֹן בֵּיתֶךָ, וּמְקוֹם מִשְׁכַּן כְּבוֹדֶךָ.
וַאֲנִי אֶשְׁתַּחֲוֶה וְאֶכְרָעָה, אֶבְרְכָה לִפְנֵי־יְיָ עֹשִׂי.

Lord, I love Your house, the place where Your glory dwells.
So I would worship with humility, I would seek blessing in the
presence of God, my Maker.

וַאֲנִי תְפִלָּתִי לְךָ, יְיָ, עֵת רָצוֹן.
אֱלֹהִים, בְּרָב־חַסְדֶּךָ, עֲנֵנִי בֶּאֱמֶת יִשְׁעֶךָ.

To You, then, Lord, does my prayer go forth. May this be a time of
joy and favor.
In Your great love, O God, answer me with Your saving truth.

✦ ✦

FOR HEALTH   אשר יצר

בָּרוּךְ אַתָּה, יְיָ אֱלֹהֵינוּ, מֶלֶךְ הָעוֹלָם, אֲשֶׁר יָצַר אֶת־הָאָדָם
בְּחָכְמָה, וּבָרָא בוֹ נְקָבִים נְקָבִים, חֲלוּלִים חֲלוּלִים.

Blessed is our Eternal God, Creator of the universe, who has
made our bodies with wisdom, combining veins, arteries, and
vital organs into a finely balanced network.

גָּלוּי וְיָדוּעַ לִפְנֵי כִסֵּא כְבוֹדֶךָ, שֶׁאִם יִפָּתַח אֶחָד מֵהֶם, אוֹ
יִסָּתֵם אֶחָד מֵהֶם, אִי אֶפְשָׁר לְהִתְקַיֵּם וְלַעֲמוֹד לְפָנֶיךָ.
בָּרוּךְ אַתָּה, יְיָ, רוֹפֵא כָל־בָּשָׂר וּמַפְלִיא לַעֲשׂוֹת.

Wondrous Fashioner and Sustainer of life, Source of our health
and our strength, we give You thanks and praise.

❖ ❖

לַעֲסוֹק בְּדִבְרֵי תוֹרה

בָּרוּךְ אַתָּה, יְיָ אֱלֹהֵינוּ, מֶלֶךְ הָעוֹלָם, אֲשֶׁר קִדְּשָׁנוּ בְּמִצְוֹתָיו
וְצִוָּנוּ לַעֲסוֹק בְּדִבְרֵי תוֹרָה.

Blessed is the Eternal, our God, Ruler of the universe, who
hallows us with His Mitzvot, and commands us to engage in
the study of Torah.

וְהַעֲרֶב־נָא, יְיָ אֱלֹהֵינוּ, אֶת־דִּבְרֵי תוֹרָתְךָ בְּפִינוּ, וּבְפִי עַמְּךָ
בֵּית יִשְׂרָאֵל, וְנִהְיֶה אֲנַחְנוּ וְצֶאֱצָאֵינוּ, וְצֶאֱצָאֵי עַמְּךָ בֵּית
יִשְׂרָאֵל, כֻּלָּנוּ יוֹדְעֵי שְׁמֶךָ וְלוֹמְדֵי תוֹרָתֶךָ לִשְׁמָהּ. בָּרוּךְ
אַתָּה, יְיָ, הַמְלַמֵּד תּוֹרָה לְעַמּוֹ יִשְׂרָאֵל.

Eternal our God, make the words of Your Torah sweet to us,
and to the House of Israel, Your people, that we and our children may be lovers of Your name and students of Your Torah.
Blessed is the Eternal, the Teacher of Torah to His people Israel.

◆

אֵלּוּ דְבָרִים שֶׁאֵין לָהֶם שִׁעוּר, שֶׁאָדָם אוֹכֵל פֵּרוֹתֵיהֶם
בָּעוֹלָם הַזֶּה וְהַקֶּרֶן קַיֶּמֶת לוֹ לָעוֹלָם הַבָּא, וְאֵלּוּ הֵן:

These are the obligations without measure, whose reward, too,
is without measure;

To honor father and mother;	כִּבּוּד אָב וָאֵם,
to perform acts of love and kindness;	וּגְמִילוּת חֲסָדִים,
to attend the house of study daily;	וְהַשְׁכָּמַת בֵּית הַמִּדְרָשׁ
	שַׁחֲרִית וְעַרְבִית,

153

to welcome the stranger; וְהַכְנָסַת אוֹרְחִים,

to visit the sick; וּבִקוּר חוֹלִים,

to rejoice with bride and groom; וְהַכְנָסַת כַּלָּה,

to console the bereaved; וּלְוָיַת הַמֵּת,

to pray with sincerity; וְעִיּוּן תְּפִלָּה,

to make peace when there is strife. וַהֲבָאַת שָׁלוֹם

בֵּין אָדָם לַחֲבֵרוֹ;

And the study of Torah is equal to them all, because it leads to them all. וְתַלְמוּד תּוֹרָה כְּנֶגֶד כֻּלָּם.

◆ ◆

FOR THE SOUL אלהי נשמה

אֱלֹהַי, נְשָׁמָה שֶׁנָּתַתָּ בִּי טְהוֹרָה הִיא! אַתָּה בְרָאתָהּ, אַתָּה יְצַרְתָּהּ, אַתָּה נְפַחְתָּהּ בִּי, וְאַתָּה מְשַׁמְּרָהּ בְּקִרְבִּי. כָּל־זְמַן שֶׁהַנְּשָׁמָה בְקִרְבִּי, מוֹדֶה אֲנִי לְפָנֶיךָ, יְיָ אֱלֹהַי וֵאלֹהֵי אֲבוֹתַי, רִבּוֹן כָּל־הַמַּעֲשִׂים, אֲדוֹן כָּל־הַנְּשָׁמוֹת.

בָּרוּךְ אַתָּה, יְיָ, אֲשֶׁר בְּיָדוֹ נֶפֶשׁ כָּל־חָי, וְרוּחַ כָּל־בְּשַׂר־אִישׁ.

The soul that You have given me, O God, is a pure one! You have created and formed it, breathed it into me, and within me You sustain it. So long as I have breath, therefore, I will give thanks to You, O Lord my God and God of all ages, Master of all creation, Lord of every human spirit.

Blessed is the Lord, in whose hands are the souls of all the living and the spirits of all flesh.

◆ ◆

FOR LIFE ברוך שאמר

בָּרוּךְ שֶׁאָמַר וְהָיָה הָעוֹלָם, בָּרוּךְ הוּא.
בָּרוּךְ עוֹשֶׂה בְרֵאשִׁית.

Blessed is the One who spoke, and the world came to be.
Blessed is the Source of creation.

בָּרוּךְ אוֹמֵר וְעוֹשֶׂה, בָּרוּךְ גּוֹזֵר וּמְקַיֵּם.

Blessed is the One whose word is deed, whose thought is fact.

154

בָּרוּךְ מְרַחֵם עַל הָאָרֶץ, בָּרוּךְ מְרַחֵם עַל הַבְּרִיּוֹת.
בָּרוּךְ מְשַׁלֵּם שָׂכָר טוֹב לִירֵאָיו.
בָּרוּךְ חַי לָעַד וְקַיָּם לָנֶצַח, בָּרוּךְ פּוֹדֶה וּמַצִּיל, בָּרוּךְ שְׁמוֹ.

Blessed is the One whose compassion covers the earth and all its creatures.

Blessed is the living and eternal God, Ruler of the universe, divine Source of deliverance and help.

בִּשְׁבָחוֹת וּבִזְמִרוֹת נְגַדֶּלְךָ וּנְשַׁבֵּחֲךָ וּנְפָאֶרְךָ, וְנַזְכִּיר שִׁמְךָ
וְנַמְלִיכְךָ, מַלְכֵּנוּ, אֱלֹהֵינוּ. יָחִיד, חֵי הָעוֹלָמִים, מֶלֶךְ, מְשֻׁבָּח
וּמְפֹאָר עֲדֵי־עַד שְׁמוֹ הַגָּדוֹל.

בָּרוּךְ אַתָּה, יְיָ, מֶלֶךְ מְהֻלָּל בַּתִּשְׁבָּחוֹת.

With songs of praise we extol You and proclaim Your sovereignty, our God and King, for You are the source of life in the universe.

Blessed is the Eternal King, to whom our praise is due.

READER'S KADDISH   חצי קדיש

יִתְגַּדַּל וְיִתְקַדַּשׁ שְׁמֵהּ רַבָּא בְּעָלְמָא דִּי־בְרָא כִרְעוּתֵהּ,
וְיַמְלִיךְ מַלְכוּתֵהּ בְּחַיֵּיכוֹן וּבְיוֹמֵיכוֹן וּבְחַיֵּי דְכָל־בֵּית
יִשְׂרָאֵל, בַּעֲגָלָא וּבִזְמַן קָרִיב, וְאִמְרוּ: אָמֵן.

יְהֵא שְׁמֵהּ רַבָּא מְבָרַךְ לְעָלַם וּלְעָלְמֵי עָלְמַיָּא.

יִתְבָּרַךְ וְיִשְׁתַּבַּח, וְיִתְפָּאַר וְיִתְרוֹמַם וְיִתְנַשֵּׂא, וְיִתְהַדָּר
וְיִתְעַלֶּה וְיִתְהַלָּל שְׁמֵהּ דְּקוּדְשָׁא, בְּרִיךְ הוּא, לְעֵלָּא מִן
כָּל־בִּרְכָתָא וְשִׁירָתָא, תֻּשְׁבְּחָתָא וְנֶחֱמָתָא דַּאֲמִירָן בְּעָלְמָא,
וְאִמְרוּ: אָמֵן.

Let the glory of God be extolled, let His great name be hallowed in the world whose creation He willed. May His kingdom soon prevail, in our own day, our own lives, and the life of all Israel, and let us say: Amen.

Let His great name be blessed for ever and ever.

Let the name of the Holy One, blessed is He, be glorified, exalted and honored, though He is beyond all the praises, songs, and adorations that we can utter, and let us say: Amen.

❖ ❖

All rise

שמע וברכותיה

בָּרְכוּ אֶת־יְיָ הַמְבֹרָךְ!

Praise the Lord, to whom our praise is due!

בָּרוּךְ יְיָ הַמְבֹרָךְ לְעוֹלָם וָעֶד!

Praised be the Lord, to whom our praise is due,
now and for ever!

◆ ◆

CREATION   יוצר

בָּרוּךְ אַתָּה, יְיָ אֱלֹהֵינוּ, מֶלֶךְ הָעוֹלָם, יוֹצֵר אוֹר וּבוֹרֵא חֹשֶׁךְ,
עֹשֶׂה שָׁלוֹם וּבוֹרֵא אֶת־הַכֹּל.

Praised be the Lord our God, Ruler of the universe, who makes
light and creates darkness, who ordains peace and fashions all
things.

הַמֵּאִיר לָאָרֶץ וְלַדָּרִים עָלֶיהָ בְּרַחֲמִים, וּבְטוּבוֹ מְחַדֵּשׁ
בְּכָל־יוֹם תָּמִיד מַעֲשֵׂה בְרֵאשִׁית.

With compassion He gives light to the earth and all who dwell
there; with goodness He renews the work of creation continually, day by day.

מָה רַבּוּ מַעֲשֶׂיךָ, יְיָ! כֻּלָּם בְּחָכְמָה עָשִׂיתָ, מָלְאָה הָאָרֶץ
קִנְיָנֶךָ.

How manifold are Your works, O Lord; in wisdom You have
made them all; the earth is full of Your creations.

תִּתְבָּרַךְ, יְיָ אֱלֹהֵינוּ, עַל־שֶׁבַח מַעֲשֵׂה יָדֶיךָ, וְעַל־מְאוֹרֵי־אוֹר
שֶׁעָשִׂיתָ: יְפָאֲרוּךָ. סֶלָה.

בָּרוּךְ אַתָּה, יְיָ, יוֹצֵר הַמְּאוֹרוֹת.

Let all bless You, O Lord our God, for the excellence of Your
handiwork, and for the glowing stars that You have made:
let them glorify You for ever. Blessed is the Lord, the Maker
of light.

◆ ◆

156

REVELATION אהבה רבה

אַהֲבָה רַבָּה אֲהַבְתָּנוּ, יְיָ אֱלֹהֵינוּ, חֶמְלָה גְדוֹלָה וִיתֵרָה חָמַלְתָּ
עָלֵינוּ. אָבִינוּ מַלְכֵּנוּ, בַּעֲבוּר אֲבוֹתֵינוּ שֶׁבָּטְחוּ בְךָ וַתְּלַמְּדֵם
חֻקֵּי חַיִּים, כֵּן תְּחָנֵּנוּ וּתְלַמְּדֵנוּ.

Deep is Your love for us, O Lord our God, and great is Your
compassion. Our Maker and King, our ancestors trusted You,
and You taught them the laws of life: be gracious now to us,
and teach us.

אָבִינוּ, הָאָב הָרַחֲמָן, הַמְרַחֵם, רַחֵם עָלֵינוּ וְתֵן בְּלִבֵּנוּ לְהָבִין
וּלְהַשְׂכִּיל, לִשְׁמֹעַ לִלְמֹד וּלְלַמֵּד, לִשְׁמֹר וְלַעֲשׂוֹת וּלְקַיֵּם
אֶת־כָּל־דִּבְרֵי תַלְמוּד תּוֹרָתֶךָ בְּאַהֲבָה.

Have compassion upon us, O Source of mercy, and guide us
to know and understand, learn and teach, observe and uphold
with love all the teachings of Your Torah.

וְהָאֵר עֵינֵינוּ בְּתוֹרָתֶךָ, וְדַבֵּק לִבֵּנוּ בְּמִצְוֹתֶיךָ, וְיַחֵד לְבָבֵנוּ
לְאַהֲבָה וּלְיִרְאָה אֶת־שְׁמֶךָ. וְלֹא־נֵבוֹשׁ לְעוֹלָם וָעֶד, כִּי בְשֵׁם
קָדְשְׁךָ הַגָּדוֹל וְהַנּוֹרָא בָּטָחְנוּ. נָגִילָה וְנִשְׂמְחָה בִּישׁוּעָתֶךָ,
כִּי אֵל פּוֹעֵל יְשׁוּעוֹת אָתָּה. וּבָנוּ בָחַרְתָּ וְקֵרַבְתָּנוּ לְשִׁמְךָ
הַגָּדוֹל סֶלָה בֶּאֱמֶת, לְהוֹדוֹת לְךָ וּלְיַחֶדְךָ בְּאַהֲבָה.

בָּרוּךְ אַתָּה, יְיָ, הַבּוֹחֵר בְּעַמּוֹ יִשְׂרָאֵל בְּאַהֲבָה.

Enlighten us with Your Teaching, help us to hold fast to Your
Mitzvot, and unite our hearts to love and revere Your name.

Then shall we never be shamed, for we shall put our trust in
You, the great, holy, and awesome One. We shall rejoice and
be glad in Your salvation, for You, O God, are the Author of
many deliverances. In love You have chosen us and drawn us
near to You to serve You in faithfulness and to proclaim Your
unity.

Blessed is the Lord, who in love has chosen His people Israel
to serve Him.

◆ ◆

שְׁמַע יִשְׂרָאֵל: יְיָ אֱלֹהֵינוּ, יְיָ אֶחָד!

Hear, O Israel: the Lord is our God, the Lord is One!

בָּרוּךְ שֵׁם כְּבוֹד מַלְכוּתוֹ לְעוֹלָם וָעֶד!

Blessed is His glorious kingdom for ever and ever!

All are seated

וְאָהַבְתָּ אֵת יְיָ אֱלֹהֶיךָ בְּכָל־לְבָבְךָ וּבְכָל־נַפְשְׁךָ וּבְכָל־מְאֹדֶךָ.
וְהָיוּ הַדְּבָרִים הָאֵלֶּה, אֲשֶׁר אָנֹכִי מְצַוְּךָ הַיּוֹם, עַל־לְבָבֶךָ.
וְשִׁנַּנְתָּם לְבָנֶיךָ, וְדִבַּרְתָּ בָּם בְּשִׁבְתְּךָ בְּבֵיתֶךָ, וּבְלֶכְתְּךָ
בַדֶּרֶךְ, וּבְשָׁכְבְּךָ וּבְקוּמֶךָ.

You shall love the Lord your God with all your mind, with all your strength, with all your being.
Set these words, which I command you this day, upon your heart. Teach them faithfully to your children; speak of them in your home and on your way, when you lie down and when you rise up.

וּקְשַׁרְתָּם לְאוֹת עַל־יָדֶךָ, וְהָיוּ לְטֹטָפֹת בֵּין עֵינֶיךָ, וּכְתַבְתָּם
עַל־מְזֻזוֹת בֵּיתֶךָ, וּבִשְׁעָרֶיךָ.

Bind them as a sign upon your hand; let them be a symbol before your eyes; inscribe them on the doorposts of your house, and on your gates.

לְמַעַן תִּזְכְּרוּ וַעֲשִׂיתֶם אֶת־כָּל־מִצְוֹתָי, וִהְיִיתֶם קְדֹשִׁים
לֵאלֹהֵיכֶם. אֲנִי יְיָ אֱלֹהֵיכֶם, אֲשֶׁר הוֹצֵאתִי אֶתְכֶם מֵאֶרֶץ
מִצְרַיִם לִהְיוֹת לָכֶם לֵאלֹהִים. אֲנִי יְיָ אֱלֹהֵיכֶם.

Be mindful of all My Mitzvot, and do them: so shall you consecrate yourselves to your God. I, the Lord, am your God who led you out of Egypt to be your God; I, the Lord, am your God.

❖ ❖

158

REDEMPTION גְּאוּלָה

אֱמֶת וְיַצִּיב, וְאָהוּב וְחָבִיב, וְנוֹרָא וְאַדִּיר, וְטוֹב וְיָפֶה הַדָּבָר
הַזֶּה עָלֵינוּ לְעוֹלָם וָעֶד.
אֱמֶת, אֱלֹהֵי עוֹלָם מַלְכֵּנוּ, צוּר יַעֲקֹב מָגֵן יִשְׁעֵנוּ.

True and enduring, beloved and precious, awesome, good, and
beautiful is this eternal teaching.
*This truth we hold to be for ever certain: the Eternal God is
our King. He is the Rock of Jacob, our protecting Shield.*

לְדֹר וָדֹר הוּא קַיָּם, וּשְׁמוֹ קַיָּם, וְכִסְאוֹ נָכוֹן, וּמַלְכוּתוֹ
וֶאֱמוּנָתוֹ לָעַד קַיֶּמֶת. וּדְבָרָיו חָיִים וְקַיָּמִים, נֶאֱמָנִים
וְנֶחֱמָדִים, לָעַד וּלְעוֹלְמֵי עוֹלָמִים.

He abides through all generations; His name is Eternal. His
throne stands firm; His sovereignty and faithfulness are everlasting.
His words live and endure, true and precious to all eternity.

מִמִּצְרַיִם גְּאַלְתָּנוּ, יְיָ אֱלֹהֵינוּ, וּמִבֵּית עֲבָדִים פְּדִיתָנוּ.

Lord our God, You redeemed us from Egypt;
You set us free from the house of bondage.

עַל־זֹאת שִׁבְּחוּ אֲהוּבִים וְרוֹמְמוּ אֵל, וְנָתְנוּ יְדִידִים זְמִירוֹת,
שִׁירוֹת וְתִשְׁבָּחוֹת, בְּרָכוֹת וְהוֹדָאוֹת לַמֶּלֶךְ, אֵל חַי וְקַיָּם.

For this the people who felt Your love sang songs of praise
to You:
The living God, high and exalted, mighty and awesome,

רָם וְנִשָּׂא, גָּדוֹל וְנוֹרָא, מַשְׁפִּיל גֵּאִים וּמַגְבִּיהַּ שְׁפָלִים, מוֹצִיא
אֲסִירִים וּפוֹדֶה עֲנָוִים, וְעוֹזֵר דַּלִּים, וְעוֹנֶה לְעַמּוֹ בְּעֵת שַׁוְּעָם
אֵלָיו.

Who humbles the proud and raises the lowly, who frees the
captive and redeems the oppressed,
who is the Answer to all who cry out to Him.

159

תְּהִלּוֹת לְאֵל עֶלְיוֹן, בָּרוּךְ הוּא וּמְבֹרָךְ. מֹשֶׁה וּבְנֵי יִשְׂרָאֵל
לְךָ עָנוּ שִׁירָה בְּשִׂמְחָה רַבָּה, וְאָמְרוּ כֻלָּם:

All praise to God Most High, the Source of blessing! Like Moses
and Israel, we sing to Him this song of rejoicing:

Who is like You, Eternal One, among the gods that are worshipped?	מִי־כָמְכָה בָּאֵלִם, יְיָ?
Who is like You, majestic in holiness,	מִי כָּמְכָה, נֶאְדָּר בַּקֹּדֶשׁ,
awesome in splendor, doing wonders?	נוֹרָא תְהִלֹּת, עֹשֵׂה פֶלֶא?

שִׁירָה חֲדָשָׁה שִׁבְּחוּ גְאוּלִים לְשִׁמְךָ עַל־שְׂפַת הַיָּם; יַחַד כֻּלָּם
הוֹדוּ וְהִמְלִיכוּ וְאָמְרוּ: "יְיָ יִמְלֹךְ לְעוֹלָם וָעֶד!"

A new song the redeemed sang to Your name. At the shore of the
Sea, saved from destruction, they proclaimed Your sovereign
power: "The Eternal will reign for ever and ever!"

צוּר יִשְׂרָאֵל, קוּמָה בְּעֶזְרַת יִשְׂרָאֵל, וּפְדֵה כִנְאֻמֶךָ יְהוּדָה
וְיִשְׂרָאֵל. גֹּאֲלֵנוּ, יְיָ צְבָאוֹת שְׁמוֹ, קְדוֹשׁ יִשְׂרָאֵל.
בָּרוּךְ אַתָּה, יְיָ, גָּאַל יִשְׂרָאֵל.

O Rock of Israel, come to Israel's help. Fulfill Your promise of redemption for Judah and Israel. Our Redeemer is the Lord of Hosts,
the Holy One of Israel. Blessed is the Lord, the Redeemer of Israel.

◆ ◆

160

All rise

תפלה

אֲדֹנָי, שְׂפָתַי תִּפְתָּח, וּפִי יַגִּיד תְּהִלָּתֶךָ.

Eternal God, open my lips, that my mouth may declare Your glory.

GOD OF ALL GENERATIONS   אבות

בָּרוּךְ אַתָּה, יְיָ אֱלֹהֵינוּ וֵאלֹהֵי אֲבוֹתֵינוּ, אֱלֹהֵי אַבְרָהָם, אֱלֹהֵי יִצְחָק, וֵאלֹהֵי יַעֲקֹב: הָאֵל הַגָּדוֹל, הַגִּבּוֹר וְהַנּוֹרָא, אֵל עֶלְיוֹן.

We praise You, Lord our God and God of all generations: God of Abraham, God of Isaac, God of Jacob; great, mighty, and awesome God, God supreme.

גּוֹמֵל חֲסָדִים טוֹבִים, וְקוֹנֵה הַכֹּל, וְזוֹכֵר חַסְדֵי אָבוֹת, וּמֵבִיא גְאֻלָּה לִבְנֵי בְנֵיהֶם, לְמַעַן שְׁמוֹ, בְּאַהֲבָה.*

Master of all the living, Your ways are ways of love. You remember the faithfulness of our ancestors, and in love bring redemption to their children's children for the sake of Your name.*

מֶלֶךְ עוֹזֵר וּמוֹשִׁיעַ וּמָגֵן. בָּרוּךְ אַתָּה, יְיָ, מָגֵן אַבְרָהָם.

You are our King and our Help, our Savior and our Shield. Blessed is the Lord, the Shield of Abraham.

* On the Ten Days of Repentance insert:

זָכְרֵנוּ לְחַיִּים, מֶלֶךְ חָפֵץ בַּחַיִּים,
וְכָתְבֵנוּ בְּסֵפֶר הַחַיִּים, לְמַעַנְךָ אֱלֹהִים חַיִּים.

Remember us unto life, for You are the King who delights in life, and inscribe us in the Book of Life, that Your will may prevail, O God of life.

◆ ◆

GOD'S POWER   גבורות

אַתָּה גִבּוֹר לְעוֹלָם, אֲדֹנָי, מְחַיֵּה הַכֹּל אַתָּה, רַב לְהוֹשִׁיעַ.

Eternal is Your might, O Lord; all life is Your gift; great is Your power to save!

מְכַלְכֵּל חַיִּים בְּחֶסֶד, מְחַיֵּה הַכֹּל בְּרַחֲמִים רַבִּים. סוֹמֵךְ
נוֹפְלִים, וְרוֹפֵא חוֹלִים, וּמַתִּיר אֲסוּרִים, וּמְקַיֵּם אֱמוּנָתוֹ
לִישֵׁנֵי עָפָר.

*With love You sustain the living, with great compassion give
life to all. You send help to the falling and healing to the sick;
You bring freedom to the captive and keep faith with those who
sleep in the dust.*

מִי כָמוֹךָ, בַּעַל גְּבוּרוֹת, וּמִי דּוֹמֶה לָּךְ, מֶלֶךְ מֵמִית וּמְחַיֶּה
וּמַצְמִיחַ יְשׁוּעָה?*

וְנֶאֱמָן אַתָּה לְהַחֲיוֹת הַכֹּל. בָּרוּךְ אַתָּה, יְיָ, מְחַיֵּה הַכֹּל.

*Who is like You, Master of Might? Who is Your equal, O
Lord of life and death, Source of salvation?* Blessed is the Lord,
the Source of life.*

* On the Ten Days of Repentance insert:

מִי כָמוֹךָ, אַב הָרַחֲמִים, זוֹכֵר יְצוּרָיו לְחַיִּים בְּרַחֲמִים?

*Who is like You, Source of mercy, who in compassion sustains the life of His
children?*

◆ ◆

SANCTIFICATION   קדושה

נְקַדֵּשׁ אֶת־שִׁמְךָ בָּעוֹלָם, כְּשֵׁם שֶׁמַּקְדִּישִׁים אוֹתוֹ בִּשְׁמֵי מָרוֹם,
כַּכָּתוּב עַל־יַד נְבִיאֶךָ: וְקָרָא זֶה אֶל־זֶה וְאָמַר:

We sanctify Your name on earth, even as all things, to the ends
of time and space, proclaim Your holiness; and in the words of
the prophet we say:

קָדוֹשׁ, קָדוֹשׁ, קָדוֹשׁ יְיָ צְבָאוֹת, מְלֹא כָל־הָאָרֶץ כְּבוֹדוֹ.

*Holy, Holy, Holy is the Lord of Hosts; the fullness of the whole
earth is His glory!*

לְעֻמָּתָם בָּרוּךְ יֹאמֵרוּ:

They respond to Your glory with blessing:

בָּרוּךְ כְּבוֹד יְיָ מִמְּקוֹמוֹ.

Blessed is the glory of God in heaven and earth.

וּבְדִבְרֵי קָדְשְׁךָ כָּתוּב לֵאמֹר:

And this is Your sacred word:

יִמְלֹךְ יְיָ לְעוֹלָם, אֱלֹהַיִךְ צִיּוֹן, לְדֹר וָדֹר, הַלְלוּיָהּ.

The Lord shall reign for ever; your God, O Zion, from genera-
tion to generation. Halleluyah!

לְדוֹר וָדוֹר נַגִּיד גָּדְלֶךָ, וּלְנֵצַח נְצָחִים קְדֻשָּׁתְךָ נַקְדִּישׁ.
וְשִׁבְחֲךָ, אֱלֹהֵינוּ, מִפִּינוּ לֹא יָמוּשׁ לְעוֹלָם וָעֶד.*

בָּרוּךְ אַתָּה, יְיָ, הָאֵל הַקָּדוֹשׁ.

To all generations we will make known Your greatness, and
to all eternity proclaim Your holiness. Your praise, O God,
shall never depart from our lips.*

Blessed is the Lord, the holy God.

On the Ten Days of Repentance conclude:
Blessed is the Lord, the holy King.　בָּרוּךְ אַתָּה, יְיָ, הַמֶּלֶךְ הַקָּדוֹשׁ.

All are seated

◆ ◆

FOR UNDERSTANDING　　　　　　　　　　　　　בינה

אַתָּה חוֹנֵן לְאָדָם דַּעַת וּמְלַמֵּד לֶאֱנוֹשׁ בִּינָה. חָנֵּנוּ מֵאִתְּךָ
דֵּעָה, בִּינָה וְהַשְׂכֵּל.

בָּרוּךְ אַתָּה, יְיָ, חוֹנֵן הַדָּעַת.

You favor us with knowledge and teach mortals understanding.
May You continue to favor us with knowledge, understanding,
and insight.

Blessed is the Lord, gracious Giver of knowledge.

◆ ◆

FOR REPENTANCE　　　　　　　　　　　　　תשובה

הֲשִׁיבֵנוּ אָבִינוּ לְתוֹרָתֶךָ, וְקָרְבֵנוּ מַלְכֵּנוּ לַעֲבוֹדָתֶךָ,
וְהַחֲזִירֵנוּ בִּתְשׁוּבָה שְׁלֵמָה לְפָנֶיךָ.

בָּרוּךְ אַתָּה, יְיָ, הָרוֹצֶה בִּתְשׁוּבָה.

Help us to return, our Maker, to Your Torah; draw us near, O Sovereign God, to Your service; and bring us back into Your presence in perfect repentance.

Blessed is the Lord, who calls for repentance.

• •

FOR FORGIVENESS סליחה

סְלַח־לָנוּ אָבִינוּ כִּי חָטָאנוּ, מְחַל־לָנוּ מַלְכֵּנוּ כִּי פָשָׁעְנוּ, כִּי מוֹחֵל וְסוֹלֵחַ אָתָּה.

בָּרוּךְ אַתָּה, יְיָ, חַנּוּן הַמַּרְבֶּה לִסְלוֹחַ.

Forgive us, our Creator, when we have sinned; pardon us, our King, when we transgress; for You are a forgiving God.

Blessed is the Lord, the gracious God, whose forgiveness is abundant.

• •

FOR REDEMPTION גאולה

רְאֵה בְעָנְיֵנוּ וְרִיבָה רִיבֵנוּ, וּגְאָלֵנוּ מְהֵרָה לְמַעַן שְׁמֶךָ, כִּי גוֹאֵל חָזָק אָתָּה.

בָּרוּךְ אַתָּה, יְיָ, גּוֹאֵל יִשְׂרָאֵל.

Look upon our affliction and help us in our need; O mighty Redeemer, redeem us speedily for Your name's sake.

Blessed is the Lord, the Redeemer of Israel.

• •

FOR HEALTH רפואה

רְפָאֵנוּ יְיָ וְנֵרָפֵא, הוֹשִׁיעֵנוּ וְנִוָּשֵׁעָה, וְהַעֲלֵה רְפוּאָה שְׁלֵמָה לְכָל־מַכּוֹתֵינוּ.

בָּרוּךְ אַתָּה, יְיָ, רוֹפֵא הַחוֹלִים.

Heal us, O Lord, and we shall be healed; save us, and we shall be saved; grant us a perfect healing from all our wounds.

Blessed is the Lord, the Healer of the sick.

• •

164

FOR ABUNDANCE   ברכת השנים

בָּרֵךְ עָלֵינוּ, יְיָ אֱלֹהֵינוּ, אֶת־הַשָּׁנָה הַזֹּאת וְאֶת־כָּל־מִינֵי
תְבוּאָתָהּ לְטוֹבָה. וְתֵן בְּרָכָה עַל־פְּנֵי הָאֲדָמָה, וְשַׂבְּעֵנוּ
מִטּוּבֶךָ.

בָּרוּךְ אַתָּה, יְיָ, מְבָרֵךְ הַשָּׁנִים.

Bless this year, O Lord our God, and let its produce bring us
well-being. Bestow Your blessing on the earth and satisfy us
with Your goodness.

Blessed is the Lord, from whom all blessings flow.

◆ ◆

FOR FREEDOM   חרות

תְּקַע בְּשׁוֹפָר גָּדוֹל לְחֵרוּתֵנוּ, וְשָׂא נֵס לִפְדּוֹת עֲשׁוּקֵינוּ, וְקוֹל
דְּרוֹר יִשָּׁמַע בְּאַרְבַּע כַּנְפוֹת הָאָרֶץ.

בָּרוּךְ אַתָּה, יְיָ, פּוֹדֶה עֲשׁוּקִים.

Sound the great horn to proclaim freedom, inspire us to strive
for the liberation of the oppressed, and let the song of liberty
be heard in the four corners of the earth.

Blessed is the Lord, Redeemer of the oppressed.

◆ ◆

FOR JUSTICE   משפט

עַל שׁוֹפְטֵי אֶרֶץ שְׁפוֹךְ רוּחֶךָ, וְהַדְרִיכֵם בְּמִשְׁפְּטֵי צִדְקֶךָ,
וּמְלוֹךְ עָלֵינוּ אַתָּה לְבַדֶּךָ, בְּחֶסֶד וּבְרַחֲמִים!

בָּרוּךְ אַתָּה, יְיָ, מֶלֶךְ אוֹהֵב צְדָקָה וּמִשְׁפָּט.

Pour Your spirit upon the rulers of all lands; guide them, that
they may govern justly. O may You alone reign over us in
steadfast love and compassion!

*Blessed is the Sovereign Lord, who loves righteousness and
justice.*

◆ ◆

FOR RIGHTEOUSNESS   צדיקים

עַל־הַצַּדִּיקִים וְעַל־הַחֲסִידִים וְעָלֵינוּ יֶהֱמוּ רַחֲמֶיךָ, יְיָ אֱלֹהֵינוּ,
וְתֵן שָׂכָר טוֹב לְכָל הַבּוֹטְחִים בְּשִׁמְךָ בֶּאֱמֶת, וְשִׂים חֶלְקֵנוּ
עִמָּהֶם לְעוֹלָם.

בָּרוּךְ אַתָּה, יְיָ, מִשְׁעָן וּמִבְטָח לַצַּדִּיקִים.

Have mercy, O Lord our God, upon the righteous and faithful
of all peoples, and upon all of us. Uphold all who faithfully
put their trust in You, and grant that we may always be num-
bered among them.

Blessed is the Lord, the Staff and Support of the righteous.

❖ ❖

FOR JERUSALEM   שלום ירושלים

וְלִירוּשָׁלַיִם עִירְךָ בְּרַחֲמִים תִּפְנֶה, וִיהִי שָׁלוֹם בִּשְׁעָרֶיהָ,
וְשַׁלְוָה בְּלֵב יוֹשְׁבֶיהָ, וְתוֹרָתְךָ מִצִּיּוֹן תֵּצֵא וּדְבָרְךָ
מִירוּשָׁלָיִם.

בָּרוּךְ אַתָּה, יְיָ, נוֹתֵן שָׁלוֹם בִּירוּשָׁלָיִם.

And turn in compassion to Jerusalem, Your city. Let there be
peace in her gates, quietness in the hearts of her inhabitants.
Let Your Torah go forth from Zion and Your word from
Jerusalem.

Blessed is the Lord, who gives peace to Jerusalem.

❖ ❖

FOR DELIVERANCE   ישועה

אֶת־צֶמַח צְדָקָה מְהֵרָה תַצְמִיחַ, וְקֶרֶן יְשׁוּעָה תָּרוּם כִּנְאֻמֶךָ,
כִּי לִישׁוּעָתְךָ קִוִּינוּ כָּל־הַיּוֹם.

בָּרוּךְ אַתָּה, יְיָ, מַצְמִיחַ קֶרֶן יְשׁוּעָה.

Cause the plant of justice to spring up soon. Let the light of deliverance shine forth according to Your word, for we await Your deliverance all the day.

Blessed is the Lord, who will cause the light of deliverance to dawn for all the world.

◆ ◆

FOR ACCEPTANCE OF PRAYER   שומע תפלה

שְׁמַע קוֹלֵנוּ, יְיָ אֱלֹהֵינוּ, חוּס וְרַחֵם עָלֵינוּ, וְקַבֵּל בְּרַחֲמִים
וּבְרָצוֹן אֶת תְּפִלָּתֵנוּ, כִּי אֵל שׁוֹמֵעַ תְּפִלּוֹת וְתַחֲנוּנִים אָתָּה.
בָּרוּךְ אַתָּה, יְיָ, שׁוֹמֵעַ תְּפִלָּה.

Hear our voice, O Lord our God; have compassion upon us, and accept our prayer with favor and mercy, for You are a God who hears prayer and supplication.

Blessed is the Lord, who hearkens to prayer.

◆ ◆

WORSHIP   עבודה

רְצֵה, יְיָ אֱלֹהֵינוּ, בְּעַמְּךָ יִשְׂרָאֵל, וּתְפִלָּתָם בְּאַהֲבָה תְקַבֵּל,
וּתְהִי לְרָצוֹן תָּמִיד עֲבוֹדַת יִשְׂרָאֵל עַמֶּךָ.
אֵל קָרוֹב לְכָל־קֹרְאָיו, פְּנֵה אֶל עֲבָדֶיךָ וְחָנֵּנוּ; שְׁפוֹךְ רוּחֲךָ
עָלֵינוּ, וְתֶחֱזֶינָה עֵינֵינוּ בְּשׁוּבְךָ לְצִיּוֹן בְּרַחֲמִים.
בָּרוּךְ אַתָּה, יְיָ, הַמַּחֲזִיר שְׁכִינָתוֹ לְצִיּוֹן.

Be gracious, O Lord our God, to Your people Israel, and receive our prayers with love. O may our worship always be acceptable to You.

Fill us with the knowledge that You are near to all who seek You in truth. Let our eyes behold Your presence in our midst and in the midst of our people in Zion.

Blessed is the Lord, whose presence gives life to Zion and all Israel.

◆ ◆

167

ON ROSH CHODESH, CHOL HAMO-EID, AND YOM HA-ATSMA-UT

אֱלֹהֵינוּ וֵאלֹהֵי אֲבוֹתֵינוּ, יַעֲלֶה וְיָבֹא וְיַגִּיעַ וְיֵרָאֶה וְיֵרָצֶה וְיִשָּׁמַע וְיִפָּקֵד וְיִזָּכֵר זִכְרוֹנֵנוּ וְזִכְרוֹן כָּל־עַמְּךָ בֵּית יִשְׂרָאֵל לְפָנֶיךָ, לְטוֹבָה, לְחֵן לְחֶסֶד וּלְרַחֲמִים, לְחַיִּים וּלְשָׁלוֹם בְּיוֹם

Our God and God of all ages, be mindful of Your people Israel on this

first day of the new month,	רֹאשׁ הַחֹדֶשׁ הַזֶּה.
day of Pesach,	חַג הַמַּצּוֹת הַזֶּה.
day of Sukkot,	חַג הַסֻּכּוֹת הַזֶּה.
day of Independence,	הָעַצְמָאוּת הַזֶּה.

and renew in us love and compassion, goodness, life and peace.

This day remember us for well-being. *Amen.*   זָכְרֵנוּ, יְיָ אֱלֹהֵינוּ, בּוֹ לְטוֹבָה. אָמֵן.

This day bless us with Your nearness. *Amen.*   וּפָקְדֵנוּ בוֹ לִבְרָכָה. אָמֵן.

This day help us to a fuller life. *Amen.*   וְהוֹשִׁיעֵנוּ בוֹ לְחַיִּים. אָמֵן.

✦ ✦

THANKSGIVING   הודאה

מוֹדִים אֲנַחְנוּ לָךְ, שָׁאַתָּה הוּא יְיָ אֱלֹהֵינוּ וֵאלֹהֵי אֲבוֹתֵינוּ לְעוֹלָם וָעֶד. צוּר חַיֵּינוּ, מָגֵן יִשְׁעֵנוּ, אַתָּה הוּא לְדוֹר וָדוֹר. נוֹדֶה לְךָ וּנְסַפֵּר תְּהִלָּתֶךָ, עַל־חַיֵּינוּ הַמְּסוּרִים בְּיָדֶךָ, וְעַל־נִשְׁמוֹתֵינוּ הַפְּקוּדוֹת לָךְ, וְעַל־נִסֶּיךָ שֶׁבְּכָל־יוֹם עִמָּנוּ, וְעַל־נִפְלְאוֹתֶיךָ וְטוֹבוֹתֶיךָ שֶׁבְּכָל־עֵת, עֶרֶב וָבֹקֶר וְצָהֳרָיִם. הַטּוֹב כִּי לֹא־כָלוּ רַחֲמֶיךָ, וְהַמְרַחֵם כִּי־לֹא תַמּוּ חֲסָדֶיךָ, מֵעוֹלָם קִוִּינוּ לָךְ.

We gratefully acknowledge that You are the Lord our God and God of our people, the God of all generations. You are the Rock of our life, the Power that shields us in every age. We thank You and sing Your praises: for our lives, which are in Your hand; for our souls, which are in Your keeping; for the signs of Your presence we encounter every day; and for

168

Your wondrous gifts at all times, morning, noon, and night.
You are Goodness: Your mercies never end; You are Compas-
sion: Your love will never fail. You have always been our hope.

וְעַל כֻּלָּם יִתְבָּרַךְ וְיִתְרוֹמַם שִׁמְךָ, מַלְכֵּנוּ, תָּמִיד לְעוֹלָם וָעֶד.

For all these things, O Sovereign God, let Your name be for
ever exalted and blessed.

On the Ten Days of Repentance insert:

וּכְתוֹב לְחַיִּים טוֹבִים כָּל־בְּנֵי בְרִיתֶךָ.

Let life abundant be the heritage of all Your children.

וְכֹל הַחַיִּים יוֹדוּךָ סֶּלָה, וִיהַלְלוּ אֶת שִׁמְךָ בֶּאֱמֶת, הָאֵל
יְשׁוּעָתֵנוּ וְעֶזְרָתֵנוּ סֶּלָה. בָּרוּךְ אַתָּה, יְיָ, הַטּוֹב שִׁמְךָ, וּלְךָ נָאֶה
לְהוֹדוֹת.

O God our Redeemer and Helper, let all who live affirm You
and praise Your name in truth. Lord, whose nature is Goodness, we give You thanks and praise.

✦ ✦

ON CHANUKAH

עַל הַנִּסִּים וְעַל הַפֻּרְקָן, וְעַל הַגְּבוּרוֹת וְעַל הַתְּשׁוּעוֹת, וְעַל
הַמִּלְחָמוֹת, שֶׁעָשִׂיתָ לַאֲבוֹתֵינוּ בַּיָּמִים הָהֵם בַּזְּמַן הַזֶּה.

בִּימֵי מַתִּתְיָהוּ בֶּן־יוֹחָנָן כֹּהֵן גָּדוֹל, חַשְׁמוֹנַי וּבָנָיו, כְּשֶׁעָמְדָה מַלְכוּת
יָוָן הָרְשָׁעָה עַל־עַמְּךָ יִשְׂרָאֵל לְהַשְׁכִּיחָם תּוֹרָתֶךָ, וּלְהַעֲבִירָם מֵחֻקֵּי
רְצוֹנֶךָ.

וְאַתָּה בְּרַחֲמֶיךָ הָרַבִּים עָמַדְתָּ לָהֶם בְּעֵת צָרָתָם. רַבְתָּ אֶת־רִיבָם,
דַּנְתָּ אֶת־דִּינָם, מָסַרְתָּ גִבּוֹרִים בְּיַד חַלָּשִׁים, וְרַבִּים בְּיַד מְעַטִּים,
וּטְמֵאִים בְּיַד טְהוֹרִים, וּרְשָׁעִים בְּיַד צַדִּיקִים, וְזֵדִים בְּיַד עוֹסְקֵי
תוֹרָתֶךָ.

וּלְךָ עָשִׂיתָ שֵׁם גָּדוֹל וְקָדוֹשׁ בְּעוֹלָמֶךָ, וּלְעַמְּךָ יִשְׂרָאֵל עָשִׂיתָ תְּשׁוּעָה
גְדוֹלָה וּפֻרְקָן כְּהַיּוֹם הַזֶּה.

וְאַחַר כֵּן בָּאוּ בָנֶיךָ לִדְבִיר בֵּיתֶךָ, וּפִנּוּ אֶת־הֵיכָלֶךָ, וְטִהֲרוּ אֶת־
מִקְדָּשֶׁךָ, וְהִדְלִיקוּ נֵרוֹת בְּחַצְרוֹת קָדְשֶׁךָ, וְקָבְעוּ שְׁמוֹנַת יְמֵי חֲנֻכָּה
אֵלּוּ לְהוֹדוֹת וּלְהַלֵּל לְשִׁמְךָ הַגָּדוֹל.

We give thanks for the redeeming wonders and the mighty deeds by which, at this season, our people was saved in days of old.

In the days of the Hasmoneans, a tyrant arose against our ancestors, determined to make them forget Your Torah, and to turn them away from obedience to Your will. But You were at their side in time of trouble. You gave them strength to struggle and to triumph, that they might serve You in freedom.

Through the power of Your spirit the weak defeated the strong, the few prevailed over the many, and the righteous were triumphant.

Then Your children returned to Your house, to purify the sanctuary and kindle its lights. And they dedicated these days to give thanks and praise to Your great name.

◆ ◆

ON PURIM

עַל הַנִּסִּים וְעַל הַפֻּרְקָן, וְעַל הַגְּבוּרוֹת וְעַל הַתְּשׁוּעוֹת, וְעַל הַמִּלְחָמוֹת, שֶׁעָשִׂיתָ לַאֲבוֹתֵינוּ בַּיָּמִים הָהֵם בַּזְּמַן הַזֶּה.

בִּימֵי מָרְדְּכַי וְאֶסְתֵּר בְּשׁוּשַׁן הַבִּירָה, כְּשֶׁעָמַד עֲלֵיהֶם הָמָן הָרָשָׁע, בִּקֵּשׁ לְהַשְׁמִיד לַהֲרֹג וּלְאַבֵּד אֶת־כָּל־הַיְּהוּדִים, מִנַּעַר וְעַד־זָקֵן, טַף וְנָשִׁים, בְּיוֹם אֶחָד, בִּשְׁלוֹשָׁה עָשָׂר לְחֹדֶשׁ שְׁנֵים־עָשָׂר, הוּא־חֹדֶשׁ אֲדָר, וּשְׁלָלָם לָבוֹז.

וְאַתָּה בְּרַחֲמֶיךָ הָרַבִּים הֵפַרְתָּ אֶת־עֲצָתוֹ, וְקִלְקַלְתָּ אֶת־מַחֲשַׁבְתּוֹ.

We give thanks for the redeeming wonders and the mighty deeds by which, at this season, our people was saved in days of old.
In the days of Mordecai and Esther, the wicked Haman arose in Persia, plotting the destruction of all the Jews. He planned to destroy them in a single day, the thirteenth of Adar, and to permit the plunder of their possessions.
But through Your great mercy his plan was thwarted, his scheme frustrated. We therefore thank and bless You, O great and gracious God!

◆ ◆

PEACE

שִׂים שָׁלוֹם, טוֹבָה וּבְרָכָה, חֵן וָחֶסֶד וְרַחֲמִים, עָלֵינוּ וְעַל־
כָּל־יִשְׂרָאֵל עַמֶּךָ.

Peace, happiness, and blessing; grace and love and mercy:
may these descend on us, on all Israel, and all the world.

בָּרְכֵנוּ אָבִינוּ, כֻּלָנוּ כְּאֶחָד, בְּאוֹר פָּנֶיךָ, כִּי בְאוֹר פָּנֶיךָ נָתַתָּ
לָנוּ, יְיָ אֱלֹהֵינוּ, תּוֹרַת חַיִּים, וְאַהֲבַת חֶסֶד, וּצְדָקָה וּבְרָכָה
וְרַחֲמִים, וְחַיִּים וְשָׁלוֹם.

Bless us, our Creator, one and all, with the light of Your presence; for by that light, O God, You have revealed to us the
law of life: to love kindness and justice and mercy, to seek
blessing, life, and peace.

וְטוֹב בְּעֵינֶיךָ לְבָרֵךְ אֶת־עַמְּךָ יִשְׂרָאֵל בְּכָל־עֵת וּבְכָל־שָׁעָה
בִּשְׁלוֹמֶךָ.*

בָּרוּךְ אַתָּה, יְיָ, הַמְבָרֵךְ אֶת־עַמּוֹ יִשְׂרָאֵל בַּשָּׁלוֹם.

O bless Your people Israel and all peoples with enduring
peace!*

Praised be the Lord, who blesses His people Israel with peace.

On the Ten Days of Repentance conclude:

בְּסֵפֶר חַיִּים וּבְרָכָה נִכָּתֵב לְחַיִּים טוֹבִים וּלְשָׁלוֹם.
בָּרוּךְ אַתָּה, יְיָ, עוֹשֵׂה הַשָּׁלוֹם.

Teach us then to find our happiness in the search for righteousness
and peace. Blessed is the Lord, the Source of peace.

❖ ❖

SILENT PRAYER

אֱלֹהַי, נְצֹר לְשׁוֹנִי מֵרָע, וּשְׂפָתַי מִדַּבֵּר מִרְמָה, וְלִמְקַלְלַי
נַפְשִׁי תִדּוֹם, וְנַפְשִׁי כֶּעָפָר לַכֹּל תִּהְיֶה. פְּתַח לִבִּי בְּתוֹרָתֶךָ,
וּבְמִצְוֹתֶיךָ תִּרְדּוֹף נַפְשִׁי, וְכָל הַחוֹשְׁבִים עָלַי רָעָה, מְהֵרָה

הָפֵר עֲצָתָם וְקַלְקֵל מַחֲשַׁבְתָּם. עֲשֵׂה לְמַעַן שְׁמֶךָ, עֲשֵׂה לְמַעַן
יְמִינֶךָ, עֲשֵׂה לְמַעַן קְדֻשָּׁתֶךָ, עֲשֵׂה לְמַעַן תּוֹרָתֶךָ. לְמַעַן
יֵחָלְצוּן יְדִידֶיךָ. הוֹשִׁיעָה יְמִינְךָ וַעֲנֵנִי.

O God, keep my tongue from evil and my lips from deceit.
Help me to be silent in the face of derision, humble in the presence of all. Open my heart to Your Torah, and I will hasten
to do Your Mitzvot. Save me with Your power; in time of
trouble be my answer, that those who love You may rejoice.

◆ ◆

יִהְיוּ לְרָצוֹן אִמְרֵי־פִי וְהֶגְיוֹן לִבִּי לְפָנֶיךָ, יְיָ, צוּרִי וְגוֹאֲלִי.

May the words of my mouth, and the meditations of my heart, be
acceptable to You, O Lord, my Rock and my Redeemer.

or

עֹשֶׂה שָׁלוֹם בִּמְרוֹמָיו, הוּא יַעֲשֶׂה שָׁלוֹם עָלֵינוּ וְעַל כָּל־
יִשְׂרָאֵל, וְאִמְרוּ אָמֵן.

May He who causes peace to reign in the high heavens let peace
descend on us, on all Israel, and all the world.

Prayers at a House of Mourning begin on page 183.

Concluding Prayers begin on page 187.

172

Weekday Evening or Morning Service

The greatness of the Eternal One surpasses our understanding, and yet at times we feel His nearness.

Overwhelmed by awe and wonder as we behold the signs of His presence, still we feel within us a kinship with the divine.

And so we turn to You, O God, looking at the world about us, and inward to the world within us, there to find You, and from Your presence gain life and strength.

◆ ◆

All rise

שמע וברכותיה

בָּרְכוּ אֶת־יְיָ הַמְבֹרָךְ!

Praise the Lord, to whom our praise is due!

בָּרוּךְ יְיָ הַמְבֹרָךְ לְעוֹלָם וָעֶד!

Praised be the Lord, to whom our praise is due,
now and for ever!

◆ ◆

Evening

בָּרוּךְ אַתָּה, יְיָ אֱלֹהֵינוּ, מֶלֶךְ הָעוֹלָם, אֲשֶׁר בִּדְבָרוֹ מַעֲרִיב עֲרָבִים. בְּחָכְמָה פּוֹתֵחַ שְׁעָרִים, וּבִתְבוּנָה מְשַׁנֶּה עִתִּים, וּמַחֲלִיף אֶת־הַזְּמַנִּים, וּמְסַדֵּר אֶת־הַכּוֹכָבִים בְּמִשְׁמְרוֹתֵיהֶם בָּרָקִיעַ

Morning

בָּרוּךְ אַתָּה, יְיָ אֱלֹהֵינוּ, מֶלֶךְ הָעוֹלָם, יוֹצֵר אוֹר וּבוֹרֵא חְשֶׁךְ, עֹשֶׂה שָׁלוֹם וּבוֹרֵא אֶת־הַכֹּל. הַמֵּאִיר לָאָרֶץ וְלַדָּרִים עָלֶיהָ בְּרַחֲמִים, וּבְטוּבוֹ מְחַדֵּשׁ בְּכָל־יוֹם תָּמִיד מַעֲשֵׂה בְרֵאשִׁית.

173

Evening   *Morning*

כִּרְצוֹנוֹ. בּוֹרֵא יוֹם וָלֵיְלָה, גּוֹלֵל
אוֹר מִפְּנֵי חֹשֶׁךְ וְחֹשֶׁךְ מִפְּנֵי
אוֹר, וּמַעֲבִיר יוֹם וּמֵבִיא לֵיְלָה,
וּמַבְדִּיל בֵּין יוֹם וּבֵין לֵיְלָה, יְיָ
צְבָאוֹת שְׁמוֹ. אֵל חַי וְקַיָּם,
תָּמִיד יִמְלוֹךְ עָלֵינוּ, לְעוֹלָם
וָעֶד.

בָּרוּךְ אַתָּה, יְיָ, הַמַּעֲרִיב עֲרָבִים.

מָה רַבּוּ מַעֲשֶׂיךָ, יְיָ! כֻּלָּם
בְּחָכְמָה עָשִׂיתָ, מָלְאָה הָאָרֶץ
קִנְיָנֶךָ. תִּתְבָּרַךְ, יְיָ אֱלֹהֵינוּ, עַל־
שֶׁבַח מַעֲשֵׂה יָדֶיךָ, וְעַל־מְאוֹרֵי־
אוֹר שֶׁעָשִׂיתָ: יְפָאֲרוּךְ. סֶלָה.
בָּרוּךְ אַתָּה, יְיָ, יוֹצֵר הַמְּאוֹרוֹת.

Heaven and earth, O Lord, are the work of Your hands. The roaring seas and the life within them issue forth from Your creative will. The universe is one vast wonder proclaiming Your wisdom and singing Your greatness.

The mysteries of life and death, of growth and decay, alike display the miracle of Your creative power. O God of life, the whole universe is Your dwelling-place, all being a hymn to Your glory!

· ·

Evening   *Morning*

אַהֲבַת עוֹלָם בֵּית יִשְׂרָאֵל עַמְּךָ
אָהָבְתָּ: תּוֹרָה וּמִצְוֹת, חֻקִּים
וּמִשְׁפָּטִים אוֹתָנוּ לִמַּדְתָּ.
עַל־כֵּן, יְיָ אֱלֹהֵינוּ, בְּשָׁכְבֵּנוּ
וּבְקוּמֵנוּ נָשִׂיחַ בְּחֻקֶּיךָ, וְנִשְׂמַח
בְּדִבְרֵי תוֹרָתְךָ וּבְמִצְוֹתֶיךָ
לְעוֹלָם וָעֶד.
כִּי הֵם חַיֵּינוּ וְאֹרֶךְ יָמֵינוּ, וּבָהֶם
נֶהְגֶּה יוֹמָם וָלֵיְלָה. וְאַהֲבָתְךָ
אַל־תָּסִיר מִמֶּנּוּ לְעוֹלָמִים!

אַהֲבָה רַבָּה אֲהַבְתָּנוּ, יְיָ
אֱלֹהֵינוּ, חֶמְלָה גְדוֹלָה וִיתֵרָה
חָמַלְתָּ עָלֵינוּ. אָבִינוּ מַלְכֵּנוּ,
בַּעֲבוּר אֲבוֹתֵינוּ שֶׁבָּטְחוּ בְךָ
וַתְּלַמְּדֵם חֻקֵּי חַיִּים, כֵּן תְּחָנֵּנוּ
וּתְלַמְּדֵנוּ. אָבִינוּ, הָאָב הָרַחֲמָן,
הַמְרַחֵם, רַחֵם עָלֵינוּ וְתֵן בְּלִבֵּנוּ
לְהָבִין וּלְהַשְׂכִּיל, לִשְׁמֹעַ לִלְמֹד
וּלְלַמֵּד, לִשְׁמֹר וְלַעֲשׂוֹת וּלְקַיֵּם
אֶת־כָּל־דִּבְרֵי תַלְמוּד תּוֹרָתְךָ

Evening   *Morning*

בְּאַהֲבָה. וְהָאֵר עֵינֵינוּ בְּתוֹרָתֶךָ, | בָּרוּךְ אַתָּה, יְיָ, אוֹהֵב עַמּוֹ
וְדַבֵּק לִבֵּנוּ בְּמִצְוֹתֶיךָ, וְיַחֵד | יִשְׂרָאֵל.
לְבָבֵנוּ לְאַהֲבָה וּלְיִרְאָה אֶת־
שְׁמֶךָ. וְלֹא־נֵבוֹשׁ לְעוֹלָם וָעֶד, כִּי בְשֵׁם קָדְשְׁךָ הַגָּדוֹל וְהַנּוֹרָא
בָּטָחְנוּ. נָגִילָה וְנִשְׂמְחָה בִּישׁוּעָתֶךָ, כִּי אֵל פּוֹעֵל יְשׁוּעוֹת אָתָּה,
וּבָנוּ בָחַרְתָּ וְקֵרַבְתָּנוּ לְשִׁמְךָ הַגָּדוֹל סֶלָה בֶּאֱמֶת, לְהוֹדוֹת לְךָ
וּלְיַחֶדְךָ בְּאַהֲבָה. בָּרוּךְ אַתָּה, יְיָ, הַבּוֹחֵר בְּעַמּוֹ יִשְׂרָאֵל בְּאַהֲבָה.

In the human heart, too, You reign supreme. Above the storms
of passion and hate that shake our world, we hear Your voice
proclaim the law of justice and love.

May our eyes be open to Your truth, our spirits alive to Your
teaching, our hearts united to serve You.

May we find the will to consecrate ourselves anew to the task
of all the generations: to speed the dawn of the new day when
all will be united in friendship and peace, and with one accord
acclaim You their Eternal God.

◆ ◆

שְׁמַע יִשְׂרָאֵל: יְיָ אֱלֹהֵינוּ, יְיָ אֶחָד!

Hear, O Israel: the Lord is our God, the Lord is One!

בָּרוּךְ שֵׁם כְּבוֹד מַלְכוּתוֹ לְעוֹלָם וָעֶד!

Blessed is His glorious kingdom for ever and ever!

All are seated

וְאָהַבְתָּ אֵת יְיָ אֱלֹהֶיךָ בְּכָל־לְבָבְךָ וּבְכָל־נַפְשְׁךָ וּבְכָל־מְאֹדֶךָ.
וְהָיוּ הַדְּבָרִים הָאֵלֶּה, אֲשֶׁר אָנֹכִי מְצַוְּךָ הַיּוֹם, עַל־לְבָבֶךָ.
וְשִׁנַּנְתָּם לְבָנֶיךָ, וְדִבַּרְתָּ בָּם בְּשִׁבְתְּךָ בְּבֵיתֶךָ, וּבְלֶכְתְּךָ
בַדֶּרֶךְ, וּבְשָׁכְבְּךָ וּבְקוּמֶךָ.

175

You shall love the Lord your God with all your mind, with all your strength, with all your being.
Set these words, which I command you this day, upon your heart. Teach them faithfully to your children; speak of them in your home and on your way, when you lie down and when you rise up.

וּקְשַׁרְתָּם לְאוֹת עַל־יָדֶךָ, וְהָיוּ לְטֹטָפֹת בֵּין עֵינֶיךָ, וּכְתַבְתָּם עַל־מְזֻזוֹת בֵּיתֶךָ, וּבִשְׁעָרֶיךָ.

Bind them as a sign upon your hand; let them be a symbol before your eyes; inscribe them on the doorposts of your house, and on your gates.

לְמַעַן תִּזְכְּרוּ וַעֲשִׂיתֶם אֶת־כָּל־מִצְוֹתָי, וִהְיִיתֶם קְדֹשִׁים לֵאלֹהֵיכֶם. אֲנִי יְיָ אֱלֹהֵיכֶם, אֲשֶׁר הוֹצֵאתִי אֶתְכֶם מֵאֶרֶץ מִצְרַיִם לִהְיוֹת לָכֶם לֵאלֹהִים. אֲנִי יְיָ אֱלֹהֵיכֶם.

Be mindful of all My Mitzvot, and do them: so shall you consecrate yourselves to your God. I, the Lord, am your God who led you out of Egypt to be your God; I, the Lord, am your God.

❖ ❖

Morning	Evening
עַל־הָרִאשׁוֹנִים וְעַל־הָאַחֲרוֹנִים	אֱמֶת וֶאֱמוּנָה כָּל־זֹאת, וְקַיָּם
דָּבָר טוֹב וְקַיָּם לְעוֹלָם וָעֶד.	עָלֵינוּ כִּי הוּא יְיָ אֱלֹהֵינוּ וְאֵין
אֱמֶת וֶאֱמוּנָה, חֹק וְלֹא יַעֲבוֹר.	זוּלָתוֹ, וַאֲנַחְנוּ יִשְׂרָאֵל עַמּוֹ.
אֱמֶת שָׁאַתָּה הוּא יְיָ אֱלֹהֵינוּ	הַפּוֹדֵנוּ מִיַּד מְלָכִים, מַלְכֵּנוּ
וֵאלֹהֵי אֲבוֹתֵינוּ, מַלְכֵּנוּ מֶלֶךְ	הַגּוֹאֲלֵנוּ מִכַּף כָּל־הֶעָרִיצִים.
אֲבוֹתֵינוּ, גּוֹאֲלֵנוּ גּוֹאֵל אֲבוֹתֵינוּ,	הָעֹשֶׂה גְדֹלוֹת עַד אֵין חֵקֶר,
יוֹצְרֵנוּ, צוּר יְשׁוּעָתֵנוּ. פּוֹדֵנוּ	וְנִפְלָאוֹת עַד־אֵין מִסְפָּר.
וּמַצִּילֵנוּ מֵעוֹלָם הוּא שְׁמֶךָ, אֵין	הָעֹשֶׂה לָנוּ נִסִּים בְּפַרְעֹה, אוֹתוֹת
אֱלֹהִים זוּלָתֶךָ.	וּמוֹפְתִים בְּאַדְמַת בְּנֵי חָם.

Evening   *Morning*

עֶזְרַת אֲבוֹתֵינוּ אַתָּה הוּא	וַיּוֹצֵא אֶת־עַמּוֹ יִשְׂרָאֵל מִתּוֹכָם
מֵעוֹלָם, מָגֵן וּמוֹשִׁיעַ לִבְנֵיהֶם	לְחֵרוּת עוֹלָם.
אַחֲרֵיהֶם בְּכָל־דּוֹר וָדוֹר. בְּרוּם	וְרָאוּ בָנָיו גְּבוּרָתוֹ; שִׁבְּחוּ וְהוֹדוּ
עוֹלָם מוֹשָׁבֶךָ וּמִשְׁפָּטֶיךָ	לִשְׁמוֹ.
וְצִדְקָתְךָ עַד אַפְסֵי־אָרֶץ.	וּמַלְכוּתוֹ בְּרָצוֹן קִבְּלוּ עֲלֵיהֶם.
אַשְׁרֵי אִישׁ שֶׁיִּשְׁמַע לְמִצְוֹתֶיךָ,	מֹשֶׁה וּבְנֵי יִשְׂרָאֵל לְךָ עָנוּ שִׁירָה
וְתוֹרָתְךָ וּדְבָרְךָ יָשִׂים עַל־לִבּוֹ.	בְּשִׂמְחָה רַבָּה, וְאָמְרוּ כֻלָּם:

Infinite God, Creator and Redeemer of all being, You are Most High, Most Near. In all generations we have cried out to You; we have put our trust in You; we have borne witness to Your truth before the nations! O now let Your light and Your truth appear to us and lead us; let them bring us to Your holy mountain.

We shall not fear, then, though earth itself should shake, though the mountains fall into the heart of the sea, though its waters thunder and rage, though the winds lift its waves to the very vault of heaven.

We shall not fear, for You are with us; we shall rejoice in Your deliverance. Then shall we know You, our Redeemer and our God, and in the shadow of Your wings we shall sing with joy:

Who is like You, Eternal One, among   מִי־כָמֹכָה בָּאֵלִם, יְיָ?
     the gods that are worshipped?

מִי כָּמֹכָה, נֶאְדָּר בַּקֹּדֶשׁ,

Who is like You, majestic in holiness,

awesome in splendor, doing wonders?   נוֹרָא תְהִלֹּת, עֹשֵׂה פֶּלֶא?

Evening   *Morning*

מַלְכוּתְךָ רָאוּ בָנֶיךָ, בּוֹקֵעַ יָם	שִׁירָה חֲדָשָׁה שִׁבְּחוּ גְאוּלִים
לִפְנֵי מֹשֶׁה; "זֶה אֵלִי!" עָנוּ	לְשִׁמְךָ עַל־שְׂפַת הַיָּם; יַחַד כֻּלָּם
וְאָמְרוּ:	הוֹדוּ וְהִמְלִיכוּ וְאָמְרוּ:
"יְיָ יִמְלֹךְ לְעֹלָם וָעֶד!"	"יְיָ יִמְלֹךְ לְעוֹלָם וָעֶד!"
וְנֶאֱמַר: "כִּי־פָדָה יְיָ אֶת־יַעֲקֹב,	צוּר יִשְׂרָאֵל, קוּמָה בְּעֶזְרַת

Evening   *Morning*

וּגְאָלוֹ מִיַּד חָזָק מִמֶּנּוּ." יִשְׂרָאֵל, וּפָדָה כִנְאֻמֶךָ יְהוּדָה
בָּרוּךְ אַתָּה, יְיָ, גָּאַל יִשְׂרָאֵל. וְיִשְׂרָאֵל. גְּאָלֵנוּ, יְיָ צְבָאוֹת שְׁמוֹ,
קְדוֹשׁ יִשְׂרָאֵל.
בָּרוּךְ אַתָּה, יְיָ, גָּאַל יִשְׂרָאֵל.

When your children perceive Your power they exclaim: "This is my God!" "The Lord will reign for ever and ever!"

◆ ◆

For an Evening Service

הַשְׁכִּיבֵנוּ, יְיָ אֱלֹהֵינוּ, לְשָׁלוֹם, וְהַעֲמִידֵנוּ, מַלְכֵּנוּ, לְחַיִּים.
וּפְרוֹשׂ עָלֵינוּ סֻכַּת שְׁלוֹמֶךָ, וְתַקְּנֵנוּ בְּעֵצָה טוֹבָה מִלְּפָנֶיךָ,
וְהוֹשִׁיעֵנוּ לְמַעַן שְׁמֶךָ, וְהָגֵן בַּעֲדֵנוּ. וְהָסֵר מֵעָלֵינוּ אוֹיֵב,
דֶּבֶר וְחֶרֶב וְרָעָב וְיָגוֹן; וְהָסֵר שָׂטָן מִלְּפָנֵינוּ וּמֵאַחֲרֵינוּ;
וּבְצֵל כְּנָפֶיךָ תַּסְתִּירֵנוּ, כִּי אֵל שׁוֹמְרֵנוּ וּמַצִּילֵנוּ אָתָּה, כִּי
אֵל מֶלֶךְ חַנּוּן וְרַחוּם אָתָּה. וּשְׁמוֹר צֵאתֵנוּ וּבוֹאֵנוּ לְחַיִּים
וּלְשָׁלוֹם, מֵעַתָּה וְעַד עוֹלָם. בָּרוּךְ אַתָּה, יְיָ, שׁוֹמֵר עַמּוֹ
יִשְׂרָאֵל לָעַד.

Let there be love and understanding among us; let peace and friendship be our shelter from life's storms. Eternal God, help us to walk with good companions, to live with hope in our hearts and eternity in our thoughts, that we may lie down in peace and rise up to find our hearts waiting to do Your will.

Blessed is the Eternal One, Guardian of Israel, whose love gives light to all the world.

◆ ◆

All rise

תפלה

אֲדֹנָי, שְׂפָתַי תִּפְתָּח, וּפִי יַגִּיד תְּהִלָּתֶךָ.

Eternal God, open my lips, that my mouth may declare Your glory.

בָּרוּךְ אַתָּה, יְיָ אֱלֹהֵינוּ וֵאלֹהֵי אֲבוֹתֵינוּ, אֱלֹהֵי אַבְרָהָם, אֱלֹהֵי
יִצְחָק, וֵאלֹהֵי יַעֲקֹב: הָאֵל הַגָּדוֹל, הַגִּבּוֹר וְהַנּוֹרָא, אֵל עֶלְיוֹן.

God of ages past and future, God of this day, as You were with
our fathers and mothers, be with us as well.

As You strengthened them, strengthen us.

גּוֹמֵל חֲסָדִים טוֹבִים, וְקוֹנֵה הַכֹּל, וְזוֹכֵר חַסְדֵי אָבוֹת, וּמֵבִיא
גְאֻלָּה לִבְנֵי בְנֵיהֶם, לְמַעַן שְׁמוֹ, בְּאַהֲבָה.

As You were their Guide, be ours as well.

*Grant that we too may be bearers of Your teaching, teachers
of Your truth.*

Then our tradition shall endure, and Israel live: from mother
and father to daughter and son, and all who follow them.

*One generation comes, one generation passes. Daughters be-
come mothers, and sons, fathers.*

מֶלֶךְ עוֹזֵר וּמוֹשִׁיעַ וּמָגֵן. בָּרוּךְ אַתָּה, יְיָ, מָגֵן אַבְרָהָם.

Students of Torah become teachers. The people and its tradition endure.

The people and its tradition will live.

❖ ❖

אַתָּה גִּבּוֹר לְעוֹלָם, אֲדֹנָי, מְחַיֵּה הַכֹּל אַתָּה, רַב לְהוֹשִׁיעַ.
מְכַלְכֵּל חַיִּים בְּחֶסֶד, מְחַיֵּה הַכֹּל בְּרַחֲמִים רַבִּים. סוֹמֵךְ
נוֹפְלִים, וְרוֹפֵא חוֹלִים, וּמַתִּיר אֲסוּרִים, וּמְקַיֵּם אֱמוּנָתוֹ
לִישֵׁנֵי עָפָר.

מִי כָמְוֹךָ, בַּעַל גְּבוּרוֹת, וּמִי דְוֹמֶה לָּךְ, מֶלֶךְ מֵמִית וּמְחַיֶּה
וּמַצְמִיחַ יְשׁוּעָה?
וְנֶאֱמָן אַתָּה לְהַחֲיוֹת הַכֹּל. בָּרוּךְ אַתָּה, יְיָ, מְחַיֵּה הַכֹּל.

Your might, O God, is everlasting;
Help us to use our strength for good and not for evil.

You are the Source of life and blessing;
Help us to choose life for ourselves and our children.

You are the Support of the falling;
Help us to lift up the fallen.

You are the Author of freedom;
Help us to set free the captive.

You are our Hope in death as in life;
Help us to keep faith with those who sleep in the dust.

Your might, O God, is everlasting;
Help us to use our strength for good.

◆ ◆

For an Evening Service

אַתָּה קָדוֹשׁ וְשִׁמְךָ קָדוֹשׁ, וּקְדוֹשִׁים בְּכָל־יוֹם יְהַלְלוּךָ סֶּלָה.
בָּרוּךְ אַתָּה, יְיָ, הָאֵל הַקָּדוֹשׁ.

You are holy, Your name is holy, and those who strive to be
holy declare Your glory day by day. Blessed is the Lord, the
holy God.

◆ ◆

For a Morning Service

SANCTIFICATION   קדושה

נְקַדֵּשׁ אֶת־שִׁמְךָ בָּעוֹלָם, כְּשֵׁם שֶׁמַּקְדִּישִׁים אוֹתוֹ בִּשְׁמֵי מָרוֹם,
כַּכָּתוּב עַל־יַד נְבִיאֶךָ: וְקָרָא זֶה אֶל־זֶה וְאָמַר:

We sanctify Your name on earth, even as all things, to the ends
of time and space, proclaim Your holiness; and in the words of
the prophet we say:

180

קָדוֹשׁ, קָדוֹשׁ, קָדוֹשׁ יְיָ צְבָאוֹת, מְלֹא כָל־הָאָרֶץ כְּבוֹדוֹ.

*Holy, Holy, Holy is the Lord of Hosts; the fullness of the whole
earth is His glory!*

לְעֻמָּתָם בָּרוּךְ יֹאמֵרוּ:

They respond to Your glory with blessing:

בָּרוּךְ כְּבוֹד יְיָ מִמְּקוֹמוֹ.

Blessed is the glory of God in heaven and earth.

וּבְדִבְרֵי קָדְשְׁךָ כָּתוּב לֵאמֹר:

And this is Your sacred word:

יִמְלֹךְ יְיָ לְעוֹלָם, אֱלֹהַיִךְ צִיּוֹן, לְדֹר וָדֹר, הַלְלוּיָהּ.

*The Lord shall reign for ever; your God, O Zion, from genera-
tion to generation. Halleluyah!*

לְדוֹר וָדוֹר נַגִּיד גָּדְלֶךָ, וּלְנֵצַח נְצָחִים קְדֻשָּׁתְךָ נַקְדִּישׁ.
וְשִׁבְחֲךָ, אֱלֹהֵינוּ, מִפִּינוּ לֹא יָמוּשׁ לְעוֹלָם וָעֶד.
בָּרוּךְ אַתָּה, יְיָ, הָאֵל הַקָּדוֹשׁ.

*To all generations we will make known Your greatness, and
to all eternity proclaim Your holiness. Your praise, O God,
shall never depart from our lips.*

Blessed is the Lord, the holy God.

All are seated

✦ ✦

A spark of the divine flame glows within us all. We give thanks for
the gift of reason that enables us to search after knowledge. May
our use of this gift make Your light burn ever more brightly within us.

Blessed is the Eternal Source of wisdom and knowledge.

May our pride of intellect never be an idol turning us away from
You. And as we grow in knowledge, may we remain aware of our
own limitations.

Blessed is the God of forgiveness and understanding.

May the beauty and mystery of the world move us to reverence and humility. O let the tree of knowledge bear good fruit for us and our children.

Blessed is our God from whom all blessings flow.

And let the consciousness of Your Presence be the glory of our lives, making joyous our days and years, and leading us to a clearer understanding of Your will.

Blessed is our God who hearkens to prayer.

✦ ✦

MEDITATION

✦ ✦

יִהְיוּ לְרָצוֹן אִמְרֵי־פִי וְהֶגְיוֹן לִבִּי לְפָנֶיךָ, יְיָ, צוּרִי וְגוֹאֲלִי.

May the words of my mouth, and the meditations of my heart, be acceptable to You, O Lord, my Rock and my Redeemer.

or

עֹשֶׂה שָׁלוֹם בִּמְרוֹמָיו, הוּא יַעֲשֶׂה שָׁלוֹם עָלֵינוּ וְעַל כָּל־יִשְׂרָאֵל, וְאִמְרוּ אָמֵן.

May He who causes peace to reign in the high heavens let peace descend on us, on all Israel, and all the world.

Prayers at a House of Mourning begin on page 183.

Concluding Prayers begin on page 187.

Havdalah for the conclusion of Shabbat is on page 62.

At a House of Mourning

One of the weekday services is read first

We are assembled with our friends in the shadow that has fallen on their home. We raise our voices together in prayer to the Source of life, asking for comfort and strength.

We need light when gloom darkens our home; to whom shall we look, but to the Creator of light? We need fortitude and courage when pain and loss assail us; where shall we find them, if not in the thought of Him who preserves all that is good from destruction?

Who among us has not passed through trials and bereavements? Some bear fresh wounds in their hearts, and therefore feel more keenly the kinship of sorrow. Others, whose days of mourning are more remote, still recall the comfort that sympathy brought to their sorrowing hearts.

All things pass; all that lives must die. All that we prize is but lent to us; and the time comes when we must surrender it. We are travellers on the same road that leads to the same end.

◆ ◆

Psalm 121

אֶשָּׂא עֵינַי אֶל־הֶהָרִים, מֵאַיִן יָבוֹא עֶזְרִי?

עֶזְרִי מֵעִם יְיָ, עֹשֵׂה שָׁמַיִם וָאָרֶץ.

I lift up my eyes to the mountains: what is the source of my help?

My help will come from the Lord, Maker of heaven and earth.

אַל־יִתֵּן לַמּוֹט רַגְלֶךָ,

אַל־יָנוּם שֹׁמְרֶךָ.

He will not allow your foot to slip;

your Guardian will not slumber.

הִנֵּה לֹא־יָנוּם וְלֹא יִישָׁן שׁוֹמֵר יִשְׂרָאֵל.
יְיָ שֹׁמְרֶךָ, יְיָ צִלְּךָ עַל־יַד יְמִינֶךָ.

Behold, the Guardian of Israel neither slumbers nor sleeps.

The Eternal is your Keeper, the Lord is your shade at your right hand.

יוֹמָם הַשֶּׁמֶשׁ לֹא־יַכֶּכָּה, וְיָרֵחַ בַּלָּיְלָה.
יְיָ יִשְׁמָרְךָ מִכָּל־רָע, יִשְׁמֹר אֶת־נַפְשֶׁךָ.
יְיָ יִשְׁמָר־צֵאתְךָ וּבוֹאֶךָ, מֵעַתָּה וְעַד־עוֹלָם.

The sun shall not harm you by day, nor the moon by night. The Lord will guard you from all evil, He will protect your being.

The Lord will guard you, coming and going, from this time forth, and for ever.

◆ ◆

MEDITATION

As in the world around us, so too in human life, darkness is followed by light and sorrow by comfort. Life and death are twins; grief and hope walk hand in hand. Although we cannot know what lies beyond the body's death, let us put our trust in the undying Spirit who calls us into life and who abides to all eternity.

◆ ◆

O Lord, God of the spirits of all flesh, You are close to the hearts of the sorrowing, to strengthen and console them with the warmth of Your love, and with the assurance that the human spirit is enduring and indestructible. Even as we pray for perfect peace for those whose lives have ended, so do we ask You to give comfort and courage to the living.

May the knowledge of Your nearness be our strength, O God, for You are with us at all times: in joy and sorrow, in light and darkness, in life and death.

◆ ◆

All rise

אֵל מָלֵא רַחֲמִים, שׁוֹכֵן בַּמְּרוֹמִים, הַמְצֵא מְנוּחָה נְכוֹנָה
תַּחַת כַּנְפֵי הַשְּׁכִינָה עִם קְדוֹשִׁים וּטְהוֹרִים כְּזֹהַר הָרָקִיעַ
מַזְהִירִים אֶת נִשְׁמַת ...... שֶׁהָלַךְ (שֶׁהָלְכָה) לְעוֹלָמוֹ
(לְעוֹלָמָהּ). בַּעַל הָרַחֲמִים יַסְתִּירֵהוּ (יַסְתִּירֶהָ) בְּסֵתֶר
כְּנָפָיו לְעוֹלָמִים. וְיִצְרוֹר בִּצְרוֹר הַחַיִּים אֶת־נִשְׁמָתוֹ
(נִשְׁמָתָהּ). יְיָ הוּא נַחֲלָתוֹ (נַחֲלָתָהּ) וְיָנוּחַ (וְתָנוּחַ) בְּשָׁלוֹם עַל
מִשְׁכָּבוֹ (מִשְׁכָּבָהּ), וְנֹאמַר אָמֵן.

O God full of compassion, Eternal Spirit of the universe, grant
perfect rest under the wings of Your Presence to our loved one
who has entered eternity. Master of Mercy, let him (her) find
refuge for ever in the shadow of Your wings, and let his (her)
soul be bound up in the bond of eternal life. The Eternal God
is his (her) inheritance. May he (she) rest in peace, and let us
say: Amen.

All are seated

◆ ◆

אָנָּא, יְיָ, הָרוֹפֵא לִשְׁבוּרֵי לֵב וּמְחַבֵּשׁ לְעַצְּבוֹתָם, שַׁלֵּם
נִחוּמִים לָאֲבֵלִים. חַזְּקֵם וְאַמְּצֵם בְּיוֹם אָבְלָם וִיגוֹנָם, וְזַכְּרֵם
לְחַיִּים טוֹבִים וַאֲרֻכִּים.

תֵּן בְּלִבָּם יִרְאָתְךָ וְאַהֲבָתְךָ לְעָבְדְּךָ בְּלֵבָב שָׁלֵם. וּתְהִי
אַחֲרִיתָם שָׁלוֹם. אָמֵן.

O Lord, Healer of the broken-hearted and Binder of their
wounds, grant consolation to those who mourn. Give them
strength and courage in the time of their grief, and restore to
them a sense of life's goodness.

Fill them with reverence and love for You, that they may
serve You with a whole heart, and let them soon know peace.
Amen.

◆ ◆

Psalm 23

מִזְמוֹר לְדָוִד. יְיָ רֹעִי, לֹא אֶחְסָר. בִּנְאוֹת דֶּשֶׁא יַרְבִּיצֵנִי,
עַל־מֵי מְנֻחוֹת יְנַהֲלֵנִי. נַפְשִׁי יְשׁוֹבֵב. יַנְחֵנִי בְמַעְגְּלֵי־צֶדֶק
לְמַעַן שְׁמוֹ. גַּם כִּי־אֵלֵךְ בְּגֵיא צַלְמָוֶת לֹא־אִירָא רָע, כִּי־
אַתָּה עִמָּדִי; שִׁבְטְךָ וּמִשְׁעַנְתֶּךָ הֵמָּה יְנַחֲמֻנִי. תַּעֲרֹךְ לְפָנַי
שֻׁלְחָן נֶגֶד צֹרְרָי. דִּשַּׁנְתָּ בַשֶּׁמֶן רֹאשִׁי, כּוֹסִי רְוָיָה. אַךְ טוֹב
וָחֶסֶד יִרְדְּפוּנִי כָּל־יְמֵי חַיָּי, וְשַׁבְתִּי בְּבֵית־יְיָ לְאֹרֶךְ יָמִים.

The Lord is my shepherd, I shall not want. He makes me lie
down in green pastures, He leads me beside still waters. He
restores my soul. He leads me in right paths for the sake of
His name. Even when I walk in the valley of the shadow of
death, I shall fear no evil, for You are with me; with rod and
staff You comfort me. You have set a table before me in the
presence of my enemies; You have anointed my head with oil,
my cup overflows. Surely goodness and mercy shall follow
me all the days of my life, and I shall dwell in the house of the
Lord for ever.

◆ ◆

Continue with Aleinu, page 189, 191, 192, or 194.

CONCLUDING PRAYERS

עָלֵינוּ

All rise

עָלֵינוּ לְשַׁבֵּחַ לַאֲדוֹן הַכֹּל, לָתֵת גְּדֻלָּה לְיוֹצֵר בְּרֵאשִׁית,
שֶׁלֹּא עָשָׂנוּ כְּגוֹיֵי הָאֲרָצוֹת, וְלֹא שָׂמָנוּ כְּמִשְׁפְּחוֹת הָאֲדָמָה;
שֶׁלֹּא שָׂם חֶלְקֵנוּ כָּהֶם, וְגוֹרָלֵנוּ כְּכָל־הֲמוֹנָם.

We must praise the Lord of all, the Maker of heaven and earth,
who has set us apart from the other families of earth, giving us a
destiny unique among the nations.

וַאֲנַחְנוּ כּוֹרְעִים וּמִשְׁתַּחֲוִים וּמוֹדִים לִפְנֵי מֶלֶךְ מַלְכֵי
הַמְּלָכִים, הַקָּדוֹשׁ בָּרוּךְ הוּא,

We therefore bow in awe and thanksgiving before the One who is
Sovereign over all, the Holy One, blessed be He.

All are seated

שֶׁהוּא נוֹטֶה שָׁמַיִם וְיוֹסֵד אָרֶץ, וּמוֹשַׁב יְקָרוֹ בַּשָּׁמַיִם מִמַּעַל,
וּשְׁכִינַת עֻזּוֹ בְּגָבְהֵי מְרוֹמִים. הוּא אֱלֹהֵינוּ, אֵין עוֹד; אֱמֶת
מַלְכֵּנוּ, אֶפֶס זוּלָתוֹ, כַּכָּתוּב בְּתוֹרָתוֹ: "וְיָדַעְתָּ הַיּוֹם וַהֲשֵׁבֹתָ
אֶל־לְבָבֶךָ, כִּי יְיָ הוּא הָאֱלֹהִים בַּשָּׁמַיִם מִמַּעַל וְעַל־הָאָרֶץ
מִתָּחַת, אֵין עוֹד."

He spread out the heavens and established the earth; He is
our God; there is none else. In truth He alone is our King, as
it is written: "Know then this day and take it to heart: the
Lord is God in the heavens above and on the earth below;
there is none else."

עַל־כֵּן נְקַוֶּה לְךָ, יְיָ אֱלֹהֵינוּ, לִרְאוֹת מְהֵרָה בְּתִפְאֶרֶת עֻזֶּךָ,
לְהַעֲבִיר גִּלּוּלִים מִן־הָאָרֶץ, וְהָאֱלִילִים כָּרוֹת יִכָּרֵתוּן,

לְתַקֵּן עוֹלָם בְּמַלְכוּת שַׁדַּי. וְכָל־בְּנֵי בָשָׂר יִקְרְאוּ בִשְׁמֶךָ, לְהַפְנוֹת אֵלֶיךָ כָּל־רִשְׁעֵי אָרֶץ.

We therefore hope, O Lord our God, soon to behold the glory
of Your might. Then will false gods vanish from our hearts,
and the world will be perfected under Your unchallenged rule.
And then will all acclaim You as their God, and, forsaking
evil, turn to You alone.

יַכִּירוּ וְיֵדְעוּ כָּל־יוֹשְׁבֵי תֵבֵל כִּי לְךָ תִּכְרַע כָּל־בֶּרֶךְ, תִּשָּׁבַע
כָּל־לָשׁוֹן. לְפָנֶיךָ, יְיָ אֱלֹהֵינוּ, יִכְרְעוּ וְיִפֹּלוּ, וְלִכְבוֹד שִׁמְךָ
יְקָר יִתֵּנוּ, וִיקַבְּלוּ כֻלָּם אֶת־עֹל מַלְכוּתֶךָ, וְתִמְלֹךְ עֲלֵיהֶם
מְהֵרָה לְעוֹלָם וָעֶד.

Let all who dwell on earth acknowledge that unto You every
knee must bend and every tongue swear loyalty. Before You,
O Lord our God, let them humble themselves. To Your glori-
ous name let them give honor. Let all accept the yoke of Your
kingdom, that You may rule over them soon and for ever.

כִּי הַמַּלְכוּת שֶׁלְּךָ הִיא, וּלְעוֹלְמֵי עַד תִּמְלוֹךְ בְּכָבוֹד,
כַּכָּתוּב בְּתוֹרָתֶךָ: "יְיָ יִמְלֹךְ לְעֹלָם וָעֶד."

For the kingdom is Yours, and to all eternity You will reign
in glory, as it is written: "The Lord will reign for ever and
ever."

וְנֶאֱמַר: "וְהָיָה יְיָ לְמֶלֶךְ עַל־כָּל־הָאָרֶץ; בַּיּוֹם הַהוּא יִהְיֶה
יְיָ אֶחָד וּשְׁמוֹ אֶחָד."

And it has been said: "The Lord shall reign over all the earth; on
that day the Lord shall be One and His name shall be One."

Continue on page 196.

עָלֵינוּ

All rise

Let us adore
the ever-living God,
and render praise
unto Him
who spread out the heavens
and established the earth,
whose glory
is revealed in the heavens above,
and whose greatness
is manifest throughout the world.
He is our God; there is none else.

עָלֵינוּ לְשַׁבֵּחַ לַאֲדוֹן הַכֹּל,
לָתֵת גְּדֻלָּה לְיוֹצֵר בְּרֵאשִׁית,
שֶׁהוּא נוֹטֶה שָׁמַיִם וְיוֹסֵד אֶרֶץ,
וּמוֹשַׁב יְקָרוֹ בַּשָּׁמַיִם מִמַּעַל,
וּשְׁכִינַת עֻזּוֹ בְּגָבְהֵי מְרוֹמִים.
הוּא אֱלֹהֵינוּ, אֵין עוֹד.

וַאֲנַחְנוּ כּוֹרְעִים וּמִשְׁתַּחֲוִים וּמוֹדִים
לִפְנֵי מֶלֶךְ מַלְכֵי הַמְּלָכִים הַקָּדוֹשׁ בָּרוּךְ הוּא.

We therefore bow in awe and thanksgiving before the One who is
Sovereign over all, the Holy One, blessed be He.

All are seated

May the time not be distant, O God, when Your name shall be
worshipped in all the earth, when unbelief shall disappear and
error be no more. Fervently we pray that the day may come
when all shall turn to You in love, when corruption and evil
shall give way to integrity and goodness, when superstition
shall no longer enslave the mind, nor idolatry blind the eye,
when all who dwell on earth shall know that You alone are
God. O may all, created in Your image, become one in spirit
and one in friendship, for ever united in Your service. Then
shall Your kingdom be established on earth, and the word of
Your prophet fulfilled: "The Lord will reign for ever and ever."

בַּיּוֹם הַהוּא יִהְיֶה יְיָ אֶחָד וּשְׁמוֹ אֶחָד.

On that day the Lord shall be One and His name shall be One.

Continue on page 196.

עָלֵינוּ

All rise

Let us revere the God of life, and
sing the praise of Nature's Lord,
who spread out the heavens and
established the earth, whose glory
is proclaimed by the starry skies,
and whose wonders are revealed
in the human heart. He is our
God; there is none else. With
love and awe we acclaim the
Eternal God, the Holy One,
blessed be He.

עָלֵינוּ לְשַׁבֵּחַ לַאֲדוֹן הַכֹּל,
לָתֵת גְּדֻלָּה לְיוֹצֵר בְּרֵאשִׁית,
שֶׁהוּא נוֹטֶה שָׁמַיִם וְיוֹסֵד אָרֶץ,
וּמוֹשַׁב יְקָרוֹ בַּשָּׁמַיִם מִמַּעַל,
וּשְׁכִינַת עֻזּוֹ בְּגָבְהֵי מְרוֹמִים.
הוּא אֱלֹהֵינוּ, אֵין עוֹד.

וַאֲנַחְנוּ כּוֹרְעִים וּמִשְׁתַּחֲוִים וּמוֹדִים לִפְנֵי מֶלֶךְ מַלְכֵי
הַמְּלָכִים הַקָּדוֹשׁ בָּרוּךְ הוּא.

All are seated

The day will come when all shall turn with trust to God, hear-
kening to His voice, bearing witness to His truth.

We pray with all our hearts: let violence be gone; let the day
come soon when evil shall give way to goodness, when war
shall be forgotten, hunger be no more, and all at last shall live
in freedom.

O Source of life: may we, created in Your image, embrace one
another in friendship and in joy. Then shall we be one family,
and then shall Your kingdom be established on earth, and the
word of Your prophet fulfilled: "The Lord will reign for ever
and ever."

בַּיּוֹם הַהוּא יִהְיֶה יְיָ אֶחָד וּשְׁמוֹ אֶחָד.

On that day the Lord shall be One and His name shall be One.

יְהִי שֵׁם יְיָ מְבֹרָךְ מֵעַתָּה וְעַד־עוֹלָם, וְיִמָּלֵא כְבוֹדוֹ אֶת־כָּל־
הָאָרֶץ. אָמֵן וְאָמֵן.

Blessed be the name of the Lord for ever; and let the whole world be filled with His glory. Amen and Amen.

Continue on page 196.

עלינו

עָלֵינוּ לְשַׁבֵּחַ לַאֲדוֹן הַכֹּל,
לָתֵת גְּדֻלָּה לְיוֹצֵר בְּרֵאשִׁית,
שֶׁהוּא שָׂם חֶלְקֵנוּ לְיַחֵד אֶת־
שְׁמוֹ, וְגוֹרָלֵנוּ לְהַמְלִיךְ מַלְכוּתוֹ.

We praise Him who gave us life. In our rejoicing He is God; He is God in our grief. In anguish and deliverance alike, we praise; in darkness and light we affirm our faith. Therefore we bow our heads in reverence, before the Eternal God of life, the Holy One, blessed be He.

וַאֲנַחְנוּ כֹּרְעִים וּמִשְׁתַּחֲוִים וּמוֹדִים לִפְנֵי מֶלֶךְ מַלְכֵי
הַמְּלָכִים, הַקָּדוֹשׁ בָּרוּךְ הוּא.

עַל־כֵּן נְקַוֶּה לְךָ, יְיָ אֱלֹהֵינוּ, לִרְאוֹת מְהֵרָה בְּתִפְאֶרֶת עֻזֶּךָ,
לְהַעֲבִיר גִּלּוּלִים מִן הָאָרֶץ, וְהָאֱלִילִים כָּרוֹת יִכָּרֵתוּן,
לְתַקֵּן עוֹלָם בְּמַלְכוּת שַׁדַּי. וְכָל־בְּנֵי בָשָׂר יִקְרְאוּ בִשְׁמֶךָ,
לְהַפְנוֹת אֵלֶיךָ כָּל־רִשְׁעֵי אָרֶץ.

Eternal God, we face the morrow with hope made stronger by the vision of Your kingdom, a world where poverty and war are banished, where injustice and hate are gone.

יַכִּירוּ וְיֵדְעוּ כָּל־יוֹשְׁבֵי תֵבֵל כִּי לְךָ תִּכְרַע כָּל־בֶּרֶךְ, תִּשָּׁבַע
כָּל־לָשׁוֹן. לְפָנֶיךָ, יְיָ אֱלֹהֵינוּ, יִכְרְעוּ וְיִפֹּלוּ, וְלִכְבוֹד שִׁמְךָ
יְקָר יִתֵּנוּ, וִיקַבְּלוּ כֻלָּם אֶת־עֹל מַלְכוּתֶךָ, וְתִמְלוֹךְ עֲלֵיהֶם
מְהֵרָה לְעוֹלָם וָעֶד.

Teach us more and more to share the pain of others, to heed Your call for justice, to pursue the blessing of peace. Help us, O God, to gain victory over evil, to bring nearer the day when all the world shall be one.

כִּי הַמַּלְכוּת שֶׁלְּךָ הִיא, וּלְעוֹלְמֵי עַד תִּמְלֹךְ בְּכָבוֹד,
כַּכָּתוּב בְּתוֹרָתֶךָ: "יְיָ יִמְלֹךְ לְעוֹלָם וָעֶד."
וְנֶאֱמַר: "וְהָיָה יְיָ לְמֶלֶךְ עַל־כָּל־הָאָרֶץ; בַּיּוֹם הַהוּא יִהְיֶה
יְיָ אֶחָד וּשְׁמוֹ אֶחָד."

On that day the age-old hope shall come true. On that day,
O God, You shall be One and Your name shall be One.

Before the Kaddish

Our thoughts turn to those who have departed this earth: our own loved ones, those whom our friends and neighbors have lost, the martyrs of our people whose graves are unmarked, and those of every race and nation whose lives have been a blessing to humanity. As we remember them, let us meditate on the meaning of love and loss, of life and death.

◆ ◆

Meditations

1. The Tradition of the Kaddish

The origins of the Kaddish are mysterious; angels are said to have brought it down from heaven. . . .

It possesses wonderful power. Truly, if there is any bond strong enough to chain heaven to earth, it is this prayer. It keeps the living together, and forms a bridge to the mysterious realm of the dead. One might almost say that this prayer is the . . . guardian of the people by whom alone it is uttered; therein lies the warrant of its continuance. Can a people disappear and be annihilated so long as a child remembers its parents?

Because this prayer does not acknowledge death, because it permits the blossom, which has fallen from the tree of humankind, to flower and develop again in the human heart, therefore it possesses sanctifying power.

2. Facing Death

The contemplation of death should plant within the soul elevation and peace. Above all, it should make us see things in their true light. For all things which seem foolish in the light of death are really foolish in themselves. To be annoyed because So-and-so has slighted us or has been somewhat more successful in social distinctions, pulled himself somehow one rung higher up the ladder than ourselves — how ridiculous all this seems when we couple it with the thought of death!

To pass each day simply and solely in the eager pursuit of money or fame, this also seems like living with shadows when one might take one's part with realities. Surely when death is at hand we should desire to say, 'I have contributed my grain to the great store of the eternal. I have borne my part in the struggle for goodness.' And let no man or woman suppose that the smallest social act of goodness is wasted for society at large. All our help, petty though it be, is needed; and though we know not the manner, the fruit of every faithful service is gathered in. Let the true and noble words of a great teacher ring in conclusion upon our ears: 'The growing good of the world is partly dependent on unhistoric acts; and that things are not so ill with you and me as they might have been, is half owing to the number who lived faithfully a hidden life and rest in unvisited tombs.'

3. In Recent Grief

When cherished ties are broken, and the chain of love is shattered, only trust and the strength of faith can lighten the heaviness of the heart. At times, the pain of separation seems more than we can bear, but if we dwell too long on our loss we embitter our hearts and harm ourselves and those about us.

The Psalmist said that in his affliction he learned the law of God. And in truth, grief is a great teacher, when it sends us back to serve and bless the living. We learn how to counsel and comfort those who, like ourselves, are bowed with sorrow. We learn when to keep silence in their presence, and when a word will assure them of our love and concern.

Thus, even when they are gone, the departed are with us, moving us to live as, in their higher moments, they themselves wished to live. We remember them now; they live in our hearts; they are an abiding blessing.

4. After a Tragic Loss

O God, help me to live with my grief!

Death has taken my beloved, and I feel that I cannot go on. My faith is shaken; my mind keeps asking: Why? Why does joy end in sorrow? Why does love exact its price in tears? Why?

O God, help me to live with my grief!

Help me to accept the mystery of life. Help me to see that even if my questions were answered, even if I did know why, the pain would be no less, the loneliness would remain bitter beyond words. Still my heart would ache.

O God, help me to triumph over my grief!

Help me to endure this night of anguish. Help me to walk through the darkness with faith in tomorrow. Give me comfort; give me courage; turn me to deeds that bless the living.

O God, help me to triumph over my grief.

5. How Can We Understand Death?

What can we know of death, we who cannot understand life?

We study the seed and the cell, but the power deep within them will always elude us.

Though we cannot understand, we accept life as the gift of God. Yet death, life's twin, we face with fear.

But why be afraid? Death is a haven to the weary, a relief for the sorely afflicted. We are safe in death as in life.

There is no pain in death. There is only the pain of the living as they recall shared loves, and as they themselves fear to die.

Calm us, O Lord, when we cry out in our fear and our grief. Turn us anew toward life and the world. Awaken us to the warmth of human love that speaks to us of You.

We shall fear no evil as we affirm Your kingdom of life.

6.   A Philosophy of Life and Death

Judaism teaches us to understand death as part of the Divine pattern of the universe. Actually, we could not have our sensitivity without fragility. Mortality is the tax that we pay for the privilege of love, thought, creative work — the toll on the bridge of being from which clods of earth and snow-peaked mountain summits are exempt. Just because we are human, we are prisoners of the years. Yet that very prison is the room of discipline in which we, driven by the urgency of time, create.

7.   The Blessing of Memory

It is hard to sing of oneness when our world is not complete, when those who once brought wholeness to our life have gone, and naught but memory can fill the emptiness their passing leaves behind.

But memory can tell us only what we were, in company with those we loved; it cannot help us find what each of us, alone, must now become. Yet no one is really alone; those who live no more, echo still within our thoughts and words, and what they did is part of what we have become.

We do best homage to our dead when we live our lives most fully, even in the shadow of our loss. For each of our lives is worth the life of the whole world; in each one is the breath of the Ultimate One. in affirming the One, we affirm the worth of each one whose life, now ended, brought us closer to the Source of life, in whose unity no one is alone and every life finds purpose.

8.   In Praise of Lives Now Gone

יִתְגַּדַּל וְיִתְקַדַּשׁ שְׁמֵהּ רַבָּא

This the profound praise of the living,
Praise for the generous gift of life.

199

Praise for the presence of loved ones,
   the bonds of friendship,
   the link of memory.

Praise for the toil and searching,
   the dedication and vision,
   the ennobling aspirations.

Praise for the precious moorings of faith,
   for courageous souls,
   for prophets, psalmists, and sages.

Praise for those who walked before us,
   the sufferers in the valley of shadows,
   the steadfast in the furnace of hate.

יִתְגַּדַּל וְיִתְקַדַּשׁ שְׁמֵהּ רַבָּא

Praise for the God of our people,
   the Source of all growth and goodness.
   the Promise on which we build tomorrow.

9.   We Live In Our Work

Eternal God, the generations come and go before You. Brief is their time. Passing, they leave many of their tasks unfinished, their plans unfulfilled, their dreams unrealized. It would be more than we could bear, but for the faith that our little day finds its permanence in Your eternity, and our work its completion in the unfolding of Your purpose for humanity.

At this sacred moment we turn our thoughts to those we love who have gone from life. We recall the joy of their companionship. We feel a pang, the echo of that intenser grief when first their death lay before our stricken eyes. Now we know that they will never vanish, so long as heart and thought remain within us. By love are they remembered, and in memory they live.

O God, grant that their memory may bring strength and blessing. May the nobility in their lives and the high ideals they cherished endure in our thoughts and live on in our deeds. May we, carrying on their work, help to redeem Your promise that life shall prevail.

10.   The Life of Eternity

The light of life is a finite flame. Like the Sabbath candles, life is kindled, it burns, it glows, it is radiant with warmth and beauty. But soon it fades; its substance is consumed, and it is no more.

In light we see; in light we are seen. The flames dance and our lives are full. But as night follows day, the candle of our life burns down and gutters. There is an end to the flames. We see no more and are no more seen. Yet we do not despair, for we are more than a memory slowly fading into the darkness. With our lives we give life. Something of us can never die: we move in the eternal cycle of darkness and death, of light and life.

11.   The Spirit Lives On

"The Lord gives; the Lord takes away; blessed be the name of the Lord."

Early or late, all must answer the summons to return to the Reservoir of Being. For we loose our hold on life when our time has come, as the leaf falls from the bough when its day is done. The deeds of the righteous enrich the world, as the fallen leaf enriches the soil beneath. The dust returns to the earth, the spirit lives on with God.

Like the stars by day, our beloved dead are not seen by mortal eyes. Yet they shine on for ever; theirs is eternal peace.

Let us be thankful for the companionship that continues in a love stronger than death. Sanctifying the name of God, we do honor to their memory.

12.   Strength for Those Who Mourn

In nature's ebb and flow, God's eternal law abides. He who is our support in the struggles of life is also our hope in death. In His care are the souls of all the living and the spirits of all flesh. His power gives us strength; His love comforts us. O Life of our life, Soul of our soul, cause Your light to shine into our hearts. Fill us with trust in You, and turn us again to the tasks of life. And may the memory of our loved ones inspire us to continue their work for the coming of Your kingdom.

13. Our Martyrs

We have lived in numberless towns and villages; and in too many of them we have endured cruel suffering. Some we have forgotten; others are sealed into our memory, a wound that does not heal. A hundred generations of victims and martyrs; still their blood cries out from the earth. And so many, so many at Dachau, at Buchenwald, at Babi Yar, and . . .

What can we say? What can we do? How bear the unbearable, or accept what life has brought to our people? All who are born must die, but how shall we compare the slow passage of our time with the callous slaughter of the innocent, cut off before their time?

They lived with faith. Not all, but many. And, surely, many died with faith; faith in God, in life, in the goodness that even flames cannot destroy. May we find a way to the strength of that faith, that trust, that sure sense that life and soul endure beyond this body's death.

They have left their lives to us: let a million prayers rise whenever Jews worship; let a million candles glow against the darkness of these unfinished lives.

◆ ◆

We recall the loved ones whom death has recently taken from us, those who died at this season in years past, and those whom we have taken into our hearts with our own. . . . The memories of all of them are with us; our griefs and sympathies are mingled as we praise God and pray for the coming of His kingdom.

◆ ◆

MOURNER'S KADDISH   קדיש יתום

יִתְגַּדַּל וְיִתְקַדַּשׁ שְׁמֵהּ רַבָּא בְּעָלְמָא דִּי־בְרָא כִרְעוּתֵהּ,

Yit·ga·dal ve·yit·ka·dash she·mei ra·ba be·al·ma di·ve·ra chi·re·u·tei,

וְיַמְלִיךְ מַלְכוּתֵהּ בְּחַיֵּיכוֹן וּבְיוֹמֵיכוֹן וּבְחַיֵּי דְכָל־בֵּית

ve·yam·lich mal·chu·tei be·cha·yei·chon u·ve·yo·mei·chon u·ve·cha·yei
de·chol beit

יִשְׂרָאֵל, בַּעֲגָלָא וּבִזְמַן קָרִיב, וְאִמְרוּ: אָמֵן.

Yis·ra·eil, ba·a·ga·la u·vi·ze·man ka·riv, ve·i·me·ru: a·mein.

יְהֵא שְׁמֵהּ רַבָּא מְבָרַךְ לְעָלַם וּלְעָלְמֵי עָלְמַיָּא.

Ye·hei she·mei ra·ba me·va·rach le·a·lam u·le·al·mei al·ma·ya.

יִתְבָּרַךְ וְיִשְׁתַּבַּח, וְיִתְפָּאַר וְיִתְרוֹמַם וְיִתְנַשֵּׂא, וְיִתְהַדָּר

Yit·ba·rach ve·yish·ta·bach, ve·yit·pa·ar ve·yit·ro·mam ve·yit·na·sei, ve·yit·ha·dar

וְיִתְעַלֶּה וְיִתְהַלָּל שְׁמֵהּ דְּקוּדְשָׁא, בְּרִיךְ הוּא, לְעֵילָא מִן־כָּל־

ve·yit·a·leh ve·yit·ha·lal she·mei de·ku·de·sha, be·rich hu, le·ei·la min kol

בִּרְכָתָא וְשִׁירָתָא, תֻּשְׁבְּחָתָא וְנֶחֱמָתָא דַּאֲמִירָן בְּעָלְמָא,

bi·re·cha·ta ve·shi·ra·ta, tush·be·cha·ta ve·ne·che·ma·ta, da·a·mi·ran be·al·ma,

וְאִמְרוּ: אָמֵן.

ve·i·me·ru: a·mein.

יְהֵא שְׁלָמָא רַבָּא מִן־שְׁמַיָּא וְחַיִּים עָלֵינוּ וְעַל־כָּל־יִשְׂרָאֵל,

Ye·hei she·la·ma ra·ba min she·ma·ya ve·cha·yim a·lei·nu ve·al kol Yis·ra·eil,

וְאִמְרוּ: אָמֵן.

ve·i·me·ru: a·mein.

עֹשֶׂה שָׁלוֹם בִּמְרוֹמָיו, הוּא יַעֲשֶׂה שָׁלוֹם עָלֵינוּ וְעַל־כָּל־

O·seh sha·lom bi·me·ro·mav, hu ya·a·seh sha·lom a·lei·nu ve·al kol

יִשְׂרָאֵל, וְאִמְרוּ: אָמֵן.

Yis·ra·eil, ve·i·me·ru: a·mein.

Let the glory of God be extolled, let His great name be hallowed, in
the world whose creation He willed. May His kingdom soon prevail,

in our own day, our own lives, and the life of all Israel, and let us say: Amen.

Let His great name be blessed for ever and ever.

Let the name of the Holy One, blessed is He, be glorified, exalted, and honored, though He is beyond all the praises, songs, and adorations that we can utter, and let us say: Amen.

For us and for all Israel, may the blessing of peace and the promise of life come true, and let us say: Amen.

May He who causes peace to reign in the high heavens, let peace descend on us, on all Israel, and all the world, and let us say: Amen.

◆ ◆

May the Source of peace send peace to all who mourn, and comfort to all who are bereaved. Amen.

ADDITIONAL PRAYERS

At the End of Mourning

Lord of spirit and flesh, we have turned to You for comfort in these days of grief. When the cup of sorrow passed into our hands, Your presence consoled us. Now we rise up to face the tasks of life once more. There will be moments of woe and hours of loneliness, for a loved one has passed from our sight. In our times of weakness may her (his) memory strengthen our spirit. Teach us, O God, to give thanks for all that was deathless in the life of our dear companion and friend, and which now is revealed to us in all its beauty. Be our support when our own strength fails us.

For the love that death cannot sever; for the friendship we shared along life's path; for those gifts of heart and mind which have now become a precious heritage; for all these and more, we are grateful. Now help us, Lord, not to dwell on sorrow and pain, but to honor our beloved by the quality of our lives. Amen.

Consecration of a Memorial

Begin with one or more of the following passages

1

From Psalm 8

יְיָ, אֲדֹנֵינוּ,

מָה־אַדִּיר שִׁמְךָ בְּכָל־הָאָרֶץ!

אֲשֶׁר תְּנָה הוֹדְךָ עַל־הַשָּׁמָיִם.

כִּי אֶרְאֶה שָׁמֶיךָ, מַעֲשֵׂה אֶצְבְּעֹתֶיךָ,

יָרֵחַ וְכוֹכָבִים אֲשֶׁר כּוֹנָנְתָּה,

מָה־אֱנוֹשׁ כִּי־תִזְכְּרֶנּוּ,

וּבֶן אָדָם כִּי תִפְקְדֶנּוּ?

וַתְּחַסְּרֵהוּ מְּעַט מֵאֱלֹהִים, וְכָבוֹד וְהָדָר תְּעַטְּרֵהוּ!

יְיָ, אֲדֹנֵינוּ,

מָה־אַדִּיר שִׁמְךָ בְּכָל־הָאָרֶץ!

Sovereign Lord, how majestic is Your presence in all the earth!
You have stamped Your glory upon the heavens!
When I consider Your heavens, the work of Your fingers;
the moon and the stars that You have established:
what are we, that You are mindful of us?
What are we mortals, that You care for us?
Yet You have made us little less than divine, and crowned us
with glory and honor.

O Sovereign Lord, how majestic is Your presence in all the earth!

◆ ◆

2

From Psalm 103

בָּרְכִי נַפְשִׁי אֶת־יְיָ, וְכָל־קְרָבַי אֶת־שֵׁם קָדְשׁוֹ!

בָּרְכִי נַפְשִׁי אֶת־יְיָ, וְאַל־תִּשְׁכְּחִי כָּל־גְּמוּלָיו!

208

הַגּוֹאֵל מִשַּׁחַת חַיָּיְכִי, הַמְעַטְּרֵכִי חֶסֶד וְרַחֲמִים.
עֹשֶׂה צְדָקוֹת יְיָ, וּמִשְׁפָּטִים לְכָל־עֲשׁוּקִים.

Praise the Lord, O my soul, and let all that is in me praise
God's holy name.
Praise the Lord, O my soul, and never forget God's blessings,
who redeems your life from destruction, and surrounds you
with love and compassion.
The Lord is just, demanding justice for all the oppressed.

רַחוּם וְחַנּוּן יְיָ, אֶרֶךְ אַפַּיִם וְרַב־חֶסֶד.
כִּי־הוּא יָדַע יִצְרֵנוּ, זָכוּר כִּי־עָפָר אֲנָחְנוּ.
אֱנוֹשׁ כֶּחָצִיר יָמָיו, כְּצִיץ הַשָּׂדֶה כֵּן יָצִיץ.
כִּי רְוּחַ עָבְרָה־בּוֹ וְאֵינֶנּוּ, וְלֹא־יַכִּירֶנּוּ עוֹד מְקוֹמוֹ.
וְחֶסֶד יְיָ מֵעוֹלָם וְעַד־עוֹלָם עַל־יְרֵאָיו, וְצִדְקָתוֹ לִבְנֵי בָנִים,
לְשֹׁמְרֵי בְרִיתוֹ, וּלְזֹכְרֵי פִקֻּדָיו לַעֲשׂוֹתָם.

The Lord is merciful and gracious, endlessly patient and full
of love.
For You know how we are made; You remember that we are
dust.
Our days are as grass, we blossom like a flower of the field.
The wind blows, and it is gone, and its place knows it no more.
But Your love, Lord, rests for ever on those who revere You,
and Your goodness on their children's children,
who keep Your covenant and remember to observe Your
precepts.

יְיָ בַּשָּׁמַיִם הֵכִין כִּסְאוֹ, וּמַלְכוּתוֹ בַּכֹּל מָשָׁלָה.
בָּרְכִי נַפְשִׁי אֶת־יְיָ!

*The Lord is enthroned in the universe; all creation is God's
domain.
Praise the Lord, O my soul!*

❖ ❖

3

Psalm 15

יְיָ, מִי־יָגוּר בְּאָהֳלֶךָ, מִי־יִשְׁכֹּן בְּהַר קָדְשֶׁךָ?
הוֹלֵךְ תָּמִים וּפֹעֵל צֶדֶק וְדֹבֵר אֱמֶת בִּלְבָבוֹ.

Lord, who may abide in Your house? Who may dwell in
Your holy mountain?

*Those who are upright; who do justly; who speak the truth
within their hearts.*

לֹא־רָגַל עַל־לְשֹׁנוֹ, לֹא־עָשָׂה לְרֵעֵהוּ רָעָה,
וְחֶרְפָּה לֹא־נָשָׂא עַל־קְרֹבוֹ.
נִבְזֶה בְּעֵינָיו נִמְאָס, וְאֶת־יִרְאֵי יְיָ יְכַבֵּד.

Who do not slander others, or wrong them, or bring shame
upon them.

Who scorn the lawless, but honor those who revere the Lord.

נִשְׁבַּע לְהָרַע וְלֹא יָמִיר.
כַּסְפּוֹ לֹא־נָתַן בְּנֶשֶׁךְ וְשֹׁחַד עַל־נָקִי לֹא־לָקָח.

Who give their word, and, come what may, do not retract.

Who do not exploit others, who never take bribes.

עֹשֵׂה אֵלֶּה לֹא יִמּוֹט לְעוֹלָם.

Those who live in this way shall never be shaken.

✦ ✦

4

From Proverbs 31

A woman of valor — seek her out,
for she is to be valued above rubies.
Her husband trusts her,
and they cannot fail to prosper.
All the days of her life
she is good to him.
She opens her hands to those in need

and offers her help to the poor.
Adorned with strength and dignity,
she looks to the future with cheerful trust.
Her speech is wise,
and the law of kindness is on her lips.
Her children rise up to call her blessed,
her husband likewise praises her:
'Many women have done well,
but you surpass them all.'
Charm is deceptive and beauty short-lived,
but a woman loyal to God has truly earned praise.
Give her honor for her work;
her life proclaims her praise.

◆ ◆

5

Psalm 23

מִזְמוֹר לְדָוִד.

יְיָ רֹעִי, לֹא אֶחְסָר.

בִּנְאוֹת דֶּשֶׁא יַרְבִּיצֵנִי, עַל־מֵי מְנֻחוֹת יְנַהֲלֵנִי.

נַפְשִׁי יְשׁוֹבֵב, יַנְחֵנִי בְמַעְגְּלֵי־צֶדֶק לְמַעַן שְׁמוֹ.

גַּם כִּי אֵלֵךְ בְּגֵיא צַלְמָוֶת לֹא אִירָא רָע, כִּי אַתָּה עִמָּדִי,

שִׁבְטְךָ וּמִשְׁעַנְתֶּךָ, הֵמָּה יְנַחֲמֻנִי.

תַּעֲרֹךְ לְפָנַי שֻׁלְחָן נֶגֶד צֹרְרָי,

דִּשַּׁנְתָּ בַשֶּׁמֶן רֹאשִׁי, כּוֹסִי רְוָיָה.

אַךְ טוֹב וָחֶסֶד יִרְדְּפוּנִי כָּל־יְמֵי חַיָּי,

וְשַׁבְתִּי בְּבֵית־יְיָ לְאֹרֶךְ יָמִים.

The Lord is my shepherd, I shall not want.
He makes me lie down in green pastures,
He leads me beside still waters. He restores my soul.
He leads me in right paths for the sake of His name.
Even when I walk in the valley of the shadow of death
I shall fear no evil, for You are with me;

With rod and staff You comfort me.
You have set a table before me in the presence of my enemies;
You have anointed my head with oil, my cup overflows.
Surely goodness and mercy shall follow me all the days of my
life, and I shall dwell in the house of the Lord for ever.

◆ ◆

6

Psalm 121

אֶשָּׂא עֵינַי אֶל־הֶהָרִים, מֵאַיִן יָבוֹא עֶזְרִי?
עֶזְרִי מֵעִם יְיָ, עֹשֵׂה שָׁמַיִם וָאָרֶץ.
אַל־יִתֵּן לַמּוֹט רַגְלֶךָ, אַל־יָנוּם שֹׁמְרֶךָ.
הִנֵּה לֹא־יָנוּם וְלֹא יִישָׁן שׁוֹמֵר יִשְׂרָאֵל.
יְיָ שֹׁמְרֶךָ, יְיָ צִלְּךָ עַל־יַד יְמִינֶךָ.
יוֹמָם הַשֶּׁמֶשׁ לֹא־יַכֶּכָּה, וְיָרֵחַ בַּלָּיְלָה.
יְיָ יִשְׁמָרְךָ מִכָּל־רָע, יִשְׁמֹר אֶת־נַפְשֶׁךָ.
יְיָ יִשְׁמָר־צֵאתְךָ וּבוֹאֶךָ, מֵעַתָּה וְעַד־עוֹלָם.

I lift up my eyes to the mountains:
what is the source of my help?
My help will come from the Lord,
Maker of heaven and earth.
He will not allow your foot to slip;
your Guardian will not slumber.
Behold, the Guardian of Israel neither slumbers nor sleeps.
the Eternal is your Keeper,
The Lord is your shade at your right hand.
The sun shall not harm you by day, nor the moon by night.
The Lord will guard you from all evil,
He will protect your being.
The Lord will guard you, coming and going,
from this time forth, and for ever.

◆ ◆

On behalf of the family of ......, and in the presence of his (her) relatives and friends, we consecrate this memorial as a sign of love undying.

תְּהִי נִשְׁמָתוֹ (נִשְׁמָתָהּ) צְרוּרָה בִּצְרוֹר הַחַיִּים.

May his (her) soul be bound up in the bond of eternal life.

◆ ◆

For an adult

God of infinite love, in whose hands are the souls of all the living and the spirits of all flesh, standing at the grave of....... we gratefully recall the goodness in her (him) and we give thanks for the consolation of memory.

Strengthen us who mourn, that, walking through the valley of the shadow of death, we may be guided by Your light. May our actions and aspirations honor our loved one as surely as does this monument, which will stand as a symbol of our abiding devotion. So will she (he) live on for blessing among us.

Continue with Kaddish on page 214.

For a child

To You, O Source of peace, we turn in our time of need. Give us strength and patience to bear our burden of sorrow. And help us to overcome our grief, that we may return to life and its tasks. Deepen our love for one another; teach us to open our hearts to all who need us; move us to reach out to them with our hands; and guide us on our path, until we find the abiding love that survives all loss and sustains us through every trial.

Grant consolation, O Lord, to sorrowing parents and to all who mourn. Heal our hurt, renew our hope and our faith. May the memory of this beloved child make all children more precious to us, and inspire us to labor for a world in which every life shall find its fulfillment.

As we dedicate this memorial to ...., we hallow and bless Your name.

◆ ◆

MOURNER'S KADDISH   קדיש יתום

יִתְגַּדַּל וְיִתְקַדַּשׁ שְׁמֵהּ רַבָּא בְּעָלְמָא דִּי־בְרָא כִרְעוּתֵהּ,

Yit·ga·dal ve·yit·ka·dash she·mei ra·ba be·al·ma di·ve·ra chi·re·u·tei,

וְיַמְלִיךְ מַלְכוּתֵהּ בְּחַיֵּיכוֹן וּבְיוֹמֵיכוֹן וּבְחַיֵּי דְכָל־בֵּית

ve·yam·llch mal·chu·tei be·cha·yei·chon u·ve·yo·mei·chon u·ve·cha·yei
de·chol beit

יִשְׂרָאֵל, בַּעֲגָלָא וּבִזְמַן קָרִיב, וְאִמְרוּ: אָמֵן.

Yis·ra·eil, ba·a·ga·la u·vi·ze·man ka·riv, ve·i·me·ru: a·mein.

יְהֵא שְׁמֵהּ רַבָּא מְבָרַךְ לְעָלַם וּלְעָלְמֵי עָלְמַיָּא.

Ye·hei she·mei ra·ba me·va·rach le·a·lam u·le·al·mei al·ma·ya.

יִתְבָּרַךְ וְיִשְׁתַּבַּח, וְיִתְפָּאַר וְיִתְרוֹמַם וְיִתְנַשֵּׂא, וְיִתְהַדָּר

Yit·ba·rach ve·yish·ta·bach, ve·yit·pa·ar ve·yit·ro·mam ve·yit·na·sei, ve·yit·ha·dar

וְיִתְעַלֶּה וְיִתְהַלַּל שְׁמֵהּ דְּקוּדְשָׁא, בְּרִיךְ הוּא, לְעֵלָּא מִן־כָּל־

ve·yit·a·leh ve·yit·ha·lal she·mei de·ku·de·sha, be·rich hu, le·ei·la min kol

בִּרְכָתָא וְשִׁירָתָא, תֻּשְׁבְּחָתָא וְנֶחֱמָתָא דַּאֲמִירָן בְּעָלְמָא,

bi·re·cha·ta ve·shi·ra·ta, tush·be·cha·ta ve·ne·che·ma·ta, da·a·mi·ran be·al·ma,

וְאִמְרוּ: אָמֵן.

ve·i·me·ru: a·mein.

יְהֵא שְׁלָמָא רַבָּא מִן־שְׁמַיָּא וְחַיִּים עָלֵינוּ וְעַל־כָּל־יִשְׂרָאֵל,

Ye·hei she·la·ma ra·ba min she·ma·ya ve·cha·yim a·lei·nu ve·al kol Yis·ra·eil,

וְאִמְרוּ: אָמֵן.

ve·i·me·ru: a·mein.

עֹשֶׂה שָׁלוֹם בִּמְרוֹמָיו, הוּא יַעֲשֶׂה שָׁלוֹם עָלֵינוּ וְעַל־כָּל־

O·seh sha·lom bi·me·ro·mav, hu ya·a·seh sha·lom a·lei·nu ve·al kol

יִשְׂרָאֵל וְאִמְרוּ: אָמֵן.

Yis·ra·eil, ve·i·me·ru: a·mein.

❖ ❖

214

אֵל מָלֵא רַחֲמִים, שׁוֹכֵן בַּמְּרוֹמִים, הַמְצֵא מְנוּחָה נְכוֹנָה
תַּחַת כַּנְפֵי הַשְּׁכִינָה עִם קְדוֹשִׁים וּטְהוֹרִים כְּזֹהַר הָרָקִיעַ
מַזְהִירִים אֶת נִשְׁמַת ..... שֶׁהָלַךְ (שֶׁהָלְכָה) לְעוֹלָמוֹ
(לְעוֹלָמָהּ). בַּעַל הָרַחֲמִים יַסְתִּירֵהוּ (יַסְתִּירֶהָ) בְּסֵתֶר
כְּנָפָיו לְעוֹלָמִים. וְיִצְרוֹר בִּצְרוֹר הַחַיִּים אֶת־נִשְׁמָתוֹ
(נִשְׁמָתָהּ). יְיָ הוּא נַחֲלָתוֹ (נַחֲלָתָהּ) וְיָנוּחַ (וְתָנוּחַ) בְּשָׁלוֹם
עַל מִשְׁכָּבוֹ (מִשְׁכָּבָהּ), וְנֹאמַר אָמֵן.

O God full of compassion, Eternal Spirit of the universe, grant
perfect rest under the wings of Your Presence to our loved one
who has entered eternity. Master of Mercy, let him (her) find
refuge for ever in the shadow of Your wings, and let his (her)
soul be bound up in the bond of eternal life. The Eternal God
is his (her) inheritance. May he (she) rest in peace, and let us
say: Amen.

For a Yahrzeit

*The family is gathered at dusk, on the eve of
the anniversary of the death.*

At this moment, which bears the memory of our beloved
. . . ., let us join hands in love and remembrance.
A link has been broken in the chain which has bound us together, yet strong bonds of home and love hold us each to
the other.

We give thanks for the blessing of life, of companionship, and
of memory. We are grateful for the strength and faith that
sustained us in the hour of our bereavement. Though sorrow
lingers, we have learned that love is stronger than death.
Though our loved one is beyond our sight, we do not despair,
for we sense our beloved in our hearts as a living presence.

*The 23rd Psalm, page 211, or another favorite passage from the Bible
or Prayerbook might now be recited.*

Sustained by words of faith, comforted by precious memories,
we kindle the Yahrzeit light in remembrance. "The human
spirit is the light of the Lord." As this light burns pure and
clear, so may the blessed memory of the goodness and nobility
of character of our dear . . . . illumine our souls.

The light is kindled

זִכְרוֹנוֹ (זִכְרוֹנָהּ) לִבְרָכָה.

Zich·ro·no (Zich·ro·na) li·ve·ra·cha.
His (her) memory is a blessing.

At the Grave of a Loved One

To this sacred place I come, drawn by the eternal ties that bind my soul to the soul of my beloved. Death has separated us. You are no longer at my side to share the beauty of the passing moment. I cannot look to you to lighten my burdens, to lend me your strength, your wisdom, your faith. And yet what you mean to me does not wither or fade. For a time we touched hands and hearts; still your voice abides with me, still your tender glance remains a joy to me. For you are part of me for ever; something of you has become a deathless song upon my lips. And so beyond the ache that tells how much I miss you, a deeper thought compels: we were together. I hold you still in mind, and give thanks for life and love. The happiness that was, the memories that do not fade, are a gift that can not be lost. You continue to bless my days and years. I will always give thanks for you.

POEMS AND PRAYERS

1

Praised be the One whose word made this world be,
this world so small and strange,
where all things begin
in the middle of their growth,
and end there;
where all things hide
from the one who longs to understand them.
Here in space and time they hide
from their beginning in time
to their eternal end.

And praised be the One who keeps a covenant
with this world,
so strange and small,
where God's good is sown to the winds,
so that hope exalts even the least of us,
so that even I find my spirit rising to redeem me.
And in my heart wells up this word:
Praised be the One whose word . . . .

2

Something is very gently,
invisibly, silently,
pulling at me — a thread
or net of threads
finer than cobweb and as
elastic. I haven't tried
the strength of it. No barbed hook
pierced and tore me. Was it
not long ago this thread
began to draw me? Or
way back? Was I
born with its knot about my
neck, a bridle? Not fear

but a stirring
of wonder makes me
catch my breath when I feel
the tug of it when I thought
it had loosened itself and gone.

3

There exists a silent, immanent language, a secret tongue,
It has no sound, syllable, only shade of hues:
Enchantments, splendid pictures, hosts of visions.
In this tongue God makes Himself known to those His spirit
chooses,
In it the Royal Emissary of the world reflects upon His
thoughts,
The Artist Creator embodies the thought of His heart,
And in it finds the solution of the unexpressed dream.
It is the language of images revealed
In a strip of blue sky and in its expanse,
In the purity of small silver clouds and in their dark mass,
In the tremor of golden wheat, in the pride of mighty cedars,
In the rustle of a dove's pure wing,
And in the eaglewing's sweep,
In the beauty of a man's body, in the aura of a glance,
In the sea's wrath, in the wave's caprice and play,
In the overflowing night, in the silence of falling stars,
In the roar of light, in the rumble of sea flaming
With sunrises and sunsets . . .

4

Lord, we will never ask that You come down
to fight our wars or make our peace or build our house
of love

like a man with magic on his sleeve to do for us
what we will not do ourselves.

Nor, O Master of Arithmetic, will we ask
that two and two make five, or three.

Only this, and this would be enough:

Let Your presence grow within us,
Your words move our weary hands.

Lord, we cannot hope at all,
unless we ground our hope in You.

How then, all hope lost, stand upright,
refusing invitations to hell?

How then could we consent to be human,
when human means divine, means free,
means all those old promises
so often glib upon our lips,
but so often only there?

And not on our lips alone, not ours alone.

Yes, we are stonyhearted, yes, we do evil, yes.

But in this too we are not alone.

Move us, then, but not us alone.
Move head and hand with the presence of Your word.
Move those who make us strangers on the earth
to see themselves in us.

So the garden planted in our wilderness be safe
from blight, and wolves, and empires.

Let us be free,
all of us,
wherever we make a home.

5

Lord, You called us
and trembling we armed ourselves
for a stony road
grown over with thorns.
Bodies aflame

and blazing pyres
were a light for our path.

And yet
above the howls of thugs
in every age,
above the screams of hate
and stones whistling murder,
we heard Your voice:
a voice men have stilled —
but not for ever.

Now You cry out to us
from the ovens.
Now Your secret
is a whisper within us,
too terrible to reveal.
Too many answers for a riddle
too hard to solve.

This people Israel:
our cries choked off by hangmen,
every road to safety blocked,
every light of rescue darkened . . .

And yet
above the noise of many throats
thirsty for our blood,
Your voice is heard —
a voice silenced
by men and their deeds:
but not for ever.

6

Wherever I go, I hear footsteps:

My brothers on the road, in swamps, in forests,
Swept along in darkness, trembling from cold,
Fugitives from flames, plagues, and terrors.

Wherever I stand, I hear rattling:

My sisters in chains, in chambers of the stricken.
They pierce the walls and burst the silence.
Through the generations their echoes cry out
In torture camps, in pits of the dead.

Wherever I lie, I hear voices:

My brothers herded to slaughter
Out of burning embers, out of ruins,
Out of cities and villages, altars for burnt offerings.
The groaning in their destruction haunts my nights.

My eyes will never stop seeing them
And my heart will never stop crying "Horror";
Every human being shall be called to account for their death.

The heavens will descend to mourn for them,
The world and all therein will be their monument.

7

Lord, we are not so arrogant as to pretend
that the trial of our lives
does not reveal our flaws.
We know ourselves,
in this moment of prayer,
to have failed ourselves and others,
the ones we love and the stranger,
again and again.
We know how often
we did not bring to the surface of our lives
the hidden goodness within.
Where we have achieved, O Lord,
we are proud of ourselves
and grateful to You;
where we have failed,
we ask forgiveness.
Remember how exposed we are

to the chances and terrors of life.
We were afraid.
We sometimes chose to fail.
And we ask:
Turn our thoughts from the hurt to its remedy.
Free us of the torments of guilt.

Forgiven, O Lord, help us to forgive others;
Failing, help us to understand failure;
Renewed and encouraged, help us to be like
those who came before us:
human. Sinners sometimes, yet a blessing.

8

Merely to have survived is not an index of excellence.
Nor, given the way things go,
Even of low cunning.
Yet we have seen the wicked in great power,
And spreading himself like a green bay tree.
And the good as if they have never been;
Their voices are blown away on the winter wind.
And again we wander the wilderness
For our transgressions
Which are confessed in the daily papers.

Except the Lord of hosts had left unto us
A very small remnant,
We should have been as Sodom,
We should have been like unto Gomorrah.
And to what purpose, as the darkness closes about
And the child screams in the jellied fire,
Had best be our present concern,
Here, in this wilderness of comfort
In which we dwell.

Shall we now consider
The suspicious posture of our virtue,
The deformed consequences of our love,
The painful issues of our mildest acts?
Shall we ask,

Where is there one
Mad, poor and betrayed enough to find
Forgiveness for us, saying,
"None does offend,
None, I say,
None?"

9

And He said: 'No longer shall your name be called Jacob, but Israel, for you have contended with gods and with men, and have prevailed.' (Genesis 32)

And so night after night, God, You come to me,
To try my strength.
And prevailing against You until dawn,
— Again I am alone,
A poor and homeless pilgrim,
Limping on my thigh.

'You have contended with gods and with men,
And have prevailed'—
Is this all the blessing You have for me,
O Hidden One?
I have prevailed over all of you,
Over all things, I know:
Except the one, except myself!

Heavy do Your blessings weigh upon me, too heavy to bear,
As I limp in lonely peril along the road.
O vanquish me once, just once, O God,
And towards morning let me know
The rest that all the vanquished know.

Night again, and again am I alone.
Again God descends. "Israel!"
Here am I, God, here I am!
Oh, why, night after night,
Do You come down to wrestle with me,
And then at dawn forsake me
As I limp along the road?

10

I think continually of those who were truly great.
Who, from the womb, remembered the soul's history
Through endless corridors of light where the hours are suns,
Endless and singing. Whose lovely ambition
Was that their lips, still touched with fire,
Should tell of the spirit clothed head to foot in song.
And who hoarded from the spring branches
The desires falling across their bodies like blossoms.

What is precious is never to forget
The delight of the blood drawn from ageless springs
Breaking through rocks in worlds before our earth;
Never to deny its pleasure in the simple morning light,
Nor its grave evening demand for love;
Never to allow the traffic to smother
With noise and fog the flowering of the spirit.

Near the snow, near the sun, in the highest fields
See how these names are fêted by the waving grass,
And by the streamers of white cloud,
And whispers of wind in the listening sky;
The names of those who in their lives fought for life,
Who wore at their hearts the fire's center.
Born of the sun they travelled a short while towards the sun,
And left the vivid air signed with their honor.

11

Not because of victories
I sing,
having none,
but for the common sunshine,
the breeze,
the largesse of the spring.

Not for the victory,
but for the day's work done
as well as I was able;
not for a seat upon the dais
but at the common table.

12

This is my prayer to You, O my God:
Let me not swerve from my life's path,
Let not my spirit wither and shrivel
In its thirst for You,
And lose the dew
With which You sprinkled it
When I was young.

Be my heart open
To every broken thing,
To orphaned life,
To every stumbler
Wandering unknown
And groping in the shadow.

Bless my eyes, purify me to see
Man's beauty rise in the world,
And my people's grandeur
In its land redeemed
Scattering its scent
Over all the earth.

Deepen and broaden my senses
To absorb a fresh,
Green, flowering world,
To take from it the secret
Of blossoming in silence.

Grant strength to yield fine fruits,
Quintessence of my life,

Steeped in my very being,
Without expectation of reward.

And when my time comes —
Let me slip into the night
Demanding nothing, God, of man,
Or of You.

13

If my days remaining on earth be few,
Let me know beauty.

Let the heat of battle sear the earth no more,
Let us live out our lives.

Let my people come back to its loved land.

Let me have a small house in a village
Hidden among the fields.

For I am weary:

My life has been a long flight
Along unmarked roads,
Unsheltered.

And let my windows be open to the world.

14

The gods we worship write their names on our faces, be sure
of that,

And we will worship something — have no doubt of
that either.

We may think that our tribute is paid in secret
in the dark recesses of the heart — but it will out.

That which dominates our imagination and our thoughts will determine our life and character.

Therefore it behooves us to be careful what we are worshipping, for what we are worshipping we are becoming. . . .

15

The sum of all known reverence I add up in you, whoever you are;
The apple-shaped earth and we upon it.
The endless pride and outstretching of man and of woman;
unspeakable joys and sorrows;
The wonder everyone sees in everyone else, and the wonders that fill each minute of time for ever;
It is for you whoever you are — it is no farther from you than your hearing and sight from you;
We consider bibles and religions divine — I do not say they are not divine; I say they have all grown out of you, and may grow out of you still;
It is not they who give the life — it is you who give the life.
Will you seek afar off? You surely come back at last, in things best known to you, finding the best, or as good as the best —
Happiness, knowledge, not in another place, but this place —
not for another hour, but this hour.

16

Where the mind is without fear and the head is held high;
Where knowledge is free;
Where the world has not been broken up into fragments by narrow domestic walls;
Where words come from the depths of truth;
Where tireless striving stretches its arms toward perfection;
Where the clear stream of reason has not lost its way in the arid desert sands of dead habit;
Where the mind is led forward by You into ever-widening thought and action —
Into that heaven of freedom, my Maker, let my people awake.

17

What does it mean to be creatures of thought and longing who live on this planet we have named the earth?
No other creature in all the universe is assembled and contained as we are.
Our history is our own, these few millions of years of evolution that have brought our conformation and countenance into being.
Only here has ensued this juncture of dust and breath.
We are the end of a long and passionate working, a slow serenity and growth.
This is our captivity and emergence, our beginning and history.
This is the fact of human oneness, one species, one living kin.
How insignificant are the differences between us, against the mountainous identities of this one family of time and earth.
Sing the family of woman and man. Sing the one home, the gentle earth, the grass, the sunlight, the eventide.
We will make this small plot of soil, this globe, a messenger of meaning and peace.

18

Let religion be to us life and joy.
Let it be a voice of renewing challenge to the best we have and may be; let it be a call to generous action.
Let religion be for us a dissatisfaction with things that are, which bids us serve more eagerly the true and right.
Let it be the sorrow that opens for us the way of sympathy, understanding, and service to suffering humanity.
Let religion be to us the wonder and lure of that which is only partly known and understood:
An eye that glories in nature's majesty and beauty, and a heart that rejoices in deeds of kindness and of courage.
Let religion be to us security and serenity because of its truth

and beauty, and because of the enduring worth and power of
the loyalties which it engenders: let it be to us hope and
purpose, and a discovering of opportunities to express our best
through daily tasks:
Religion, uniting us with all that is admirable in human beings
everywhere;
Holding before our eyes a prospect of the better life for humankind, which each may help to make actual.

19

Master of the universe,
let there be no good hope that is not a command,
let there be no prayer that does not ask to become a deed,
let there be no promise unless it be kept.

Upon this earth may just and reverent nations arise:
needing no challenge like war,
no more undone by poverty and injustice.
Let them be places where every person matters.
So shall the human community,
rich in beginnings and poor in conclusions,
grow mature in wisdom and ripe in understanding.

Upon this earth may women of spirit arise,
men of integrity and compassion,
creators of God-seeking peoples;
slow to judge others,
quick to judge themselves:
so may they be all their days and years.
We ask for messiahs,
a new age of the spirit,
Your kingdom on earth.

Let the Eternal be King over all the earth.

20

Who are happy?
Those who see a blossoming world
and give their blessing.

Who are strong?
Those who restrain their grief
and teach it to smile.

21

This is the discipline that withstood the siege of every Jew;
these are the prayer-shawls that have proved
stronger than armor.

Let us begin then humbly. Not by asking:
Who is this you pray to? Name Him;
define Him. For the answer is:
We do not name Him.
Once out of a savage fear, perhaps;
now out of knowledge — of our ignorance.

Begin then humbly. Not by asking:
Shall I live for ever?
Hear again the dear dead greeting me gladly
as they used to
when we were all among the living?
For the answer is:
If you think we differ from all His other creatures,
say only if you like with the Pharisees, our teachers,
those who do not believe in an eternal life
will not have it.

In the morning I arise and match again
my plans against my cash.
I wonder now if the long morning prayers
were an utter waste of an hour,

weighing, as they do, hopes and anguish,
and sending the believer out into the street
with the sweet taste of prayer on his lips.

How good to stop
and look out upon eternity a while;
and daily
in the morning, afternoon, and evening
be at ease in Zion.

22

Divine sanctuary of my youth,
my venerable house of study,
not empty-handed did you send me
forth from your peaceful shade.
I was dispatched on my way by
your good angels —
fruitful thought, luxuriant meditation,
a true and confident heart against
the time when knees might falter.
Truly, my foe prevailed over me.
He reduced me to an empty vessel,
but I saved my God — and He saved me.

You shall not be moved, O tent of Shem!
I will build you and you shall be rebuilt.
From the heaps of your dust
I will restore your walls.
When I heal the shattered sanctuary of God
light will dispel the darkness of its
outstretched shadows.
When the cloud lifts, the glory of
the Lord will descend.
And all flesh small and great shall see
that the grass fades, the flower withers —
but God is everlasting!

23

Where has this week vanished?
Is it lost for ever?
Will I ever recover anything from it?
The joy of life, the unexpected victory,
the realized hope, the task accomplished?
Will I ever be able to banish the memory of pain,
the sting of defeat, the heaviness of boredom?
On this day let me keep for a while what must drift away.
On this day let me be free of the burdens that must return.
On this day, Shabbat, abide.

And now Shabbat has come,
can it help me to withdraw for a while
from the flight of time?
Can it contain the retreat of the hours and days from the
grasp of a frantic life?
When all days abandon me, Shabbat, abide.

Let me learn to pause, if only for this day.
Let me find peace on this day.
Let me enter into a quiet world this day.
On this day, Shabbat, abide.

24

Now from the world the light of God is gone,
And men in darkness move and are afraid,
Some blaming heaven for the evil done,
And some each other for the part they played.
And all their woes on Him are strictly laid,
For being absent from these earthly ills,
Who set the trees to be the noonday shade,
And placed the stars in beauty on the hills.
Turn not away, and cry that all is lost;
It is not so, the world is still in His hands,
As once it was when Egypt's mighty host

Rode to the sea and vanished in the sands.
For still the heart, by love and pity wrung,
Finds the same God as when the world was young.

25

When the departing, great sun stands
    And plants, on the last hill, his feet,
He comes; likewise to morning lands,
    Or down a dim and crowded street.

Today I knew that ecstasy;
    A soaring light was all my blood,
And in me, voices, like the sea,
    Shouted and my heart understood.

Today He smote earth with the flame
    That clothes His presence when He comes.
And earth grew vibrant with His name,
    Like hidden trumpets, answering drums.

26

They list for me the things I may not know:
Whence came the world? Whose hand flung out the light
Of yonder stars? How could a God of Right
Ordain for earth an ebbless tide of woe?

Their word is right; I would not scorn their doubt
Who press their questions of the how and why.
But this I know: that from the star-strewn sky
There comes to me a peace that puts to rout

All brooding thoughts of dread, abiding death;
And, too, I know with every fragrant dawn
That Life is Lord, that, with the Winter gone,
There cometh Spring, a great reviving breath.

It is enough that Life means this to me.
What death shall bring, some sunny morn shall see.

27

It may be so with us, that in the dark
When we have done with time and wander space,
Some meeting of the blind may strike a spark,
And to death's empty mansion give a grace.
It may be that the loosened soul may find
Some new delight in living without limbs,
Bodiless joy of flesh-untrammeled mind,
Peace like a sky where starlike spirit swims.
It may be that the million cells of sense,
Loosed from their seventy years' adhesion, pass
Each to some joy of changed experience,
Weight in the earth or glory in the grass;
It may be that we cease; we cannot tell.
Even if we cease, life is a miracle.

28

What fills the heart of man
Is not that his life must fade,
But that out of his dark there can
A light like a rose be made,
That seeing a snowflake fall
His heart is lifted up,
That hearing a meadow-lark call
For a moment he will stop
To rejoice in the musical air
To delight in the fertile earth
And the flourishing everywhere
Of spring and spring's rebirth.
And never a woman or man
Walked through their quickening hours
But found for some brief span
An intervale of flowers,
Where love for a man or a woman
So captured the heart's beat

That they and all things human
Danced on rapturous feet.
And though, for each man, love dies,
The rose to his children's eyes
Will flower again, again,
Will flower again out of shadow
To make the brief heart sing
And the meadow-lark from the meadow
Will call again in spring.

29

Mourn not the dead that in the cool earth lie —
Dust unto dust —
The calm sweet earth that mothers all who die
As all men must;

Mourn not your captured comrades who must dwell —
Too strong to strive —
Each in his own steel-bound coffin of a cell, buried alive;
But rather mourn the apathetic throng —
The coward and the meek —
Who see the world's great anguish and its wrong
And dare not speak.

30

They are not gone from us. O no! they are
The inmost essence of each thing that is
Perfect for us; they flame in every star;
The trees are emerald with their presences.
They are not gone from us; they do not roam
The flaw and turmoil of the lower deep,
But now have made the whole wide world their home,
And in its loveliness themselves they steep.

They fail not ever; theirs is the diurn
Splendor of sunny hill and forest grave;

In every rainbow's glittering drop they burn;
They dazzle in the massed clouds' architrave;
They chant on every wind, and they return
In the long roll of any deep blue wave.

31

Shall I cry out in anger, O God,
Because Your gifts are mine but for a while?
Shall I forget the blessing of health
The moment there is pain?

Shall I be ungrateful for the laughter,
the seasons of joy, the days of gladness,
when tears cloud my eyes and darken the world
and my heart is heavy within me?

Shall I blot from mind the love
I have rejoiced in when fate
leaves me bereft of shining presences
that have lit my way through years
of companionship and affection?

Shall I, in days of adversity, fail to recall
the hours of glory You once did grant me?

Shall I, in turmoil of need and anxiety,
Cease blessing You for the peace of former days?
Shall the time of darkness put out for ever
The glow of the light in which once I walked?

Give me the vision, O God, to see
that embedded in each of Your gifts
is a core of eternity, undiminished and bright,
an eternity that survives the dread hours of affliction.

Those I have loved, though now beyond my view,
Have given form and quality to my being.
They have led me into the wide universe
I continue to inhabit, and their presence
is more real to me than their absence.

What You give to me, O Lord,
You never take away.
And bounties granted once
Shed their radiance evermore.

32

Will there yet come days of forgiveness and grace,
When you will walk in the field as the innocent wayfarer
walks?
And the soles of your feet caress the clover leaves:
Though stubble will sting you, sweet will be their stalks.
Or rain will overtake you, its thronging drops tapping
On your shoulder, your chest, your throat, your gentle head
bowed.
And you walk in the wet field, the quiet in you expanding
Like light in the hem of a cloud.

And you will breathe the odor of furrow, breathing and quiet,
And you will see mirrored in the gold puddle the sun above,
And simple will be these things and life, permitted to touch,
Permitted, permitted to love.

Slowly you will walk in the field. Alone. Unscorched by flame
Of conflagrations on roads that bristled with horror and blood.
Again
You will be peaceful in heart, humble and bending
Like one of the grasses, like one of man.

33

i thank You God for most this amazing
day:for the leaping greenly spirits of trees
and a blue true dream of sky;and for everything
which is natural which is infinite which is yes

(i who have died am alive again today,
and this is the sun's birthday;this is the birth

day of life and of love and wings:and of the gay
great happening illimitably earth)

how should tasting touching hearing seeing
breathing any—lifted from the no
of all nothing—human merely being
doubt unimaginable You?

(now the ears of my ears awake and
now the eyes of my eyes are opened)

34

I will lift up my hands unto thee, O my God!
So shall I praise thee.
As the flower breaketh from the bud
And from the blind earth riseth fast
The stem, and pusheth from the root
The eager shoot — upwards and upwards —
So shall I praise thee, Lord of light,
With lifted hands.

Deep planted is the soul — alone
It dwelleth in a secret place
And sleepeth until the spring;
Then it hungereth and thirsteth,
And thou art rain and sunshine
And the voice of birds at dawn.
So will I praise thee, Lord,
With lifted hands.

35

("And though after my skin worms destroy this body, yet in my
flesh shall I see God." — Job 19.26)

O the chimneys
On the ingeniously devised habitations of death

When Israel's body drifted as smoke
Through the air —
Was welcomed by a star, a chimney sweep,
A star that turned black
Or was it a ray of sun?

O the chimneys!
Freedom way for Jeremiah and Job's dust —
Who devised you and laid stone upon stone
The road for refugees of smoke?

O the habitations of death,
Invitingly appointed
For the host who used to be a guest —
O you fingers
Laying the threshold
Like a knife between life and death —

O you chimneys
O you fingers
And Israel's body as smoke through the air!

36

The first ones to be destroyed were the children,
    orphans, abandoned upon the face of the earth,
they who were the best in the world,
the acme of grace on the dark earth!
From them, the bereaved of the world,
in a house of shelter we drew consolation;
From the mournful faces, mute and dark,
we said the light of day will yet break upon us!

. . . .

They, the children of Israel, were the first in doom and
    disaster,
most of them without father and mother,
were consumed by frost, starvation and lice;

holy messiahs sanctified in pain. . . .
Say then, how have these lambs sinned?
Why in days of doom were they the first victims of
    wickedness,
the first in the trap of evil!

The first were they detained for death;
the first into the wagons of slaughter,
they were thrown into the wagons, the huge wagons,
like heaps of refuse, like the ashes of the earth —
They killed them,
and they transported them,
exterminated them
without remnant or remembrance. . . .
The best of my children were all wiped out!
O woe unto me —
Doom and desolation!

37

But who emptied your shoes of sand
When you had to get up, to die?
The sand which Israel gathered,
Its nomad sand?
Burning Sinai sand,
Mingled with throats of nightingales,
Mingled with wings of butterflies,
Mingled with the hungry dust of serpents;
Mingled with all that fell from the wisdom of Solomon,
Mingled with what is bitter in the mystery of wormwood.
O you fingers
That emptied the deathly shoes of sand.
Tomorrow you will be dust
In the shoes of those to come.

38

We orphans
We lament to the world:
Our branch has been cut down
and thrown in the fire —
Kindling was made of our protectors —
We orphans lie stretched out on the fields of loneliness.
We orphans
We lament to the world:
At night our parents play hide and seek —
From behind the black folds of night
The faces gaze at us.
Their mouths speak:
Kindling we were in a woodcutter's hand —
But our eyes have become angel eyes
And regard you.
Through the black folds of night
They penetrate —
We orphans
We lament to the world:
Stones have become our playthings,
Stones have faces, father and mother faces
They wilt not like flowers, nor bite like beasts —
and burn not like tinder when tossed into the ovens —
We orphans we lament to the world:
World, why have you taken our soft mothers from us
And the fathers who say: My child, you are like me!
We orphans are like no one in this world any more!
O world
We accuse you!

39

Why the black answer of hate
to your existence, Israel?

You stranger

from a star one farther away
than the others.

Sold to this earth
that loneliness might be passed on.

Your origin entangled in weeds —
your stars bartered
for all that belongs to moths and worms,
and yet: fetched away from dreamfilled sandy shores of time
like moonwater into the distance.

In the others' choir
you always sang
one note lower
or one note higher —

you flung yourself into the blood of the evening sun
like one pain seeking the other.
Long is your shadow
and it has become late for you
Israel!

How far your way from the blessing
along the aeon of tears
to the bend of the road
where you turned to ashes

and your enemy with the smoke
of your burned body
engraved your mortal abandonment
on the brow of heaven!

O such a death!
When all helping angels
with bleeding wings
hung tattered
in the barbed wire of time!

Why the black answer of hate
to your existence
Israel?

40

The heaviest wheel rolls across our foreheads
To bury itself deep somewhere inside our memories.

We've suffered here more than enough,
Here in this clot of grief and shame,
Wanting a badge of blindness
To be a proof for their own children.

A fourth year of waiting, like standing above a swamp
From which any moment might gush forth a spring.

Meanwhile, the rivers flow another way,
Another way,
Not letting you die, not letting you live.

And the cannons don't scream and the guns don't bark
And you don't see blood here.
Nothing, only silent hunger.
Children steal the bread here and ask and ask

and ask

And all would wish to sleep, keep silent and just to go to
sleep again . . .

The heaviest wheel rolls across our foreheads
To bury itself deep somewhere inside our memories.

41

Black milk of dawn we drink it at even
we drink it at noon and mornings we drink it at night
we drink and we drink
we are digging a grave in the skies there one lies uncrowded.

A man lives in the house he plays with the serpents he writes
he writes when the dark comes to Germany your golden hair
    Margarete
he writes it and steps from the house and the stars flash he
    whistles up his dogs

he whistles out his Jews let a grave be dug in the earth
he commands us now play for the dance.

Black milk of dawn we drink you at night
we drink you mornings and noon we drink you at even
we drink and we drink.

A man lives in the house he plays with the serpents he writes
he writes when the dark comes to Germany your golden hair
    Margarete
your ashen hair Shulamith we are digging a grave in the
    skies there one lies uncrowded.
He calls stab deeper into the earth you there you others sing
    sing and play
he reaches for the iron in his belt he swings it his eyes are blue
stab deeper your spades you there you others play on for the
    dance.

Black milk of dawn we drink you at night
we drink you noon and mornings we drink you at even
    we drink and we drink
a man lives in the house your golden hair Margarete
your ashen hair Shulamith he plays with the serpents.

He calls play sweeter of death death is a master from Germany
he calls stroke darker the violins then you will climb as smoke
    into the sky
then you will have a grave in the clouds there one lies
    uncrowded

Black milk of dawn we drink you at night
we drink you at noon death is a master from Germany
we drink you at even and mornings we drink and we drink
death is a master from Germany his eye is blue
he hits you with a lead bullet his aim is true
a man lives in the house your golden hair Margarete
he sets his dogs upon us he gives us a grave in the sky
he plays with the serpents and dreams death is a master from
    Germany
your golden hair Margarete
your ashen hair Shulamith.

42

Would that I were a stone
like all the stones of Jerusalem,
and how blessed,
were my bones joined to the Wall!
Why should my body be spared more than
my soul, which endured
fire and water with my people?

Take me with the Jerusalem stone
and place me in the walls
and set me in with plaster,
and out of the very walls my bones
will sing,
that pine to greet the messiah.

43

The earth grows still.
The lurid sky slowly pales
Over smoking borders.
Heartsick but still alive
A people stands by
To greet the miracle
Second to none.
Readied, they wait beneath the moon,
Wrapped in awestruck joy,
Before the light.
And now
A girl and boy step out,
And slowly walk
Before the waiting nation.
In workday clothes and heavy shoes,
Dressed for battle still,
They climb in silence.
Their dress unchanged,
Their hands still show

The filth of day's battle
And the night of fire.
Infinitely weary,
But vowing not to rest,
They wear their youth
Like dewdrops on the hair.
Silent the two approach
And stand unmoving.
No sign tells:
Do they live,
Or are they dead?
Through wondering tears,
The people asks:
Who are you?
And the silent two reply:
"We are the silver platter,
Upon which the Jewish State
Was served to you."
This said,
They fall in shadow
At the nation's feet.
In Israel's chronicles
Will the rest be told.

44

Go slowly, go slowly, O moon, upon your way. We are
sowing by your light.
Enemies rise against us from all sides, the roaring human
desires close in upon us —
And we go out to sow at night,
For we want only to sow and our soul longs for grain.

Go slowly, go slowly, O moon, upon your way.
Divided and cleft are the fields of Galilee, precious and holy
is the seed we scatter . . .
We need your light, we need your light.
Let us go, seeing but ourselves unseen.

Let our seed sprout, let not the cruel uproot it.
Make our night-sown grain grow, for the sun has surely
betrayed us,
And the days are given to destruction.

Go slowly, go slowly, O moon, on your way, do not be
alarmed by our moving shadows.
We are Hebrews who must sow our fields at night.
There is no sound in our horses' hoofs and our wagon wheels
are muffled.
Secretly, secretly we walk, the surrounding mountains do
not understand us.
You, understand our deed. Let them not plunder us.
Guard us from the stray bullet, from the knife in ambush.
Guard us from war's battle cry, from blood spilled on the
furrows.

Guard the seed we have sown, guard it from theft and from
scorching wind,
So our children eat and are satisfied.
May they rise lofty and remember us for good.
Only for them do we sow at night, for their sake our steps
anxious.
For we are Hebrews who must sow our fields at night.
Go slowly, go slowly, O moon, upon your way.

45

You have kept us alive and sustained us and brought us to
this day —
Every prophet's dream,
Every seer's vision:
A dream no more,
No longer a will-of the-wisp.
The vision is real.

With my own eyes I see
where those few,
gaunt with hunger,

so thin they cast no shadow,
dropped the seed
in the Valley of Jezreel,
And, lo!
The grain rises and grows —
The State of Israel!

46

Working is another way of praying.
You plant in Israel the soul of a tree.
You plant in the desert the spirit of gardens.

Praying is another way of singing.
You plant in the tree the soul of lemons.
You plant in the gardens the spirit of roses.

Singing is another way of loving.
You plant in the lemons the spirit of your son.
You plant in the roses the soul of your daughter.

Loving is another way of living.
You plant in your daughter the spirit of Israel.
You plant in your son the soul of the desert.

NOTES

Notes

INTRODUCTION

THE PURPOSE of the Notes is to identify the sources of the prayers, readings, and meditations contained in *Shaarei Habayit, Gates of the House*, and to draw attention to, and explain, any textual changes that have been made as well as features of the translations which require special comment. Since much in this volume derives from *Shaarei Tefillah, Gates of Prayer* (C.C.A.R., 1975), the reader of these Notes will find that they contain many references to the Notes to *Shaarei Tefillah*. The Notes to the latter volume may be found in *Shaarei Binah, Gates of Understanding*, also published by the C.C.A.R., in cooperation with the Union of American Hebrew Congregations.

In addition to the prayers and readings which *Shaarei Habayit* has borrowed from *Shaarei Tefillah*, it owes to that volume (of which it had been intended originally to be a part) its basic design and English style. Other main sources of the present volume include *Service of the Heart* (edited by Rabbis John D. Rayner and Chaim Stern for the Union of Liberal and Progressive Synagogues, London, 1967) and *The Union Home Prayerbook* (C.C.A.R., 1951), which this volume replaces. In addition, many items have been written specially for this volume by the Editor.

The Notes that follow owe much to Rabbi John D. Rayner, who compiled the Notes to *Service of the Heart*, and to Rabbi A. Stanley Dreyfus, Chairman of the C.C.A.R.'s Committee on Liturgy.

Chaim Stern

Abbreviations

BOOKS OF THE BIBLE

N.B. The references are to the Hebrew (Masoretic) division into chapters and verses, as maintained in Jewish translations of the Bible; Christian translations differ slightly in this respect.

BOOKS OF THE BIBLE

DEUT.	Deuteronomy	LEV.	Leviticus
EXOD.	Exodus	NEH.	Nehemiah
GEN.	Genesis	NUM.	Numbers
ISA.	Isaiah	PROV.	Proverbs
JER.	Jeremiah	PS., PSS.	Psalm, Psalms
	SAM.	Samuel	

OTHER ABBREVIATIONS

ABRAHAMS Dr. Israel Abrahams (1858–1925), *A Companion to the Authorised Daily Prayer Book*, Hermon Press, N. Y., 1966 (first published 1922).

ASD Rabbi A. Stanley Dreyfus

B. Babylonian Talmud

b. ben (son of)

BAER Seligman Baer: *Seder Avodat Yisrael*, Roedelheim, 1868, and often reprinted.

BER. Berachot (tractate of Mishnah, Tosefta, or Talmud)

C. Century (Common Era, unless otherwise stated)

CCAR Central Conference of American Rabbis

C.E. Common Era

CF. compare

CS Rabbi Chaim Stern

E English

ED. edited, edition, editor

E.G. for example

F., FF. following (one or two pages)

H Hebrew

IBID. in the same place

J. 'Jerusalem' Talmud

JE *The Jewish Encyclopedia*, Funk and Wagnalls Company, N. Y. and London, 1901

JR	Rabbi John D. Rayner
LOC. CIT.	in the passage cited
M.	Mishnah
MV	Machzor Vitry
P., PP.	page, pages
PB	Prayerbook
R.	Rabbi, Rav
R.H.	Rosh Hashanah (tractate of Mishnah, Tosefta, or Talmud)
SB	Rabbi Sidney Brichto
SOFERIM	'Minor Tractate' Soferim
SOH	*Service of the Heart* (1967), ed. CS and JR
SPJH	*Services and Prayers for Jewish Homes* (ULPS, 1955 ed.)
SRA	*Seder Rav Amram Gaon*, ed. Daniel Goldschmidt, Hotza'at ha-Rav Kook, Jerusalem, 1971
ST	*Shaarei Tefillah* (*Gates of Prayer*)
TRAD.	tradition, traditional, traditionally
TRSL.	translated by, translation, translator
ULPS	Union of Liberal and Progressive Synagogues (London)
UPB	*The Union Prayerbook for Jewish Worship*, Newly Revised, Part I, 1940
V., VV.	verse, verses
VOL.	volume
Y.K.	Yom Kippur (tractate of Mishnah, Tosefta, or Talmud)

Prayers and Readings

dictions. The introductory formula derives from M. Ber. 7.2;
B. Ber. 45b; 49b–50a. All four benedictions are mentioned in
B. Ber. 48b.

10   7 *Blessed is the Lord ... for all who live.* B. Ber. 48b. Contains an allusion to Ps. 136.25. See, too, Ps. 145.15f.

11   7 *For leading us out of Egypt ...* Quotes Deut. 8.10 (See B. Ber. 48b). Our version of this, the second benediction, is slightly abridged. The insertions for Chanukah and Purim are trad. See Notes to ST, Nos. 78 and 79.

12   8 *Lord our God, show compassion ...* Our version of this benediction is slightly abridged, and our trsl. somewhat free. The benediction is mentioned in B. Ber. 49a. It includes both a Sabbath ('O Lord our God, strengthen our resolve') and a Festival ('Our God ... be mindful ...') insertion, both alluded to in B. Pesachim 105a. The Festival insertion comes from the Festival *Kedushat Hayom* (See ST Notes Nos. 76 and 800). Here we add Yom Ha-atsma-ut to the insertions for the Day, and we include part of the final sentence of the '*Ya-aleh Veyavo*,' omitted elsewhere. The Hebrew which underlies our English phrase, 'Your open and generous bounty,' contains the word הגדושה, 'overflowing,' while other versions of the *Ashkenazi* liturgy print, incorrectly, הקדושה, 'holy.'

13 10 *Blessed is the Lord ... mighty Creator and Redeemer ...* A slightly abridged version of the last benediction of the Grace after Meals. This benediction is said to have been introduced at the end of the Bar Kochba revolt, 135 C.E. (B. Ber. 48b; B. Ta-anit 31a). Some parts of this benediction are, however, medieval. The phrase 'may divine and human grace and favor ...' alludes to Prov. 3.4. We have added an insertion for *Yom Ha-atsma-ut* to the other insertions in this benediction. It is derived from the trad. *Yotser.* See ST Notes Nos. 258 and 100. We have added a number of (optional) insertions to this benediction. The first four and the sixth derive from the *Sefardi* liturgy. The fifth is a composite, the first half coming from the *Sefardi* liturgy and the conclusion from SRA, p. 46. In the penultimate sentence we have added, in English, 'and all the world' (See ST Notes No. 83). The last sentence is Ps. 29.11.

14 17 *Grace after Meals (short form) ...* The *Birkat Hamazon* ('Grace after meals') was formerly much shorter than the present versions, and only grew longer in the course of time as additional passages were included. The trad. knows of a number of 'short forms' designed for particular purposes — for use by working men (B. Ber. 16a), mourners (SRA, p. 187), and for general use (Singer, *The Authorised Daily Prayer Book*, 14th ed., London, 1929, p. 286). Our version is simi-

lar to but not identical with the latter one, which is based on one which first appeared in Venice in 1603, by R. Naftali b. David Zechariah Mendel.

BLESSINGS IN PRAISE OF LIFE AND ITS CREATOR

15 19 *Blessed is the Lord our God, Ruler of the universe* ... " 'The earth is the Lord's, and all its fullness (Ps. 24.1),' but when consecrated by a benediction it becomes our privilege to enjoy it (R. Levi, in B. Ber. 36a)." We offer here a number of trad. benedictions in the light of that statement. The trad. benediction is distinguished by a formula which calls upon God and proclaims God's sovereignty (B. Ber. 40b), and which is a Rabbinic composition made up of Scriptural phrases: Ps. 119.12; Deut. 6.4; Jer. 10.10. A longer form of the benediction (adding *asher kideshanu bemitzvotav, vetzivanu*) is recited before the performance of a Mitzvah (e. g., kindling Sabbath lights); it adds these Scriptural allusions: Deut. 28.9/26.19; 33.4. We omit some trad. benedictions, especially those that occur elsewhere with some regularity in the present PBs. The sources of our benedictions are: 'bread,' M. Ber. 6.1; 'wine,' *ibid.*; 'many kinds of food,' B. Ber. 36b; 'fruit of the tree,' M. Ber. 6.1; 'fruit of the earth,' *ibid.*; 'by whose word,' M. Ber. 6.3; 'for giving us life,' B. Pesachim 7b; 'Source of creative power,' 'power and might;' 'the great sea,' M. Ber. 9.2; 'filled with beauty,' B. Ber. 58b; 'keep faith with us,' B. Ber. 59a; 'lovely trees,' B. Ber. 43b; 'You share Your wisdom,' B. Ber. 58a; 'You give of Your wisdom,' *ibid.*

16 22 *I offer You my tribute* ... The benediction of thanksgiving after recovery from illness or escape from danger is trad. recited after the completion of the Reading of the Torah and before the return of the Scroll to the Ark. It is partially cited in B. Ber. 54b. Our version of the benediction ('who bestows great goodness') is abridged. To the benediction and its response ('May the One who has been gracious ...'), we add Ps. 116.17 and *Shehecheyanu* (See ST Notes No. 661). Cf. Maimonides, *Mishneh Torah, Hilchot Berachot* 10.8.

17 22 *Blessed is the Lord* ... *the righteous Judge.* M. Ber. 9.2. *Blessed is the Lord* ... *the Source of good. Ibid.*

18 23 *The Lord shall guard* ... Freely adapted by CS from a prayer in the *Union Home Prayerbook*, p. 41. The quotations are Pss. 121.7; 139.8ff. The concluding paragraph begins with an allusion to Ps. 119.105.

No. Page

FOR A PILGRIMAGE TO ISRAEL

19 24 *I rejoiced* . . . Ps. 122.1–3, 5–9. Verse 3 is repeated to take advantage of the difference in emphasis derived from the two trsls. of that verse. Love of Zion, manifested (among other things) in pilgrimages, has been a feature of Jewish life since early times.

FOR THE NEW MOON

20 25 *Praise the Lord! Praise God* . . . Ps. 148.1, 3, 7–13, 5b–6a. *Blessed is the Lord* . . . *who renews the months.* B. Sanhedrin 42a. The ceremony of reciting a benediction upon the appearance of the new moon, also called *Kiddush Levanah,* 'Sanctification of the Moon,' is ancient. Trad., it is preferably recited at the conclusion of the Sabbath. In B. Sanhedrin 42a, it is lauded as tantamount to greeting the Divine Presence. Various Scriptural passages accompany the benediction — the practice is not uniform. Ours is a somewhat untrad. arrangement of a trad. passage.

Sabbaths, Festivals, Holy Days

WELCOMING SHABBAT

21 29 *Happy are those* . . . New, by CS. The quotation is slightly adapted from Ps. 41.2. Cf. *The Authorised Daily Prayer Book,* ed. by S. Singer, 14th Ed., London, 1929, p. 311. We include this prayer to encourage the observance of the ancient tradition of giving *tzedakah* before Sabbaths and Holidays.

22 29 *Peace be to you* . . . See ST Notes No. 294.

23 30 *As these Shabbat candles* . . . See ST Notes No. 225.

24 30 *Blessed is the Lord* . . . *the lights of Shabbat.* See ST Notes No. 190. Abrahams (p. 119) remarks that "Light and joy are a natural association . . . and as the Sabbath was a day of joy, light was its obvious concomitant." One may add that light is a basic symbol of the human soul and the divine reality, both of which are explored on Shabbat.

25 30 *May we be blessed* . . . See ST Notes No. 462.

26 30 *We thank You, O God* . . . Adapted by CS from SOH, p. 400, where it was adapted from SPJH, p. 12. It alludes to Malachi 3.24.

27   31 *A woman of valor* ... Prov. 31.10ff., 20, 25f., 28ff. Based on a new trsl. by JR, adapted by CS. A selection from the passage (Prov. 31.10–31, an alphabetical acrostic extolling the ideal wife and mother) trad. recited Friday eve by the husband, in honor of the wife. The custom seems to have originated among the mystics of sixteenth C. Safed, who recited this passage in honor of the *Shechinah* ('Divine Presence'). Only later did it come to be applied to the wife. *Blessed is the man* ... Ps. 112.1f., 4, 7–8a, 9. Ours is a somewhat free trsl., though based on the *Revised Standard Version* of the Bible. This alphabetical acrostic extols the ideal man in terms similar to those of the passage from Prov. 31 discussed above. Its use here as the reciprocal of Prov. 31 is an innovation of the present PB (Ps. 112 is not found in the trad. liturgy). Either of these passages might, in the absence of a parent, be recited by a son or daughter. *May God bless you* ... Though the concept of the parental blessing plays an important part already in the Bible (e. g., Gen. 27 and 48f.), as a regular practice on the eve of the Sabbath and of Festivals it is first attested in an ethical treatise (*Brautspiegel*) of the year 1602 (David Philipson in JE, Vol. III, p. 243). There is, however, a reference to the custom in Soferim 18.5. Our first passage is from SOH, p. 401, which adapted it from SPJH, p. 13. Our second is trad. (See Gen. 48.20). Our third passage is Num. 6.24ff.; cf. ST Notes No. 843.

28   33 *Six days shall you labor* ... New, by CS. Based on UPB, p. 93 (Cf. SOH, p. 401). The quotation is Exod. 20.9f.

29   33 *Now the whole universe* ... Gen. 2.1ff. Trad. recited before the Kiddush only at home. See ST Notes No. 214.

30   34 *Blessed is the Lord* ... *Creator of the fruit of the vine.* The benediction to be said before drinking wine (M. Ber. 6.1). Wine is a symbol of joy (Cf. Ps. 104.15); and since the Sabbath is a day of joy (Cf. Isa. 58.13), wine became associated especially with the Sabbath. Thus the commandment: 'Remember the Sabbath day and sanctify it' (Exod. 20.8), was taken by the Rabbis to mean 'Remember it over wine' (B. Pesachim 106a). So originated the ritual of the *Kiddush*, which is short for *Kiddush Hayom*, 'the Sanctification of the Day.' It consists of the blessing over the wine, followed by a prayer giving thanks for the Sabbath and proclaiming its sanctity. The Mishnah (e. g., M. Ber. 8.1) testifies to its antiquity. It was and is essentially a *home* rite, preceding the evening meal; but the practice of reciting *Kiddush* also in the synagogue (originally for the benefit of travellers who might eat and sleep there) began already in Talmudic times (B. Pesachim 101a). Rav Amram quotes

his predecessor, Natronai Gaon, to the effect that 'they make *Kiddush* in the synagogues even when no travellers are present who eat there' (SRA, p. 65). Today this is the general practice.

31 34 *Blessed is the Lord ... for the Sabbath and its holiness.* See preceding Note. The essential themes of this prayer are stipulated in B. Pesachim 117b. The full text, practically as now, appears in SRA, p. 66.

32 34 *Blessed is the Lord ... from the earth.* See No. 7.

33 35 *For the Morning of Shabbat ...* See Notes to ST, No. 1150.

SONGS FOR SHABBAT

34 36 *Songs for Shabbat ...* See Notes to ST, Notes to Songs, Nos. 8, 13, 14, 15, 17, 22, 29, 43, 39, and 44.

WELCOMING YOM TOV

35 41 *Happy are those ...* See No. 29.

36 41 *We praise You ... the Source of light ...* SOH, p. 403, where it was slightly adapted from SPJH, p. 9.

37 41 *Blessed is the Lord ... Yom Tov.* See ST Notes No. 765. The kindling of light to inaugurate a Festival follows naturally from the similar custom of kindling light to welcome the Sabbath. See No. 24.

38 42 *We thank You, O God ...* See No. 26.

39 42 *May God bless you ...* See No. 27 (last nine lines).

40 43 *Pesach teaches us ...* Slightly adapted from SOH, p. 404, where it is new, by SB, and based on SPJH, pp. 65 and 77.

41 43 *Shavuot teaches us ...* Adapted by CS from a prayer by SB in SOH, pp. 404f.

42 43 *Sukkot teaches us ...* Adapted from SOH, p. 405, where it is new, by SB.

43 44 *This festival teaches us ...* Adapted from SOH, pp. 406f., where it is new, by SB.

44 45 *Now the whole universe ...* Gen. 2.1ff. See No. 29.

45 45 *Blessed is the Lord ... and the Festivals.* The custom of reciting *Kiddush* over a cup of wine on the eve of Festivals, as on Sabbath eve (See No. 30), was well established in the days of the Talmud (Cf. B. Pesachim 105a). The prescribed text is partly cited in Soferim 19.3 and is found fully (almost as now) in SRA, p. 173.

46 46 *Blessed is the Lord ... this season.* See ST Notes No. 661.

47 46 *Blessed is the Lord ... from the earth.* See No. 7.

48 46 *Blessed is the Lord ... in the Sukkah.* Cited in B. Sukkah 46a. Alludes to Lev. 23.42.

49 47 *For the morning of Yom Tov ...* See ST Notes No. 1152.

No. Page

WELCOMING ROSH HASHANAH

50 49 *Happy are those* ... See No. 21.

51 49 *With the setting* ... A revision by CS of a prayer by Malcolm Stern and CS in *Gate of Repentance*, ed. CS and JR, London, 1973, p. 15. It alludes to Ps. 43.3.

52 49 *Blessed is the Lord* ... *Yom Tov*. See No. 37.

53 50 *May God bless you* ... See No. 39.

54 51 *The observance of Rosh Hashanah* ... Slightly adapted from *Gate of Repentance* (ULPS, London, 1973), where it is new, by CS. It introduces the *Kiddush*, 'Sanctification.' *Kiddush* is essentially a domestic rite, preceding the meal on the eve of Rosh Hashanah, though the practice of reciting it also in the Synagogue, preceding the *Aleinu* (See Notes to ST, No. 978) is ancient (Cf. No. 30). It is, however, not essential that it be recited in the Synagogue, and some authorities have actually opposed it on that ground that *Kiddush* should be recited only where one eats. It follows, however, that the recitation of *Kiddush* in the home is regarded by the tradition as mandatory. *Now the whole universe* ... Gen. 2.1ff. See No. 29. *Blessed is the Lord* ... See No. 30. *Blessed is the Lord* ... *the Day of Remembrance.* The R.H. *Kiddush* is largely identical with the version for other Festivals that is already mentioned in the Talmud (B. Pesachim 105a). The earliest reference specifically to the R.H. version is Soferim 19.4. Our text is virtually the trad. one, omitting two words that are trad. inserted when R.H. coincides with Shabbat. *Blessed is the Lord* ... *this season.* See ST Notes No. 661. *Blessed is the Lord* ... *from the earth.* See No. 7. *Blessed is the Lord* ... *fruit of the tree.* See No. 15. The custom of eating sweet things on R.H. eve, as a 'good omen,' goes back to Gaonic times (See H. Schauss, *The Jewish Festivals*, p. 158 and Note 167). According to MV, the Jews of France used to eat red apples. The custom of eating sweet apples with honey is first mentioned in *Sefer Maharil* (a compendium of laws and customs by R. Jacob Moellin, who lived in the Rhineland, 1365–1427), p. 38a. Cf. also Neh. 8.10. *Lord our God* ... Also first cited in *Sefer Maharil, loc. cit.*

55 54 *For the Morning of Rosh Hashanah* ... Our version of the R.H. morning *Kiddush* is slightly more full than the trad. one, to whose contents we add Num. 10.10. The other (and trad.) Scriptural vv. are Exod. 31.16f. and Ps. 81.4f. *Blessed is the Lord* ... *fruit of the vine.* See No. 30. *Blessed is the Lord* ... *from the earth.* See No. 7.

No. Page

THE SUKKAH

86 75 *Lord, who may abide* ... See ST Note No. 292. The ritual for building a Sukkah is an innovation of this pb.

87 76 *Eternal Lord* ... New, by CS. It refers to a prayer trad. recited in
the Sukkah deriving from a compendium of mystical prayers
called *Shaarei Zion* by Nathan b. Moses Hannover, Prague, 1662.
See Singer, *op. cit.*, p. 232.

88 76 *Blessed is the Lord* ... *of the Sukkah.* New, by CS.

89 76 *Blessed is the Lord* ... *this season.* See Notes to ST, No. 661.

WELCOMING GUESTS IN THE SUKKAH

90 77 *Lord our God* ... Adapted from the prayer by Nathan b. Moses
cited in No. 87.

91 77 *Abraham, exalted guest* ... By Isaac Luria (1534–1572; known as
the holy *Ari*, 'Lion,' Luria was the leading Safed Kabbalist). To
the seven male 'guests' of the trad. passage, we have added seven
equivalent female guests. On each day, all are 'invited,' but a different pair receives the first invitation and serves, as it were, as
the leader.

92 78 *I take Lulav and Etrog* ... Based on a meditation in *Shaarei Zion*
(See No. 87). *Blessed is the Lord* ... *the Lulav.* See ST Note No. 847.

THANKSGIVING DAY

93 79 *Lord of the universe* ... Adapted by CS from a prayer in the *Union
Home Prayerbook*, pp. 29f. *Hamotsi* ... *We give thanks* ... *Blessed
is the Lord* ... *from the earth.* See No. 7.

CHANUKAH

94 80 *The lights of Chanukah* ... See Notes to ST, No. 1019.

95 80 *Blessed is the match* ... See Notes to ST, No. 675.

96 80 *Zion hears and is glad* ... Ps. 97.8.

97 80 *Within living memory* ... See Notes to ST, No. 1022.

98 80 *Let the lights we kindle* ... See Notes to ST, No. 1023.

99 81 *Blessed is the Lord* ... *the Chanukah lights.* Cited in B. Shabbat 23a.

100 81 *Blessed is the Lord* ... *who performed wondrous deeds* ... See Notes
to ST, No. 1025.

101 81 *Blessed is the Lord* ... *this season.* See Notes to ST, No. 1026.

102 81 *The people who walked in darkness* ... See Notes to ST, No. 1027.

The Path of Life

PSALMS FOR REFLECTION

105 89 *Lord, how many* . . . Ps. 3.2–7a, 8a, 9. In a number of instances we trsl. 3rd person H by 2nd person E. This results in a somewhat more 'normal' English style, and it enables us, in these instances, to avoid the unnecessary use of the masculine pronoun.

106 89 *When I call* . . . Ps. 4.2–9. In v. 7, we trsl. נסה as 'fled,' in agreement with the New English Bible. Others have 'lift up,' presumably from נשא.

107 90 *Lord, give ear* . . . Ps. 5.2–13. In v. 7, we render the 3rd person H by a 2nd person E trsl., to make it conform to the rest of the Psalm. See No. 105.

108 91 *In the Lord* . . . Ps. 11 (with the superscription omitted). Several 3rd person H words are trsl. in the 2nd person. See No. 105.

109 91 *Help, Lord* . . . Ps. 12.2–9. Several 3rd person H words are trsl. in the 2nd person (See No. 105). Verses 8 and 9 have been reversed to make for smoother English.

110 92 *Lord, must I still* . . . Ps. 13.2–6.

111 92 *Sin speaks* . . . Ps. 36.2–13. The trsl. is somewhat free, a device to make sense out of H that is sometimes obscure. In vv. 2–5, we trsl. a number of H singular words by plural E (See No. 105). Verses 2f. are obscure, and the trsl. presupposes an emendation of לבי to לבו (which we then render in the plural in accordance with our general pattern in these Psalm trsls.). In v. 9, our trsl. uses a 1st person plural pronoun in place of the 3rd person plural, to effect a smooth transition from v. 8.

BEGINNING A NEW ENTERPRISE

112 94 *Unless the Lord* . . . Adapted by CS from a prayer in the *Union Home Prayerbook*, pp. 43f. The quotation is from Ps. 127.1.

AT A TIME OF SUCCESS

113 95 *You are the strength of my hands* . . . Adapted by CS from the *Union Home Prayerbook*, pp. 188f., 131.

AT A TIME OF DISAPPOINTMENT

114 96 *O God of love* ... New, by CS. It is based on two prayers in the *Union Home Prayerbook*, pp. 102, 184.

ON LIFE WITH OTHERS

115 97 *O God, when I am estranged* ... New, by CS. It is based on two prayers in the *Union Home Prayerbook*, pp. 139, 157ff.

ON REACHING THE AGE OF RETIREMENT

116 98 *As I look back* ... New, by CS. Based on a meditation by Morris Lazaron in UPB II, pp. 215ff. In the penultimate paragraph, the conclusion ('... the spirit of wisdom ... reverence for God.') is a quotation from Isa. 11.2. The Isa. passage is utilized in a prayer trad. recited during the Torah Ritual on Sabbaths and Festivals, deriving from *Shaarei Zion* (See No. 87).

MARRIAGE PRAYERS

117 100 *I am about to enter* ... New, by CS. Based in part on two prayers in the *Union Home Prayerbook*, pp. 45f.

118 100 *In mercy* ... New, by CS. We offer this prayer especially for those who, their first marriage having failed, are about to remarry.

119 101 *How can I give thanks enough* ... New, by CS. Based on two prayers in the *Union Home Prayerbook*, pp. 47–50.

120 101 *I am my beloved's* ... New, by CS. Based on a prayer in the *Union Home Prayerbook*, p. 32. The quotation is from Song of Songs 2.16, slightly adapted.

121 102 *In the fullness* ... Slightly adapted by CS from a prayer in the *Union Home Prayerbook*, pp. 32f. *We give thanks ... day of joy. Amen.* See ST Notes No. 661.

CONSECRATION OF A HOUSE

122 103 *In the spirit of our Jewish faith* ... SOH, p. 425, where it comes, slightly adapted, from SPJH, p. 143. The practice of consecrating a new house may have existed already in Biblical times; see Deut. 20.5. According to the Mishnah (M. Ber. 9.3) a person who builds a new house says the *Shehecheyanu* (ST Notes No. 661). The Palestinian Talmud (J. Ber. 9.4) mentions a benediction, similar to the

trad. one, to be recited when affixing a Mezuzah. Both ideas are combined in our service.

123 103 *Hear, O Israel* ... See ST Notes No. 55. Included here, following SOH (although it does not trad. belong to this ceremony) because it stresses the duty to 'speak of them in your home,' and because it alludes to the Mezuzah.

124 104 *Our homes have always been the dwelling place* ... Freely adapted by CS from *Rabbi's Manual*, CCAR, pp. 50f. The quotation is an adaptation of M. Avot 3.3. On the benediction, see No. 7.

125 104 *Wine is a symbol of joy* ... Adapted from *Rabbi's Manual*, CCAR, beginning with an allusion to Ps. 104.15. On the benediction, see No. 30.

126 104 *The Torah has been our life* ... New, by CS (Cf. *Rabbi's Manual*, CCAR, p. 52). On the benediction, see ST Notes No. 93.

127 105 *Lord, who may abide* ... Ps. 15. See ST Notes No. 292.

128 106 *This ancient symbol* ... Adapted by CS from SOH, p. 426, where it is adapted from *Rabbi's Manual*, CCAR, pp. 52f. On the benediction itself, see No. 122. The word *Mezuzah* means 'doorpost,' but it has come mainly to signify the scroll containing Deut. 6.4–9; 11.13–21 which is placed in a cylindrical case. The word *Shaddai*, 'Almighty' is inscribed on the back of the scroll, so that it can be seen through an aperture in the case, or it is inscribed on the case itself. *Shaddai* is, in its present use, sometimes interpreted as an acronym for *Shomeir Daletot Yisrael*, 'Guardian of the doors (i. e., dwellings) of Israel.' According to Maimonides (*Mishneh Torah, Hilchot Mezuzah* 6.13), the sole purpose of the *Mezuzah* is to serve as a reminder of the unity of God.

129 106 *Blessed is the Lord* ... *this happy day.* See ST Notes No. 661.

130 106 *Unless the Lord* ... Ps. 127.1a.

131 106 *In this awareness* ... Slightly adapted from SOH, p. 428, where it was adapted from A. Minda, *The Sanctuary of the Home*, pp. 7f., and from SPJH, p. 143. The quotations are Num. 24.5 and Ps. 121.8.

ON BEHALF OF A WOMAN IN CHILDBIRTH

132 108 *Lord of all generations* ... Adapted by CS from a prayer in the *Union Home Prayerbook*, p. 50.

ON THE BIRTH OR ADOPTION OF A CHILD

133 109 *We give thanks* ... Freely adapted by CS from two prayers in the *Union Home Prayerbook*, pp. 51f. On the opening benediction, see ST Notes No. 661.

No. Page

ON THE BIRTH OR ADOPTION OF
A GRANDCHILD

134 110 *Blessed is the Lord ... We are thankful ...* New, by CS. Suggested by a prayer in SPJH, pp. 198f. On the opening benediction, see ST Notes No. 661.

THE COVENANT OF MILAH

135 111 *May he who comes be blessed ...* From Ps. 118.26. The opening words of the circumcision service since the 14th C.

136 111 *The rite of circumcision ...* Partly adapted by CS from *Rabbi's Manual*, CCAR, p. 9, and incorporating Gen. 17.9, 12a; Gen. 17.1, and an allusion to Deut. 30.6.

137 111 *Lord, You established a testimony ...* Ps. 78.5–6a. *You are for ever mindful ...* Ps. 105.8ff. (The trsls. of both of the preceding passages are slightly adapted.) *O give thanks to the Lord ...* Ps. 118.1.

138 112 *Blessed is the Lord ... Mitzvah of circumcision ... Covenant of Abraham.* Both of these benedictions are found in Tosefta Ber. 7.12. *Blessed is the Lord ... fruit of the vine.* Already in SRA, p. 179. Cf. No. 30.

139 112 *Our God and God of our people ...* Attested since the 14th C. Cf. Baer, p. 583.

140 113 *May the One who blessed ...* From *Rabbi's Manual*, CCAR, p. 12. The trsl. is influenced by the latter and by SOH, pp. 430f.

141 113 *The Lord bless you ...* Num. 6.24ff. Cf. ST Notes No. 843.

142 113 *O God, we give thanks ...* Freely adapted by CS from *Rabbi's Manual*, CCAR, pp. 12f.

THE COVENANT OF LIFE

In accordance with the principle of the equality of the sexes, for which Reform Judaism has long stood, and which has most recently been affirmed by the CCAR at its convention in June, 1975, we offer a ceremony prepared by CS, entitled 'The Covenant of Life' (ברית חיים) as the feminine equivalent of The Covenant of Milah, above.

143 114 *May she who comes be blessed ...* Ps. 118.28, adapted. Cf. No. 135.

144 114 *Reverence for life ...* New, by CS, quoting Deut. 30.19.

145 114 *Joyfully I bring ...* New, by CS. *Blessed is the Lord ... to sanctify life.* New, by CS.

146 114 *I, the Lord, have made you ...* Isa. 42.6, slightly adapted.

147 114 *For the Mitzvah* ... Prov. 6.23a.

148 114 *Blessed ... world.* The concluding eulogy of a bed-time prayer cited in B. Ber. 60b.

149 115 *Blessed is the Lord ... this day of joy.* See ST Notes No. 661.

150 115 *This is the day ...* Ps. 118.24. The use of this and the preceding passage in the present context was suggested by Michael Isaacson.

151 115 *Lord, You established a testimony ...* Ps. 78.5–6a. *You are for ever mindful ...* Ps. 105.8ff. The trsls. of both the preceding passages are slightly adapted. *O give thanks to the Lord ...* Ps. 118.1. Cf. No. 137.

152 116 *Blessed is the Lord ... fruit of the vine.* See No. 30. Cf. No. 138.

153 116 *Our God, God of all the generations ...* See No. 139. Here we have changed the masculine references to the feminine.

154 116 *May the One who blessed ...* See No. 140. Here we have changed the masculine references to the feminine.

155 116 *The Lord bless you ...* Num. 6.22ff. Cf. ST Notes No. 843.

156 117 *O God, we give thanks ...* See No. 142. Here we have changed the masculine references to the feminine.

FOR THE NAMING OF A CHILD

157 118 *God and Creator ...* Very slightly adapted from SOH, p. 432, where it is adapted from *Rabbi's Manual*, CCAR, p. 14, and SPJH, p. 151. The custom of having such a service of thanksgiving after childbirth has been known since the 15th C.; cf. Abrahams, p. 223. The underlying idea can be traced back to Lev. 12.6ff. and I Sam. 1.24. On the *naming* of a child, see H. Schauss, *The Lifetime of a Jew*, pp. 12f., 27ff., 43f., 51ff. Trad. a boy is named at his circumcision, and a girl on the first or fourth Sabbath after birth. In Reform congregations both girls and boys (even though the boy was previously named at his circumcision, and the girl at her *Berit Chayim*) are named and blessed in the synagogue shortly after birth. If desired, the ceremony may be conducted in the home.

158 118 *Blessed is the Lord ... whose love and kindness ...* The present version of this benediction differs from the trad. text; for that text (and a correspondingly different trsl.), see No. 16.

159 118 *Blessed is the Lord ... this happy day.* See ST Notes No. 661.

160 118 *O God, for the gift ...* Adapted by CS from SOH, p. 433, where it is adapted from SPJH, pp. 150f.

161 119 *May the One who blessed ...* Adapted by CS from SOH, pp. 434f., where it is adapted from *Rabbi's Manual*, CCAR, p. 14. It is a somewhat condensed version of the Hebrew that precedes it.

No. Page

162 120 *The Lord bless you* ... Num. 6.24ff. Cf. ST Notes No. 843.
163 120 *Blessed is the Lord* ... *fruit of the vine.* See No. 30.

AT A BIRTHDAY CELEBRATION

164 121 *God of days and years* ... Slightly adapted by CS from a prayer in the *Union Home Prayerbook*, p. 31. *Blessed is the Lord* ... *this day.* See Notes to ST, No. 661. *Blessed is the Lord* ... *many kinds of food.* B. Ber. 36b. See No. 15.

ON THE BEGINNING OF A CHILD'S RELIGIOUS EDUCATION

165 122 *Set these words* ... Adapted by CS from a prayer in the *Union Home Prayerbook*, pp. 55f. The quotations are from Deut. 6.6f.; Ps. 8.3a (slightly adapted).

AT BAR MITZVAH, BAT MITZVAH, OR CONFIRMATION

166 123 *And all your children* ... Adapted by CS from a prayer in the *Union Home Prayerbook*, pp. 57f. The quotation is from Isa. 54.13. On *Blessed is the Lord* ... *this great day*, see Notes to ST, No. 661.

ON ENTERING COLLEGE

167 124 *You favor us with knowledge* ... New, by CS. On the opening quotation, see ST Notes No. 63. In the second paragraph, "Teach me ... our own age," is based on UPB, p. 34. The final sentence alludes to Ps. 119.103.

IN ILLNESS AND ON RECOVERY

These prayers are adapted by CS and ASD from a series issued on cards by the CCAR, 1963. For the concluding eulogy, see ST Notes No. 67.

168 125 *In sickness I turn to You* ... Card No. 8.
169 125 *My God and God of all generations* ... Card No. 14. The quotation is Ps. 118.17.
170 126 *Loving God, Your healing power* ... Card No. 21.
171 126 *For health of body and of spirit* ... Card No. 20.
172 127 *O God, help me* ... Card No. 25.

Weekday Services

MORNING SERVICE

EVENING OR MORNING SERVICE

Concluding Prayers

Additional Prayers

Poems and Prayers

No. Page

334 234 *This is the discipline* . . . By Charles Reznikoff, *By The Waters of Manhattan, op. cit.*, pp. 97f.

335 235 *Divine Sanctuary* . . . By Chaim Nachman Bialik (See ST Notes No. 319), from *Al Saf Beit Hamidrash*, in *Kol Kitvei C. N. Bialik* (Dvir, Tel Aviv, 5711), pp. 6f. Trsl. David Polish.

336 236 *Where has this week vanished* . . . By David Polish.

337 236 *Now from the world* . . . By Robert Nathan, from *A Winter Tide* (Alfred A. Knopf, Inc., N. Y., 1935).

338 237 *When the departing* . . . By Kenneth Slade Alling, 'A Presence,' from *The Bowling Green, an Anthology of Verse*, selected by C. Morley (Doubleday, Page & Co., N. Y., 1924).

339 237 *They list for me* . . . Anonymous.

340 238 *It may be so* . . . A Sonnet, by John Masefield, in *Collected Poems* (MacMillan Co., Publishers, London).

341 238 *What fills the heart* . . . From 'Heritage,' by Theodore Spencer, in *An Act of Life* (Harvard University Press).

342 239 *Mourn not the dead* . . . By Ralph Chaplin, in *Bars and Shadows*, 1921.

343 239 *They are not gone* . . . 'Sonnet: Our Dead,' by Robert Nichols, in *Ardours and Endurance* (Chatto & Windus, 1917; now Collins-Publishers, London).

344 240 *Shall I cry out* . . . Slightly adapted from a reading by Morris Adler. Suggested by Roland B. Gittelsohn.

345 241 *Will there yet come* . . . By Leah Goldberg (1911–); Lithuania-Palestine/Israel), trsl. R. F. Mintz, in *Modern Hebrew Poetry*, p. 248.

346 241 *i thank You God* . . . By e. e. cummings, from *Selected Poems, 1923–1958*.

347 242 *I will lift up my hands* . . . By Amy K. Blank.

348 242 *O the Chimneys* . . . By Nelly Sachs (See ST Notes No. 918). She begins by quoting Job 19.26, in the trsl. of the *Authorised* (King James) *Version* of the Bible. The JPS trsl. renders this difficult v. as follows: "And when after my skin this [dust] is destroyed, then without my flesh shall I see God."

349 243 *The first ones* . . . By Yitzchak Katzenelson.

350 244 *But who emptied* . . . By Nelly Sachs, *op. cit.*, p. 9.

351 245 *We orphans* . . . By Nelly Sachs, *ibid.*, pp. 29f.

352 245 *Why the black answer of hate* . . . By Nelly Sachs, *ibid.*, pp. 65f.

353 247 *The heaviest wheel* . . . Attributed to MIF in *I Never Saw Another Butterfly: Children's Drawings and Poems from Terezin Concentration Camp, 1942–1944*. McGraw-Hill, Inc., Publishers, N. Y., 1964.

354 247 *Black milk of dawn* . . . 'Death Fugue,' by Paul Celan (1920–1970, Russia-France). Trsl. by Albert Friedlander, in *Pointer* (quarterly journal of the ULPS), Vol. VII, No. 1.

Scriptural Readings

SCRIPTURAL READINGS

A Table of Scriptural Readings

THE READINGS given in this Table for the fifty-four sidrot into which the Torah is divided, and for the corresponding haftarot, are those prescribed by tradition. Occasionally the Sefardi rite differs from the Ashkenazi in the choice of haftarah. In those instances the Sefardi reading is given in parentheses. Alternative readings are suggested for the haftarot and for several sidrot.

On Shabbat afternoon, and Monday and Thursday mornings, the first parasha of the sidra for the coming Shabbat is read. This parasha is indicated in the Table by an asterisk.

In some years several or all of the following sidrot are combined: Vayak-heil-Pikudei, Tazria-Metsora, Acharei-Kedoshim, Behar-Bechukotai, Chukat-Balak, Matot-Masei, Nitsavim-Vayeilech. When this occurs, read the haftarah assigned to the second sidra, except that when Nitsavim-Vayeilech are joined, Isaiah 61.10–63.9 (the haftarah for Nitsavim) is the traditional reading.

The readings given for holidays are in accordance with the practice of the Reform synagogue.

For those congregations which conduct daily services, readings have been suggested for the intermediate days of Sukkot and Pesach, as well as for Chanukah, Pruim, and Tish'a be-Av.

In the traditional synagogue, appropriate selections from two Sifrei Torah are read on holidays and special Sabbaths, and, on rare occasions, selections from three are read. Some of these selections have been indicated in the Table. Choice may be made from the regular weekly portion, from the special reading or readings for the day, or excerpts from all may be read.

Reform Jews throughout the world observe Pesach and Sukkot for seven days, and Shavuot and Shemini Atzeret-Simchat Torah for one day. This is also the practice in traditional congregations in Israel. Traditional Jews in the Diaspora add an extra day to these festivals. When, in the Diaspora, the eighth day of Pesach or the second day of Shavuot falls on Shabbat, Reform congregations read the sidra assigned to the following week in the standard religious calendars. However, in order to preserve uniformity in the reading of the Torah throughout the entire community, it is suggested that on these occasions, the sidra be spread over two weeks, one portion to be read while traditional congregations are observing the festival, and another portion to be read the following Shabbat.

	Torah	Haftarah
בראשית	Genesis 1.1–6.8	Isaiah 42.5–43.11 (42.5–21) Psalm 19.1–15 Psalm 104.1–30 Psalm 139.1–18 Job 38.1–11
	*Genesis 1.1–13	
נח	Genesis 6.9–11.32	Isaiah 54.1–55.5 (54.1–10) Isaiah 14.12–20 Isaiah 44.1–8 Jeremiah 31.31–36 Zephaniah 3.9–20 Psalm 104.24–35
	*Genesis 6.9–22	
לך לך	Genesis 12.1–17.27	Isaiah 40.27–41.16 Joshua 24.1–14 Isaiah 51.1–16 Joel 2.21–3.2 Psalm 105.1–15
	*Genesis 12.1–13	
וירא	Genesis 18.1–22.24	II Kings 4.1–37 (4.1–23) Ezekiel 18.1–32 Micah 6.1–8 Psalm 111.1–10 Job 5.17–27
	*Genesis 18.1–14	
חיי שרה	Genesis 23.1–25.18	I Kings 1.1–31 Jeremiah 32.1–27 Psalm 15.1–5 Psalm 45.1–18 Proverbs 31.10–31
	*Genesis 23.1–16	

	Torah	*Haftarah*
תולדות	Genesis 25.19–28.9	*Malachi 1.1–2.7* *I Kings 5.15–26* *Psalm 5.1–13* *Proverbs 4.1–23*
	*Genesis 25.19–26.5	
ויצא	Genesis 28.10–32.3	*Hosea 12.13–14.10* *(11.7–12.12)* *I Samuel 1.1–28* *I Kings 19.1–12* *Jeremiah 31.1–17* *Psalm 27.1–14* *Psalm 62.1–9* *Psalm 139.1–18* *Proverbs 2.1–9* *Ruth 4.9–17*
	*Genesis 28.10–22	
וישלח	Genesis 32.4–36.43	*Hosea 11.7–12.12* *(Obadiah 1.1–21)* *Isaiah 44.6–21* *Isaiah 45.1–7* *Jeremiah 10.1–16* *Jeremiah 31.10–26* *Psalm 27.1–14* *Psalm 37.1–40*
	*Genesis 32.4–13	
וישב	Genesis 37.1–40.23	*Amos 2.6–3.8* *I Kings 3.5–15* *Psalm 34.1–23* *Psalm 63.1–12*
	*Genesis 37.1–11	
מקץ	Genesis 41.1–44.17	*I Kings 3.15–4.1* *Judges 7.2–23* *Isaiah 19.19–25* *Psalm 67.1–8* *Proverbs 10.1–7* *Daniel 2.1–23*
	*Genesis 41.1–14	

	Torah	*Haftarah*
ויגש	Genesis 44.18–47.27	*Ezekiel 37.15–28*
		Amos 8.4–11
		Psalm 71.1–24
		Psalm 72.1–20
	*Genesis 44.18–30	
ויחי	Genesis 47.28–50.26	*I Kings 2.1–12*
		Psalm 22.24–32
		Job 5.17–27
		Ecclesiastes 12.1–14
		I Chronicles 28.1–10
	*Genesis 47.28–48.9	
שמות	Exodus 1.1–6.1	*Isaiah 27.6–28.13; 29.22–23*
		(Jeremiah 1.1–2.3)
		I Samuel 3.1–21
		Isaiah 6.1–13
		Joel 2.21–3.2
	*Exodus 1.1–17	
וארא	Exodus 6.2–9.35	*Ezekiel 28.25–29.21*
		Isaiah 42.5–17
		Isaiah 52.1–10
		Jeremiah 1.1–10
		Ezekiel 31.1–12
		Psalm 78.38–55
	*Exodus 6.2–13	
בא	Exodus 10.1–13.16	*Jeremiah 46.13–28*
		Isaiah 19.19–25
		Psalm 105.7–45
		Ezra 6.16–22
	*Exodus 10.1–11	
בשלח	Exodus 13.17–17.16	*Judges 4.4–5.31*
		(5.1–31)
		Joshua 4.4–18
		Isaiah 63.7–16
		Psalm 78.1–29
		Psalm 106.1–12
		Psalm 124.1–8
	*Exodus 13.17–14.8	

	Torah	*Haftarah*
יתרו	Exodus 18.1–20.23	*Isaiah 6.1–7.6; 9.5–6*
		(6.1–13)
		I Kings 3.3–15
		Isaiah 43.1–12
		Jeremiah 7.1–23
		Jeremiah 31.23–36
		Psalm 19.1–15
	*Exodus 18.1–12	
משפטים	Exodus 21.1–24.18	*Jeremiah 34.8–22; 33.25–26*
		Jeremiah 17.5–14
		Amos 5.6–24
	*Exodus 21.1–19	
תרומה	Exodus 25.1–27.19	*I Kings 5.26–6.13*
		I Kings 7.51–8.21
		I Kings 8.22–43
		I Chronicles 22.1–13
	*Exodus 25.1–16	
תצוה	Exodus 27.20–30.10	*Ezekiel 43.10–27*
		Joshua 24.1–28
		Isaiah 61.1–11
		Isaiah 65.17–66.2
		Psalm 42.1–12
		Psalm 43.1–5
	*Exodus 27.20–28.12	
כי תשא	Exodus 30.11–34.35	*I Kings 18.1–39*
		(18.20–39)
		Jeremiah 31.31–36
		Ezekiel 20.1–20
		Psalm 27.1–14
		Psalm 81.1–17
		Psalm 106.1–23
	*Exodus 30.11–22	

	Torah	*Haftarah*
ויקהל	Exodus 35.1–38.20	*I Kings 7.40–50*
		(7.13–26)
		I Chronicles 29.9–20
	*Exodus 35.1–20	
פקודי	Exodus 38.21–40.38	*I Kings 7.51–8.21*
		(7.40–50)
		I Kings 8.10–30
		II Chronicles 5.1–14
	*Exodus 38.21–39.1	
ויקרא	Leviticus 1.1–5.26	*Isaiah 43.21–44.23*
		Isaiah 1.10–20, 27
		Isaiah 33.13–22
		Psalm 50.1–23
	*Leviticus 1.1–13	
צו	Leviticus 6.1–8.36	*Jeremiah 7.21–8.3; 9.22–23*
		Hosea 6.1–6
		Malachi 1.6–14; 2.1–7
		Malachi 3.1–6
	*Leviticus 6.1–11	
שמיני	Leviticus 9.1–11.47	*II Samuel 6.1–7.17*
		(6.1–19)
		Isaiah 61.1–11
		Psalm 39.1–14
		Psalm 51.1–21
		Psalm 73.1–28
		Daniel 1.1–21
	*Leviticus 9.1–16	
תזריע	Leviticus 12.1–13.59	*II Kings 4.42–5.19*
		Job 2.1–10
	*Leviticus 12.1–13.5	
	Deuteronomy 12.28–13.5	

	Torah	*Haftarah*
מצרע	Leviticus 14.1–15.33	*II Kings 7.3–20* *Psalm 103.1–22* *Proverbs 10.11–23*
	*Leviticus 14.1–12 Deuteronomy 26.12–19	
אחרי מות	Leviticus 16.1–18.30	*Ezekiel 22.1–19* *(22.1–16)* *Isaiah 58.1–14* *Isaiah 59.1–21* *Ezekiel 22.17–31*
	*Leviticus 16.1–17	
קדשים	Leviticus 19.1–20.27	*Amos 9.7–15* *(Ezekiel 20.2–20)* *Jeremiah 22.1–9, 13–16* *Psalm 15.1–5* *Job 29.1–17*
	*Leviticus 19.1–14	
אמר	Leviticus 21.1–24.23	*Ezekiel 44.15–31* *Isaiah 56.1–8* *Ezekiel 36.16–28* *Malachi 1.1–14* *Nehemiah 8.1–18*
	*Leviticus 21.1–15	
בהר	Leviticus 25.1–26.2	*Jeremiah 32.6–27* *Jeremiah 31.1–13* *Jeremiah 34.8–16* *Nehemiah 5.1–13*
	*Leviticus 25.1–13	
בחקתי	Leviticus 26.3–27.34	*Jeremiah 16.19–17.14* *Zephaniah 3.1–20* *Psalm 116.1–19* *Job 36.1–15*
	*Leviticus 26.3–13	

289

	Torah	*Haftarah*
במדבר	Numbers 1.1–4.20	Hosea 2.1–22
		II Samuel 24.1–14
		Malachi 2.4–10
		Psalm 107.1–16
		I Chronicles 15.1–15
	*Numbers 1.1–19	
נשא	Numbers 4.21–7.89	Judges 13.2–25
		Judges 16.4–21
		Jeremiah 35.1–19
		Psalm 67.1–8
		Ezra 3.8–13
	*Numbers 4.21–33	
בהעלתך	Numbers 8.1–12.16	Zechariah 2.14–4.7
		Joel 2.21–3.5
		Psalm 68.1–11, 33–36
		Psalm 77.1–21
		Psalm 81.1–11
		II Chronicles 5.1–14
	*Numbers 8.1–14	
שלח לך	Numbers 13.1–15.41	Joshua 2.1–24
		Joshua 14.6–14
		Jeremiah 17.19–18.8
		Ezekiel 20.1–22
		Psalm 106.1–27, 44–48
	*Numbers 13.1–20	
קרח	Numbers 16.1–18.32	I Samuel 11.14–12.22
		Judges 9.1–21
		Isaiah 56.1–8
		Psalm 106.13–46
	*Numbers 16.1–13	
חקת	Numbers 19.1–22.1	Judges 11.1–33
		Ezekiel 36.21–38
		Psalm 42.1–12
		Psalm 78.1–24
	*Numbers 19.1–17	

	Torah	Haftarah
בלק	Numbers 22.2–25.9	Micah 5.6–6.8
		Joshua 24.1–14
		Isaiah 54.11–17
		Habakkuk 3.1–19
	*Numbers 22.2–12	
פינחס	Numbers 25.10–30.1	I Kings 18.46–19.21
		Joshua 17.1–5
		Joshua 22.11–34
		Joshua 23.1–14
		Judges 1.1–15
		Ezekiel 45.18–25
	*Numbers 25.10–26.4	
מטות	Numbers 30.2–32.42	Jeremiah 1.1–2.3
		Joshua 22.1–10
		Joshua 22.11–34
	*Numbers 30.2–17	
מסעי	Numbers 33.1–36.13	Jeremiah 2.4–28; 3.4; 4.1–2
		(2.4–28; 4.1–2)
		Joshua 20.1–9
		Jeremiah 33.1–27
	*Numbers 33.1–10	
דברים	Deuteronomy 1.1–3.22	Isaiah 1.1–27
		Amos 2.1–11
		Lamentations 3.19–41
	*Deuteronomy 1.1–11	
ואתחנן	Deuteronomy 3.23–7.11	Isaiah 40.1–26
		Jeremiah 7.1–23
	*Deuteronomy 3.23–4.8	
עקב	Deuteronomy 7.12–11.25	Isaiah 49.14–51.3
		Isaiah 50.1–10
		Jeremiah 2.1–9
		Jeremiah 26.1–16
		Zechariah 8.7–23
	*Deuteronomy 7.12–21	

	Torah	*Haftarah*
ראה	Deuteronomy 11.26–16.17	*Isaiah 54.11–55.5*
		Joshua 8.30–35
		I Kings 22.1–14
		Isaiah 26.1–12
		Jeremiah 23.13–32
		Jeremiah 34.8–17
		Psalm 15.1–5
		Psalm 24.1–10
	*Deuteronomy 11.26–12.10	
שפטים	Deuteronomy 16.18–21.9	*Isaiah 51.12–52.12*
		I Samuel 8.1–22
		Jeremiah 23.13–32
		Ezekiel 34.1–31
	*Deuteronomy 16.18–17.13	
כי תצא	Deuteronomy 21.10–25.19	*Isaiah 54.1–10*
		Isaiah 5.1–16
		Isaiah 59.1–21
		Proverbs 28.1–14
		Proverbs 30.1–9
	*Deuteronomy 21.10–21	
כי תבוא	Deuteronomy 26.1–29.8	*Isaiah 60.1–22*
		Joshua 4.1–24
		Isaiah 35.1–10
		Isaiah 49.14–26
	*Deuteronomy 26.1–15	
נצבים	Deuteronomy 29.9–30.20	*Isaiah 61.10–63.9*
		Joshua 24.1–28
		Isaiah 51.1–16
		Jeremiah 31.27–36
	*Deuteronomy 29.9–28	
וילך	Deuteronomy 31.1–30	*Isaiah 55.6–56.8*
		On Shabbat Shuvah: Hosea
		14.2–10, Micah 7.18–20,
		Joel 2.15–27
	*Deuteronomy 31.1–3	

	Torah	*Haftarah*

האזינו	Deuteronomy 32.1–52	*II Samuel 22.1–51*
		Psalm 78.1–38
		On Shabbat Shuvah: Hosea
		  14.2–10, Micah 7.18–20,
		  Joel 2.15–27

	*Deuteronomy 32.1–12	
וזאת הברכה	Deuteronomy 33.1–34.12	*Joshua 1.1–18* *(1.1–9)*
	*Deuteronomy 33.1–7	

Shabbat Shuvah	Weekly portion	*Hosea 14.2–10; Micah*
		  7.18–20; Joel 2.15–27
		  (Hosea 14.2–10; Micah
		  7.18–20)

Sukkot

1st day	Leviticus 23.33–44	*Zechariah 14.7–9, 16–21* *Isaiah 35.1–10* *Isaiah 32.1–8, 14–20*
2nd day	Leviticus 23.39–44	
3rd day		
(*if Shabbat*)	Exodus 33.12–34.26	*Ezekiel 38.18–39.7*
(*if weekday*)	Exodus 23.14–17	
4th day	Exodus 34.21–24	
5th day		
(*if Shabbat*)	See readings for 3rd day	
(*if weekday*)	Deuteronomy 16.13–17	
6th day		
(*if Shabbat*)	See readings for 3rd day	
(*if weekday*)	Deuteronomy 31.9–13	

	Torah	*Haftarah*
7th day	Deuteronomy 11.10–15	

NOTE: *The Book of Ecclesiastes is read on the Shabbat during Sukkot.*

Atzeret-Simchat Torah	Deuteronomy 34.1–12 Genesis 1.1–2.3	*Joshua 1.1–18* *(1.1–9)*

Chanukah		
1st day	Numbers 6.22–7.17	
2nd day	Numbers 7.18–29	
3rd day	Numbers 7.24–35	
4th day	Numbers 7.30–41	
5th day	Numbers 7.36–47	
6th day	Numbers 7.42–53	
7th day	Numbers 7.48–59	
8th day	Numbers 7.54–8.4	
1st Shabbat during Chanukah	Weekly portion	*Zechariah 4.1–7*
2nd Shabbat during Chanukah	Weekly portion	*I Kings 7.40–50* *I Kings 8.54–66*

NOTE: *The first day of Tevet falls on the sixth or seventh day of Chanukah. The special reading for Rosh Chodesh may be added to that for Chanukah or substituted for it. If Rosh Chodesh and Shabbat coincide, three Sifrei Torah may be taken from the Ark. A selection from the regular weekly portion is read first.*

Shabbat Shekalim	Weekly portion Exodus 30.11–16	*II Kings 12.5–16* *(11.17–12.17)*
Shabbat Zachor	Weekly portion Deuteronomy 25.17–19	*Esther 7.1–10; 8.15–17,* *or 9.20–28*

	Torah	*Haftarah*
Purim	Exodus 17.8–16	

NOTE: *The Book of Esther is read on Purim.*

Shabbat Parah	Weekly portion Numbers 19.1–9	*Ezekiel 36.22–36*
Shabbat Hachodesh	Weekly portion Exodus 12.1–20	*Ezekiel 45.16–25*
Shabbat Hagadol	Weekly portion	*Malachi 3.4–24*
Pesach		
1st day	Exodus 12.37–42; 13.3–10	*Isaiah 43.1–15*
2nd day	Exodus 13.14–16	
3rd day		
(*if Shabbat*)	Exodus 33.12–34.26	*Ezekiel 37.1–14* *Song of Songs 2.7–17*
(*if weekday*)	Exodus 23.14–17	
4th day	Exodus 34.18–23	
5th day		
(*if Shabbat*)	See readings for 3rd day	
(*if weekday*)	Numbers 9.1–5	
6th day	Leviticus 23.1–8	
7th day	Exodus 14.30–15.21	*II Samuel 22.1–51* *Isaiah 11.1–6, 9; 12.1–6*

NOTE: *The Song of Songs is read on the Shabbat during Pesach.*

Yom Hasho-ah	Deuteronomy 4.30–40	*II Samuel 1.17–27* *Psalm 9.1–21* *Psalm 116.1–19* *Psalm 118.5–24*
Yom Ha-atsma-ut	Deuteronomy 8.1–18 Deuteronomy 11.8–21 Deuteronomy 26.1–11 Deuteronomy 30.1–16	*Isaiah 60.1–22* *Isaiah 10.32–12.6* *Isaiah 65.17–25*
Shavuot	Exodus 19.1–8; 20.1–14	*Isaiah 42.1–12*

NOTE: *The Book of Ruth is read on Shavuot.*

	Torah	*Haftarah*
Tish'a be-Av		
Morning	Deuteronomy 4.25–41	*Jeremiah 8.13–9.23*
Afternoon	Exodus 32.11–14; 34.1–10	*Isaiah 55.6–56.8*
		(Hosea 14.2–10, Micah
		7.18–20)

NOTE: *The Book of Lamentations is read on Tish'a be-Av.*

Rosh Chodesh		
Weekday	Numbers 28.11–15	
Shabbat and Rosh Chodesh	Weekly portion	*Isaiah 66.1–13, 23*
Shabbat when Rosh Chodesh is next day	Weekly portion	*I Samuel 20.18–42*

NOTE: *In the traditional calendar, when a month has thirty days, the thirtieth day and the first day of the new month are observed as Rosh Chodesh. It is suggested that in the Reform synagogue Rosh Chodesh should be observed on the first day of the new month.*

LITURGY COMMITTEE

OF THE

CENTRAL CONFERENCE OF AMERICAN RABBIS

A. Stanley Dreyfus,
Chairman

JAY R. BRICKMAN	NORMAN D. HIRSH
HERBERT BRONSTEIN	GUNTER HIRSCHBERG
HARVEY J. FIELDS	LAWRENCE A. HOFFMAN

FREDRIC S. POMERANTZ

JOSEPH B. GLASER, *ex-officio*

W. GUNTHER PLAUT, *ex-officio*

MALCOLM H. STERN, *ex-officio*

GEORGE WEINFLASH, *for the American Conference of Cantors*

*   *

Chaim Stern,
Editor